AZ-104
AZURE ADMINISTRATOR
MASTERY

4 BOOKS IN 1

BOOK 1
AZURE ESSENTIALS: A BEGINNER'S GUIDE TO NAVIGATING AZ-104

BOOK 2
MASTERING IDENTITY & RESOURCE MANAGEMENT IN AZURE: A
COMPREHENSIVE GUIDE TO AZ-104

BOOK 3
AZURE NETWORKING AND STORAGE MASTERY: ADVANCED TECHNIQUES
FOR AZ-104 ADMINISTRATORS

BOOK 4
AZURE ADMINISTRATOR EXPERTISE: PRO-LEVEL AUTOMATION AND
OPTIMIZATION FOR AZ-104

ROB BOTWRIGHT

Published by Rob Botwright
Library of Congress Cataloging-in-Publication Data
ISBN 978-1-83938-540-7
Cover design by Rizzo

Disclaimer

The contents of this book are based on extensive research and the best available historical sources. However, the author and publisher make no claims, promises, or guarantees about the accuracy, completeness, or adequacy of the information contained herein. The information in this book is provided on an "as is" basis, and the author and publisher disclaim any and all liability for any errors, omissions, or inaccuracies in the information or for any actions taken in reliance on such information.

The opinions and views expressed in this book are those of the author and do not necessarily reflect the official policy or position of any organization or individual mentioned in this book. Any reference to specific people, places, or events is intended only to provide historical context and is not intended to defame or malign any group, individual, or entity.

The information in this book is intended for educational and entertainment purposes only. It is not intended to be a substitute for professional advice or judgment. Readers are encouraged to conduct their own research and to seek professional advice where appropriate.

Every effort has been made to obtain necessary permissions and acknowledgments for all images and other copyrighted material used in this book. Any errors or omissions in this regard are unintentional, and the author and publisher will correct them in future editions.

TABLE OF CONTENTS – BOOK 1 - AZURE ESSENTIALS: A BEGINNER'S GUIDE TO NAVIGATING AZ-104

TABLE OF CONTENTS – BOOK 2 - MASTERING IDENTITY & RESOURCE MANAGEMENT IN AZURE: A COMPREHENSIVE GUIDE TO AZ-104

TABLE OF CONTENTS – BOOK 3 - AZURE NETWORKING AND STORAGE MASTERY: ADVANCED TECHNIQUES FOR AZ-104 ADMINISTRATORS

TABLE OF CONTENTS – BOOK 4 - AZURE ADMINISTRATOR EXPERTISE: PRO-LEVEL AUTOMATION AND OPTIMIZATION FOR AZ-104

Introduction

In the rapidly evolving landscape of cloud computing, Microsoft Azure has emerged as a dominant force, offering a vast array of services and solutions to empower organizations in their digital transformation journey. For IT professionals, administrators, and aspiring cloud enthusiasts, Azure represents both an opportunity and a challenge. To harness the full potential of this cloud platform, one needs not only knowledge but also mastery.

Welcome to "AZ-104: Azure Administrator Mastery," a comprehensive book bundle designed to guide you on a transformative journey through the intricacies of Microsoft Azure. This bundle consists of four distinct yet interconnected books, each tailored to equip you with the skills and expertise needed to navigate Azure with confidence and proficiency.

Book 1 - Azure Essentials: A Beginner's Guide to Navigating AZ-104: Embark on your Azure journey as a beginner and build a strong foundation in Azure fundamentals. This book is your compass, helping you navigate the Azure portal, create and manage resources, and grasp the core concepts that form the bedrock of the Azure ecosystem. Whether you're new to cloud computing or seeking to refine your Azure basics, this book will be your trusted guide.

Book 2 - Mastering Identity & Resource Management in Azure: A Comprehensive Guide to AZ-104: Identity management and resource governance are pivotal in the Azure realm. This book delves deep into these critical aspects, providing you with the knowledge and skills to secure access to Azure resources, implement robust identity solutions, and enforce compliance through resource management. As you master these fundamentals, you'll become a steward of security and governance in the Azure cloud.

Book 3 - Azure Networking and Storage Mastery: Advanced Techniques for AZ-104 Administrators: Azure's networking and storage capabilities are at the heart of many cloud solutions. In this book, you'll advance your expertise by exploring the intricacies of Azure networking, designing resilient network architectures, optimizing connectivity, and harnessing the power of Azure Storage for diverse data needs. With these advanced techniques, you'll be equipped to architect and manage high-performance Azure solutions.

Book 4 - Azure Administrator Expertise: Pro-Level Automation and Optimization for AZ-104: As you progress through your Azure journey, automation and optimization become your allies. This book takes you to the level of a pro-level administrator, guiding you to streamline operations, optimize resources for cost, performance, and security, and master the art of Azure PowerShell and Azure CLI. Armed with automation and optimization skills, you'll be prepared to take on complex Azure challenges with confidence.

The "AZ-104: Azure Administrator Mastery" bundle is more than just a collection of books; it's a roadmap to Azure excellence. Whether you're an IT professional seeking to upskill, an administrator looking to enhance your Azure proficiency, or an aspiring cloud architect eager to embark on your Azure journey, this bundle is your comprehensive guide.

Azure Administrator Mastery is about more than acquiring knowledge; it's about gaining a mindset of continuous learning and adaptability in the ever-evolving cloud landscape. The world of Azure is vast and dynamic, filled with boundless opportunities waiting for you to explore and conquer.

So, fasten your seatbelt and prepare for a transformative journey through the world of Azure. "AZ-104: Azure Administrator Mastery" is your ticket to unlocking the full potential of Microsoft Azure, and your destination is nothing less than mastery itself. Let's embark on this Azure adventure together, and may your Azure journey be a voyage of discovery, growth, and achievement.

BOOK 1
AZURE ESSENTIALS
A BEGINNER'S GUIDE TO NAVIGATING AZ-104

ROB BOTWRIGHT

Chapter 1: Embracing the Cloud Revolution

The evolution of cloud computing is a fascinating journey that has redefined the way we interact with technology and data. In the early days of computing, individuals and businesses relied heavily on mainframes and physical servers to store and process data. These systems were often cumbersome, expensive, and required extensive infrastructure and management. The need for more flexible and scalable solutions led to the emergence of cloud computing, which brought a revolutionary change in the field of information technology.

Cloud computing emerged as a means to provide users with access to computing resources over the internet, eliminating the need for owning and maintaining physical hardware. The concept of delivering computing power as a utility, akin to electricity or water, was a breakthrough. This paradigm shift allowed for computing resources to be accessed and scaled on-demand, giving businesses unprecedented flexibility and agility. The transformative power of cloud computing quickly became evident as companies realized the cost savings and efficiency gains they could achieve by migrating to the cloud.

The adoption of cloud computing was not an overnight phenomenon; it was driven by the convergence of several technological advances. The development of virtualization technology, which allowed multiple virtual machines to run on a single physical server, was one such catalyst. Virtualization paved the way for resource pooling and led to the creation of data centers that could serve many users simultaneously.

In the early stages, cloud computing models were largely focused on providing infrastructure services. Infrastructure as a Service (IaaS) solutions offered virtualized computing resources over the internet, allowing users to rent processing power, storage, and networking components. This was a transformative moment, as businesses no longer needed to invest in expensive hardware and could instead pay for only what they used.

Platform as a Service (PaaS) soon followed, providing developers with a platform and environment to build, deploy, and manage applications without worrying about the underlying infrastructure. This abstracted away even more complexity, allowing developers to focus solely on their code and applications.

Then came Software as a Service (SaaS), which delivered software applications over the internet on a subscription basis. SaaS eliminated the need for installing, maintaining, and updating software on individual computers, simplifying the user experience tremendously.

The rise of cloud computing also led to the emergence of big data and analytics. The cloud's ability to store and process vast amounts of data quickly and efficiently opened new doors for businesses to gain insights and make data-driven decisions. Analytics and data visualization tools began to flourish in the cloud environment, empowering organizations to extract valuable information from their data.

Security and privacy concerns, which were initial roadblocks in the adoption of cloud computing, saw continuous improvement as cloud providers invested heavily in building secure and compliant platforms. Data encryption, identity management, and compliance certifications became integral components of cloud offerings, enhancing trust among users.

The proliferation of mobile devices and the growth of the internet of things (IoT) further fueled the adoption of cloud computing. The need to access data and applications from anywhere, at any time, made the cloud an indispensable asset for businesses and individuals alike.

One of the key aspects that propelled the growth of cloud computing was the embrace of open-source technologies. Open-source software and frameworks allowed for rapid innovation and created vibrant communities of developers and enterprises contributing to and benefiting from shared resources.

As cloud computing matured, the focus shifted towards optimizing for performance, reliability, and cost-effectiveness. Organizations began adopting multi-cloud and hybrid cloud strategies to leverage the best offerings from different cloud providers and to avoid vendor lock-in. These strategies enabled businesses to create flexible and resilient architectures tailored to their specific needs.

The evolution of cloud computing continues to this day, with new advancements like serverless computing, edge computing, and artificial intelligence services becoming integral parts of the cloud ecosystem. Serverless computing, for instance, allows developers to build and run applications without managing servers, further simplifying the development process.

Edge computing, on the other hand, seeks to bring computing resources closer to the location where data is generated, reducing latency and bandwidth use. This is particularly crucial in applications such as autonomous vehicles, smart cities, and IoT devices where real-time data processing is essential.

The integration of artificial intelligence and machine learning services within cloud platforms has unlocked new possibilities in automation, data analysis, and intelligent applications. Cloud providers now offer a myriad of AI services that can be easily integrated into applications, allowing businesses to harness the power of AI without the need for specialized expertise.

Through all these advancements, the evolution of cloud computing has fundamentally altered the way we think about technology. It has democratized access to computing resources, fostered innovation, and catalyzed digital transformation across industries.

As we look to the future, the continuous evolution of cloud computing promises to bring forth even more groundbreaking developments. Innovations in quantum computing, augmented reality, and distributed ledger technologies may find their homes in the cloud, paving the way for new possibilities and applications.

In reflecting upon this journey, it is evident that cloud computing is not merely a technological shift but a cultural and organizational one as well. The cloud has changed not just how we manage and deploy technology, but also how we work, collaborate, and innovate.

In essence, the story of cloud computing is one of continuous evolution, a narrative of transformation and progress. As we continue to explore and embrace the cloud, we become active participants in this unfolding story, contributing to and shaping the future of this dynamic and ever-evolving landscape.

The transition to cloud technologies has brought about a multitude of benefits that have revolutionized the way organizations operate, innovate, and deliver value. By harnessing the power of the cloud, companies of all sizes have experienced unprecedented growth, agility, and competitiveness. Let's delve into the myriad advantages that the adoption of cloud technologies bestows upon organizations.

One of the most compelling benefits of cloud adoption is cost savings. Traditional on-premises solutions often necessitate significant upfront capital investment in hardware, software, and infrastructure. In contrast, the cloud operates on a pay-as-you-go model, where businesses can rent computing resources and only pay for what they use. This shift from capital expenditure to operational expenditure can significantly reduce costs and make technology more accessible to a wider range of organizations.

The scalability and flexibility afforded by cloud technologies are equally transformative. Organizations can swiftly scale up or down based on demand, ensuring that resources are used efficiently. The ability to adapt to changing workloads means that businesses can respond promptly to market shifts, seasonal fluctuations, or sudden opportunities, thus staying ahead of the competition.

Enhanced collaboration and accessibility are additional perks that come with embracing cloud technologies. With data and applications hosted in the cloud, team members can access resources from virtually anywhere, using any device with an internet connection. This facilitates seamless collaboration among geographically dispersed teams, fostering creativity and enhancing productivity.

The cloud also excels in terms of reliability and availability. Cloud service providers invest heavily in building resilient and redundant infrastructure, ensuring that services remain accessible even in the face of hardware failures or other disruptions. This high level of availability is often accompanied by service level agreements that guarantee uptime, providing organizations with peace of mind.

Data backup, disaster recovery, and business continuity are areas where cloud technologies shine brightly. Traditional methods of data backup can be cumbersome and prone to errors. However, cloud-based solutions automate this process, ensuring that data is regularly backed up and can be easily restored in case of a system failure or data loss incident. The cloud thus acts as a safety net, safeguarding valuable data and ensuring business continuity.

Security is a paramount concern for organizations, and cloud technologies have made significant strides in this domain. Cloud providers implement rigorous security protocols and practices, such as data encryption, identity management, and regular security audits. By leveraging the expertise and resources of cloud providers, organizations can benefit from robust security measures that may otherwise be beyond their reach.

Innovation and speed to market are other areas where cloud technologies make a substantial impact. The cloud provides a conducive environment for experimentation, allowing organizations to test new ideas and deploy applications swiftly. By reducing the time and resources required to bring a product or service to market, the cloud empowers organizations to stay innovative and responsive to customer needs.

Cloud technologies also contribute to sustainability and environmental conservation. By sharing resources in a cloud environment, organizations can achieve higher utilization rates of hardware, thereby reducing the overall environmental footprint. The efficient use of energy and resources in large data centers operated by cloud providers further contributes to a more sustainable and eco-friendly approach to computing.

Interoperability and integration are additional benefits that arise from cloud adoption. Cloud services are often designed to work seamlessly with other cloud-based and on-premises solutions. This ease of integration enables organizations to build cohesive and streamlined workflows, improving efficiency and reducing manual intervention.

The cloud is also an enabler of new business models and revenue streams. With the ease of deploying and scaling applications, organizations can explore new markets and opportunities more readily. Subscription-based models, e-commerce platforms, and digital services are just a few examples of the innovative business models facilitated by cloud technologies.

Customer experience is another area that stands to gain from cloud adoption. By leveraging cloud-based analytics, artificial intelligence, and customer relationship management tools, businesses can gain insights into customer behavior and preferences. This data-driven approach enables organizations to tailor their offerings and interactions to enhance customer satisfaction and loyalty.

Furthermore, the cloud provides an avenue for continuous learning and skill development. With a plethora of educational resources, training platforms, and community forums available, professionals can continuously upgrade their skills and stay abreast of the latest developments in cloud technologies.

The agility conferred by cloud technologies extends beyond IT departments and permeates the entire organization. The ease and speed of deploying new applications or scaling existing ones mean that departments such as marketing, sales, and customer service can respond swiftly to changing conditions and opportunities.

In essence, the benefits of adopting cloud technologies are multifaceted and transformative. Organizations that embrace the cloud find themselves better positioned to navigate the complexities of the modern business landscape. They are equipped to respond to change with agility, innovate with speed, and operate with efficiency.

As we reflect on these advantages, it is evident that cloud technologies are not just tools or platforms but catalysts for organizational transformation. The cloud has the potential to redefine the way businesses operate, fostering a culture of innovation, collaboration, and continuous improvement.

By adopting cloud technologies, organizations are making a strategic investment in their future. They are laying the foundation for a resilient, agile, and innovative enterprise that is capable of navigating the challenges and opportunities of the digital age. The journey to the cloud is, therefore, a journey towards achieving sustainable competitive advantage, operational excellence, and lasting success.

As we continue to explore and harness the capabilities of cloud technologies, we are charting a course towards a more connected, efficient, and innovative future. The cloud beckons us with promises of transformation, and it is up to us to seize these opportunities and chart a path towards progress and prosperity.

Chapter 2: The Azure Landscape

Navigating the realm of Microsoft Azure can be akin to exploring a vast and varied landscape, each service a unique landmark with its own purpose and functionality. Azure, as one of the world's leading cloud platforms, offers a multitude of core services designed to address a wide spectrum of needs for businesses and individuals alike. Let's embark on a journey to understand these services and how they fit together to create powerful, scalable, and efficient solutions.

At the heart of Azure lies its computing services, providing the virtual muscle to power applications, data processing, and much more. Azure Virtual Machines, for instance, offer on-demand scalable computing resources that can run a variety of operating systems and applications. The ease with which these virtual machines can be deployed, managed, and scaled allows organizations to focus on innovation while leaving infrastructure management to Azure.

Azure's computing prowess extends beyond virtual machines with services like Azure Functions, a serverless compute service that enables users to run event-driven functions without having to manage infrastructure. Serverless computing allows for code execution in response to triggers, such as changes in data or a user's actions, creating dynamic and responsive applications.

Another pillar of Azure's offerings is its data storage services, ensuring that data is securely and efficiently stored, retrieved, and managed. Azure Blob Storage, for instance, provides scalable and cost-effective object storage for unstructured data such as documents, images, and videos. With its high availability and redundancy, Blob Storage ensures that data is accessible when needed, while keeping it secure and durable.

Azure also offers relational database services like Azure SQL Database, a fully-managed relational database service that provides seamless integration with SQL Server and advanced features such as automated backups, updates, and scaling. By handling much of the management overhead, Azure SQL Database allows developers to concentrate on crafting applications rather than managing databases.

Azure's networking services are designed to connect, protect, and enhance communication within applications. Azure Virtual Network allows users to create isolated and secure cloud-based networks where resources can communicate in a controlled and private environment. With features like Network Security Groups and Virtual Network Peering, Azure Virtual Network ensures that resources are securely connected and traffic is efficiently routed.

Delving further into security, Azure offers a suite of services to ensure applications and data are protected against threats. Azure Security Center provides unified security management, advanced threat protection, and intelligent recommendations to secure resources and data. With its ability to adapt to an ever-evolving threat landscape, Azure Security Center acts as a vigilant guardian for assets deployed in Azure.

Monitoring and management are crucial aspects of any robust system, and Azure does not disappoint in this regard. Azure Monitor offers full-stack monitoring, advanced analytics, and intelligent insights to ensure performance and availability. By collecting, analyzing, and acting on telemetry data, Azure Monitor enables users to gain insights, spot trends, and diagnose issues swiftly.

Azure's identity and access management services, such as Azure Active Directory, provide secure identity services enabling the right people to access the right information. It offers features like single sign-on and multi-factor authentication to secure and streamline user access to applications.

Integration and automation are pivotal in creating cohesive and efficient workflows. Azure Logic Apps is a service that helps design and automate workflows, integrating apps, data, systems, and services across enterprises or organizations. By visually designing workflows, users can create complex processes that can be easily managed and scaled.

Artificial intelligence and machine learning hold transformative potential, and Azure provides tools and services to harness these technologies. Azure Machine Learning is a comprehensive service that allows developers and data scientists to build, train, and deploy machine learning models efficiently. It simplifies the process of creating models, enabling organizations to incorporate intelligent features and analytics into their applications.

Azure's content delivery and media services, such as Azure Media Services, allow for the delivery of streaming content and provide capabilities for encoding, encryption, and content protection. This ensures a smooth and high-quality experience for end-users regardless of their location.

DevOps practices and principles are integral to modern development, and Azure DevOps Services provide a set of cloud-based collaboration tools for software development. These services aim to streamline the development process, fostering a culture of continuous integration, continuous delivery, and rapid feedback.

Azure's Internet of Things (IoT) services, such as Azure IoT Hub, enable the connection, management, and data ingestion from IoT devices seamlessly and securely. By integrating devices and back-end services, Azure IoT Hub facilitates the creation of innovative and responsive IoT solutions.

In the realm of mobile applications, Azure offers services like Azure Mobile Apps, which simplifies the backend processes of mobile application development, providing essential functionalities such as data storage, offline synchronization, and authentication.

When we consider the cloud's role in modernizing traditional applications, Azure's container and microservices offerings, such as Azure Kubernetes Service, come to the fore. By facilitating the deployment, management, and scaling of containerized applications using Kubernetes, Azure allows organizations to build agile and scalable solutions.

In essence, the array of services offered by Azure is akin to a well-stocked toolbox, each tool designed to address specific needs while working seamlessly with others. Azure's commitment to flexibility, scalability, and innovation is evident in the continuous evolution and expansion of its services.

Exploring Azure's core services provides a glimpse into the vast possibilities that the platform offers. From computing to data storage, networking to security, and beyond, Azure stands as a testament to the transformative power of the cloud. By weaving these services together, organizations can craft solutions that are not just responsive and scalable but also secure and innovative.

In our journey through Azure's core services, we uncover a tapestry of interconnected capabilities, each contributing to the realization of an organization's objectives. The versatility of Azure ensures that regardless of the challenge at hand, there is likely a service or combination of services ready to address it.

The beauty of Azure lies in its ability to evolve and adapt, ensuring that it remains relevant and valuable in an ever-changing technological landscape. By understanding and leveraging Azure's core services, organizations equip themselves to navigate the complexities and opportunities of the digital era. Through this exploration, we gain not just knowledge but also an appreciation for the possibilities that Azure unlocks, setting the stage for innovation, growth, and success.

Embarking on a journey through the cloud computing landscape, one cannot help but notice the distinct features that set Microsoft Azure apart from its counterparts. With an array of services, tools, and innovations, Azure has established itself as a compelling choice for organizations of all sizes seeking to harness the power of the cloud. Let's delve into the key differentiators that make Azure such a compelling option in the world of cloud computing.

A striking aspect of Azure is its integration capabilities with the myriad of products and services under the Microsoft ecosystem. For organizations that rely heavily on Microsoft software such as Windows Server, Active Directory, and SQL Server, transitioning to Azure can be remarkably seamless. The compatibility between Azure and other Microsoft products ensures a cohesive experience, reducing friction during migration and subsequent operations.

Azure's commitment to hybrid flexibility is another distinctive feature that warrants attention. While many cloud providers focus primarily on public cloud offerings, Azure extends its embrace to hybrid environments, allowing organizations to seamlessly operate across on-premises data centers, multi-cloud environments, and the edge. Azure Arc, for instance, brings Azure services and management to virtually any infrastructure, underscoring Microsoft's commitment to meeting organizations where they are.

Security, always a paramount concern, is addressed head-on by Azure with an approach that is deeply ingrained in its fabric. Azure offers a comprehensive suite of security features and compliance certifications that are designed to protect data and applications. The robust security measures span identity, network, information, and threat protection, ensuring that organizations can operate with confidence in a secure environment.

Azure's commitment to fostering innovation is evident in its support for a wide range of programming languages, frameworks, and operating systems. Developers are not confined to a particular language or toolset but can use the technologies they are most comfortable with, including open-source solutions. By providing a versatile platform, Azure encourages creativity and productivity among developers and architects alike.

A standout differentiator of Azure is its extensive global footprint. With a vast network of data centers spanning multiple regions across the globe, Azure ensures low latency, high availability, and resilience. Organizations can deploy their applications and services close to their customer base, ensuring optimal performance and reliability.

One of Azure's hallmarks is its comprehensive approach to data and artificial intelligence. Azure provides a rich set of services and tools designed to harness the power of data, ranging from traditional databases to advanced machine learning solutions. Azure Synapse Analytics, for instance, brings together big data and data warehousing, while Azure Machine Learning provides tools for building, training, and deploying machine learning models.

The commitment to sustainability and responsible cloud computing is another area where Azure shines. Microsoft has made significant strides in its efforts to minimize the environmental impact of its data centers and has ambitious goals for sustainability. By choosing Azure, organizations align themselves with a cloud provider that is conscious of its environmental responsibilities.

Understanding the budget constraints and financial planning needs of organizations, Azure provides cost management and optimization tools that set it apart. The Azure Cost Management and Billing suite offers a detailed view into resource usage and costs, along with recommendations for optimizing expenditures. This transparency and guidance empower organizations to make informed financial decisions regarding their cloud usage.

Azure's emphasis on providing industry-specific solutions is another distinguishing feature. Recognizing that different industries have unique requirements and challenges, Azure offers tailored solutions for sectors such as healthcare, finance, retail, and manufacturing. By aligning its services to meet the regulatory, compliance, and operational needs of different industries, Azure ensures a more customized and relevant experience.

The spirit of continuous improvement and innovation runs deep in Azure's ethos. Microsoft consistently invests in research and development, ensuring that Azure remains at the cutting edge of cloud technology. Regular updates, new features, and enhancements are testament to Azure's commitment to delivering value and staying ahead of evolving needs.

In terms of developer support and community engagement, Azure stands tall with a vibrant community of developers, architects, and enthusiasts. Azure's documentation is extensive, and its community forums, blogs, and social media channels are teeming with discussions, tutorials, and advice. This supportive ecosystem ensures that users can find answers to their questions and engage in collaborative problem-solving.

Azure also demonstrates its versatility through its robust offerings in the Internet of Things (IoT) space. With services like Azure IoT Hub, which facilitates the secure connection and management of IoT devices, Azure ensures that organizations can harness the potential of connected devices and intelligent edge computing.

In the realm of app development, Azure provides a plethora of tools and services that cater to both traditional and modern application architectures. Azure App Service offers a platform for building, deploying, and scaling web applications, while Azure Kubernetes Service caters to those looking to leverage container orchestration for microservices-based applications.

In the pursuit of digital transformation, businesses often find themselves grappling with legacy systems and applications. Azure recognizes this challenge and offers pathways for modernizing existing applications, ensuring that organizations can transition smoothly to the cloud without discarding their investments in legacy systems.

Through its diverse suite of services, global presence, security focus, and commitment to innovation and sustainability, Azure has crafted a unique identity in the cloud computing space. Its compatibility with existing Microsoft products, coupled with its emphasis on flexibility, developer choice, and industry-specific solutions, makes it a compelling choice for organizations charting their path in the cloud.

In essence, Azure's key differentiators lie in its ability to blend tradition with innovation, offer choices while ensuring security, and provide global scale coupled with industry-specific attention. By doing so, it stands out as a cloud platform that is not just robust and versatile, but also attuned to the nuanced and evolving needs of organizations.

As we reflect on the distinctive features of Azure, we realize that it is more than just a cloud platform; it is a testament to Microsoft's vision of empowering organizations to achieve more. In the constantly evolving landscape of technology, Azure's differentiators position it as a beacon guiding organizations through their cloud journey, ensuring they are well-equipped to navigate the challenges and opportunities that lie ahead.

Chapter 3: Setting the Stage: Azure Subscriptions and Accounts

Creating and managing Azure subscriptions is an integral step in your journey to harnessing the cloud's power through Microsoft's Azure platform. Let's delve into how you can go about creating these subscriptions and managing them effectively. Azure subscriptions are essentially agreements with Microsoft to use one or more cloud services, including access to cloud-based resources such as virtual machines, storage, and databases.

To begin creating an Azure subscription, you would need to have a Microsoft account. Once you have that, you can sign up for Azure through the Azure portal. The process of creating a subscription is smooth and straightforward, guiding you through steps such as selecting your subscription plan and setting up payment details. It is important to choose the right type of subscription based on your needs, as Azure offers a range of options, from pay-as-you-go to more extensive enterprise agreements.

When you've successfully created a subscription, it becomes your gateway to deploying and managing resources in Azure. Each subscription is associated with an Azure AD directory which allows you to control access and permissions. Effective management of your subscriptions is crucial, as it not only impacts your billing but also ensures that your resources are organized and secure.

The Azure portal becomes your go-to hub for managing your subscriptions. It's a comprehensive interface that provides insights into your usage, billing, and management settings. Azure subscriptions are also versatile in that they allow you to segment and allocate resources based on your organizational structure or projects. For example, you can create different subscriptions for different departments or phases of a project, ensuring more granular control over costs and resources.

Now, let's delve into how Azure Resource Manager (ARM), Azure's deployment and management service, plays a pivotal role in managing your subscriptions. ARM allows you to organize resources by grouping them into resource groups within your subscriptions. This logical grouping facilitates efficient resource management and simplifies the task of tracking billing costs.

Understanding role-based access control (RBAC) is crucial for managing Azure subscriptions effectively. RBAC allows you to define who has access to what within your Azure environment. By assigning roles to users or groups, you can dictate who can create, modify, or delete resources within your subscriptions. This granularity in permissions ensures security and compliance.

When managing multiple subscriptions, the Azure Management Groups feature comes to the fore. Management groups allow you to organize your subscriptions into hierarchical structures, applying policies, and access controls at a broad level. This can be particularly useful for large organizations where multiple subscriptions need to be governed under a unified set of rules and policies.

Policies in Azure play a critical role in ensuring compliance and standardization across your subscriptions. By defining policies, you can specify certain rules and standards that every deployed resource must adhere to. For instance, you can enforce specific configurations, naming conventions, or regions for resource deployment through policies, ensuring consistency across your environment.

Another aspect to consider while managing subscriptions is cost management and budgeting. Azure provides tools that allow you to monitor your spending and set up budgets for your subscriptions. By leveraging the Azure Cost Management and Billing features, you can gain insights into your expenditure, forecast future costs, and ensure that your cloud journey stays within financial bounds.

Effective management of subscriptions also entails regularly reviewing and optimizing your resource usage. Azure Advisor is a personalized cloud consultant that helps you follow best practices to optimize your Azure deployments. It provides recommendations that can help you improve the performance, security, and cost-effectiveness of your Azure resources.

Let's also touch upon the importance of staying vigilant regarding the security of your subscriptions. Azure Security Center is a unified infrastructure security management system that strengthens the security posture of your data and services. By continuously monitoring your subscriptions and resources, it helps you detect and respond to potential threats swiftly.

In the realm of Azure subscriptions, understanding service health and staying informed about updates and incidents is crucial. Azure provides a Service Health dashboard that gives you a view into the health of your resources and notifies you about any incidents or maintenance updates that might impact your services.

As you delve deeper into managing your subscriptions, you might find the need to automate certain repetitive tasks. Azure Automation allows you to automate frequent, time-consuming, and error-prone cloud management tasks. This automation ensures that your resources are managed efficiently, freeing up time for more strategic endeavors.

Given the dynamic nature of cloud environments, continuous monitoring and logging of your subscriptions' activity is also imperative. Azure Monitor and Azure Activity

Log provide detailed insights into operations that were performed on resources in your account. This data is instrumental in understanding the state and health of your resources, and it aids in identifying areas for improvement and optimization.

Creating and managing Azure subscriptions may seem like a daunting task, but with the array of tools and features provided by Azure, the process can be streamlined and efficient. From the initial setup of your subscription to implementing policies, access controls, cost management, and ensuring security and compliance, Azure provides a comprehensive environment that is both robust and user-friendly.

The key to effective subscription management lies in understanding the unique features and tools at your disposal and leveraging them to create an organized, secure, and cost-effective cloud environment. Regularly reviewing your configurations, staying abreast of the latest features and updates, and proactively optimizing your resources can lead to a seamless and productive Azure experience.

As your organization evolves, so too will your needs and requirements for Azure subscriptions. Adapting to these changes, consistently optimizing your deployments, and ensuring that your management practices evolve in tandem are crucial aspects of the cloud journey. By doing so, you ensure that your Azure subscriptions are always aligned with your organizational goals and needs.

In summary, creating and managing Azure subscriptions is a journey that encompasses thoughtful planning, meticulous organization, regular optimization, and continuous monitoring. By embracing the tools and practices that Azure provides, you ensure a streamlined, secure, and efficient cloud experience. So, as you navigate your Azure journey, remember that effective subscription management is a cornerstone for building and maintaining a successful cloud environment.

Embarking on the path to understanding and configuring account settings is a nuanced endeavor that requires a grasp of the various components and functionalities that a platform or service offers. Let's take a moment to explore this landscape and untangle the complexities that surround account settings. In most online platforms, the process of setting up and managing an account is a user's first interaction with the service, and it sets the tone for the entire experience.

Understanding your account settings begins with the basics, such as personal information, security preferences, and notification settings. Personal information is typically where you set up your profile, including your name, contact details, and any personal preferences. It's essential to ensure that this information is accurate and up to date, as it can often be used for verification purposes or personalization of the service.

Security settings are another crucial aspect of account configuration. These include password settings, two-factor authentication, and other security measures designed to protect your account from unauthorized access. When configuring security settings, it's important to strike a balance between convenience and protection. Employing strong, unique passwords and enabling two-factor authentication where possible can add an extra layer of security to your account.

Notification settings are where you can manage how and when a platform communicates with you. These can include email notifications, text messages, or push notifications on your devices. It's vital to adjust these settings to ensure that you receive important updates and information without being overwhelmed by unnecessary alerts.

Privacy settings are equally significant and allow you to control who can see your information and how it is used. Many platforms provide options to adjust your privacy preferences, allowing you to determine how much of your information is visible to others and how it may be used by the service.

Now, let's shift our focus to platforms that are more business-oriented, such as cloud service providers or enterprise-level applications. In these environments, account settings can extend to encompass aspects such as user roles, permissions, and access levels. Understanding and configuring these settings is paramount to ensuring that users have the right level of access to perform their roles effectively.

User roles and permissions define what actions a user can take within a system. For example, an administrator may have broad access to create, modify, and delete resources, while a regular user may only be able to view or edit specific items. Configuring these roles and permissions with precision ensures that the principle of least privilege is followed, which is a best practice in security.

Access levels and restrictions can also be part of the account settings, dictating which parts of a system or service a user can access. This could include restrictions based on location, device, or network, adding another layer of security to the account.

In collaborative environments, account settings may also include options to manage teams or groups. Here, administrators can create groups of users, assign roles, and manage access to resources collectively. This streamlines the process of managing large teams and ensures that everyone has access to the tools and resources they need.

Billing and subscription settings are another aspect to consider. These settings allow you to manage your payment information, view invoices, and monitor usage and costs. Keeping a close eye on these settings and understanding the billing model of the service you're using is crucial to avoid any unexpected charges.

In the realm of cloud services, account settings can also extend to service-specific configurations. This could include settings related to compute resources, storage, network configurations, and more. These settings are crucial to optimize based on your needs and can have a direct impact on performance and costs.

Customization settings allow users to tailor the look and feel of a platform to their preferences. This can include themes, layouts, and other user interface adjustments that enhance the user experience and make interaction with the platform more pleasant and productive.

Understanding and configuring account settings may also involve integrating with other services and platforms. Integration settings allow you to connect different applications and services, facilitating seamless data flow and enhanced functionality.

In platforms that involve content creation or data management, account settings can include preferences related to content visibility, sharing options, and data retention policies. These settings are vital for ensuring that your data is managed, stored, and shared in accordance with your preferences and any regulatory requirements.

Support and help settings are also an integral part of account configurations. These settings provide access to customer support, help documentation, and resources that can assist in troubleshooting or optimizing your use of the service.

As we explore the intricacies of understanding and configuring account settings, it's clear that each setting serves a purpose and contributes to the overall experience of using a platform or service. Whether it's ensuring the security of your account, optimizing your notification preferences, or managing your user roles and permissions, each setting plays a pivotal role.

To navigate this complex landscape effectively, it's important to take the time to familiarize yourself with the various settings available and understand how they impact your interaction with the service. Regularly reviewing and updating your account settings ensures that your account remains secure, your preferences are respected, and your interactions with the service are as seamless and productive as possible.

In the ever-evolving world of technology, where new features and settings are continually being introduced, staying abreast of changes and understanding how to configure your account settings is an ongoing journey. By approaching this task with curiosity and diligence, you can ensure that you're making the most of the tools and services at your disposal.

Chapter 4: Exploring Azure Portal: A First Look

Navigating the Azure dashboard can be likened to steering a ship through a sea of possibilities, where every click opens up a new horizon filled with potential and opportunities. The Azure dashboard is a user's gateway to all the services and resources offered by Microsoft's cloud platform, and understanding how to move through this interface is key to a smooth and productive experience. When you first log in to the Azure portal, you are greeted by a customizable space designed to put everything you need right at your fingertips.

The dashboard is akin to a personal workspace where you can pin, organize, and have quick access to different Azure services, resources, and other essential tools. It's a canvas where you can visualize and access data and resources most relevant to your tasks, thereby increasing efficiency and minimizing time spent in search. Your initial interaction with the dashboard may seem overwhelming due to the multitude of options available, but once you become acquainted with its nuances, navigating becomes second nature.

One of the first elements you may notice is the sidebar, which is akin to a well-organized toolbox. This sidebar holds icons that represent different Azure services, and clicking on any of these icons opens up a world of functionalities specific to that service. For example, clicking on the 'Virtual Machines' icon takes you to a space where you can manage and monitor your VMs.

The Azure dashboard is not just a static space but is highly customizable, allowing you to create an environment tailored to your needs. You can pin frequently used services or specific resources to your dashboard, ensuring that they are always just a click away. This level of customization ensures that your workspace stays clutter-free and focused on your priorities.

Search functionality is another aspect of the Azure dashboard that warrants attention. With a search bar conveniently located at the top, you can quickly find and access resources, services, and documentation. It's like having a compass that points you directly to what you need amidst a sea of options.

The dashboard also offers insights and quick metrics that can be incredibly valuable. For instance, you might find widgets displaying the health of your resources or the consumption of your allocated budgets. These insights act as a pulse check, allowing you to monitor and adjust your usage as needed.

Moreover, the Azure dashboard isn't merely about accessing resources but also about management and control. From this central hub, you can start, stop, and configure resources, monitor their performance, and even troubleshoot issues. This centralized management capability ensures that you can govern your resources effectively without having to jump between different interfaces.

When it comes to organization, the Azure dashboard excels in providing tools and features to streamline your workflow. Resource groups, for example, can be used to logically arrange related resources, making it easier to manage and navigate through them. It's like having a well-organized filing system where everything is grouped and labeled according to your preferences.

Azure's dashboard also focuses on enhancing the user experience through features like the Cloud Shell, which offers a command-line interface right within the portal. This allows users to run commands and scripts to manage their

Azure resources, offering a level of control and flexibility that is appreciated by many seasoned administrators.

Accessibility and ease of use are also central to the design of the Azure dashboard. Options to adjust the visual appearance, such as changing themes or modifying the display settings, ensure that the dashboard is accessible and comfortable for everyone to use. These adjustments can transform the dashboard into a space that feels familiar and intuitive, making navigation and interaction a pleasant experience.

Moreover, the Azure dashboard evolves with the needs of its users. Regular updates and enhancements mean that new features, services, and optimizations are continuously being added. This ensures that the dashboard remains a dynamic and evolving space that aligns with the current trends and requirements of cloud computing.

One of the subtle yet powerful aspects of the Azure dashboard is its ability to educate while facilitating tasks. Integrated help options and tooltips provide context and assistance, subtly guiding users through various functionalities. This integration of support and learning resources ensures that users have the help they need without having to leave the task at hand.

Collaboration is another aspect where the Azure dashboard shines. Users can share dashboards, ensuring that teams have a unified view of the resources and metrics that matter to them. This collaborative approach ensures that everyone is on the same page, fostering teamwork and collective problem-solving.

Security and compliance are embedded into the Azure dashboard, allowing users to manage access, set permissions, and ensure that all activities align with organizational policies and standards. From configuring role-based access control to monitoring activity logs, the dashboard provides the tools needed to ensure a secure and compliant environment.

As we delve deeper into the nuances of the Azure dashboard, it's clear that it is designed to be much more than just a launchpad for resources. It is an intelligent, customizable, and user-centric interface that aims to streamline, simplify, and enhance the way users interact with Azure services.

The Azure dashboard is an ever-evolving space that adapts and grows with the needs of its users. From the customizable layout to the intuitive navigation, every aspect is designed to offer a seamless and enriching experience. By understanding the intricacies of this interface, users can unlock its full potential and navigate the vast and exciting world of Azure with ease and confidence.

Embarking on a journey through Microsoft Azure, you'll find that customizing and organizing the portal interface is akin to tailoring a suit to fit perfectly, ensuring that every element aligns with your preferences and needs. The Azure portal is designed to be a highly customizable space, allowing users to tailor their experiences and streamline their workflows. By diving into the customization options available, one can transform the Azure portal into a personalized command center that enhances productivity and simplifies navigation.

The first aspect you might notice when you log into the Azure portal is the dashboard, a central area that serves as your home base. Here, you can pin various resources, services, and other elements to have them readily accessible. Think of it as placing your favorite tools on a workbench, ready to be used at a moment's notice. Customizing this space ensures that you have immediate access to the tools and resources you use most frequently.

A key feature that enhances the customization experience is the ability to create multiple dashboards. Each dashboard can be dedicated to a specific project or task, allowing you to compartmentalize your work and focus on one thing at a time. For example, you might have a dashboard dedicated to virtual machines and another for monitoring and analytics. This level of organization can be incredibly beneficial in maintaining a clear and focused workspace.

An interesting aspect of customizing the Azure portal is the freedom to change the visual appearance according to your preferences. The portal offers theme options that let you adjust the colors and layout, ensuring a comfortable and visually appealing experience. Subtle adjustments, such as switching to a dark theme or changing the menu positioning, can make a significant difference in how you interact with the platform.

The flexibility of the Azure portal extends to the way you interact with data and information. You can resize, reposition, and modify the tiles on your dashboard, ensuring that the most critical information is always front and center. This customization ensures that you're not overwhelmed with data but instead are presented with what is most relevant to your tasks.

Customizing the sidebar is another way to streamline your navigation experience. By organizing the services and resources in an order that suits your workflow, you can minimize the time spent searching for specific items. This level of personalization ensures that the portal feels intuitive and familiar, aligning with your unique way of working.

The portal also allows for the creation of personalized views for various resources. For example, you can customize the columns in your resources list to display information that is pertinent to your tasks. This way, you can quickly glance at your resources and gather the information you need without delving into detailed pages.

The Azure portal also shines when it comes to collaborative customization. You can share your personalized dashboards with your team, ensuring that everyone has access to the same information and tools. This shared workspace fosters collaboration and ensures that teams can work cohesively and efficiently.

Customizing notifications and alerts is another aspect that can enhance your experience with the Azure portal. By setting up alerts and notifications that align with your priorities, you ensure that you're always informed about the status of your resources and services. This proactive approach ensures that you can respond quickly to any changes or issues that may arise.

Understanding and utilizing the Cloud Shell within the Azure portal can also enhance your customization experience. The Cloud Shell offers a command-line interface that allows you to manage your resources directly. Customizing your Cloud Shell experience, such as selecting your preferred shell or setting up persistent storage, can significantly boost your productivity.

The portal also offers a wealth of extensions and add-ons that can be integrated to further enhance and customize your experience. These extensions can range from additional monitoring tools to integrations with third-party services. By carefully selecting and integrating these extensions, you can build an environment that perfectly caters to your needs and preferences.

Customizing and organizing the Azure portal is not just about aesthetics and layout; it's also about optimizing your workflow and boosting your productivity. By taking the time to understand and utilize the customization options available, you can transform the portal into a space that feels uniquely yours.

This personalized environment not only simplifies navigation but also fosters a sense of familiarity and ease of use. The Azure portal becomes an ally in your cloud journey, adapting to your needs and preferences. The time and effort invested in customizing the interface pay off by allowing you to work more efficiently and effectively.

As you continue to explore and use the Azure portal, your needs may evolve, and the portal is ready to evolve with you. The customization options are not set in stone but are flexible and can be adjusted as your projects and preferences change. This dynamic and adaptable nature ensures that the Azure portal remains a valuable and personalized tool throughout your cloud journey.

In essence, the ability to customize and organize the Azure portal is a testament to Microsoft's commitment to providing a user-centric experience. By empowering users to tailor the interface to their needs, Azure ensures that each individual can navigate the cloud in a way that feels intuitive and natural. Through customization, the portal becomes an extension of your workspace, a tailored environment where you can thrive and excel in your cloud endeavors.

Chapter 5: Building Blocks of Azure: Understanding Resource Groups and Resources

Defining and creating resource groups in Microsoft Azure is a process akin to organizing a toolbox, ensuring that each tool is placed thoughtfully for ease of access and optimal use. In Azure, a resource group is a logical container that holds related resources for an Azure solution. Just like a well-organized toolbox, a resource group ensures that you can find, manage, and organize your resources efficiently.

When you think about a resource group, consider it as a strategy to manage and organize your Azure resources coherently. By grouping related resources that share a similar lifecycle, you create an environment that is easy to monitor, manage, and maintain. The concept of resource groups stems from the need for simplicity and cohesiveness in cloud management.

The process of defining a resource group begins with understanding the resources that need to be grouped together. These could be virtual machines, databases, web apps, or other services that work in tandem to deliver a solution. By identifying the resources that share a commonality in purpose and lifecycle, you lay the foundation for an effective resource group.

Once you've identified the resources, creating a resource group is a straightforward process within the Azure portal. The portal provides an intuitive interface that guides you through the steps of creating a new resource group. During this process, you'll need to specify details such as the resource group's name, its subscription, and the region it will be associated with.

The name you choose for a resource group should be descriptive and indicative of the resources it contains or the solution it represents. This ensures that when you or your colleagues look at the resource group, its purpose is immediately clear. Just like naming a file folder on your computer, choosing a clear and descriptive name keeps things organized and easy to navigate.

The subscription and region are equally important aspects to consider while creating a resource group. By associating the resource group with a specific subscription, you ensure that the costs and usage are tracked accurately. The choice of region determines where the metadata about the resource group will be stored, although it's important to note that the resources within the group can reside in different regions.

Defining the resources that will be part of your resource group also involves considering factors such as dependencies, access control, and policies. By thoughtfully categorizing resources that have similar dependencies, you can simplify management tasks and streamline deployments. For instance, a web app and its associated database could be placed in the same resource group because of their interdependence.

Access control is another aspect that is simplified by effective resource group creation. By defining access policies at the resource group level, you ensure a consistent and secure approach to managing permissions. This approach allows you to grant, modify, or revoke access to all resources within a group, thus maintaining security and compliance.

One of the appealing aspects of resource groups is that they facilitate the application of policies uniformly across all contained resources. This means that if you have specific compliance requirements or need to enforce certain rules, these can be applied at the resource group level. This uniformity ensures consistency and can significantly reduce the chances of oversight or misconfiguration.

Creating a resource group also offers opportunities for optimizing cost management. By grouping resources that share a lifecycle, you can manage costs effectively by monitoring the collective usage and expenditure for that group. This method provides a consolidated view of costs and can be helpful in budgeting and optimizing resource utilization.

Resource groups also simplify the process of deploying, updating, or deleting resources. When you deploy a template to a resource group, Azure takes care of orchestrating the deployment of the individual resources in the correct order. If you need to update or delete resources, doing so at the resource group level ensures that the changes are propagated uniformly, saving time and reducing complexity.

Beyond the technical aspects, defining and creating resource groups is also about adopting best practices for cloud management. By thoughtfully structuring your resources and organizing them into coherent groups, you foster a culture of clarity and efficiency. The resource groups become a reflection of your approach to cloud management, emphasizing organization and strategic grouping.

The beauty of resource groups lies in their flexibility and the ease with which they can be modified. As your project evolves, you may find that the composition of a resource group needs to change. Azure allows you to easily add or remove resources from a group, ensuring that your resource groups can adapt and evolve alongside your projects.

In essence, resource groups are a manifestation of the principle that good organization is a precursor to efficiency and effectiveness. By defining and creating resource groups thoughtfully, you create an environment that is not only technically sound but also easy to navigate and manage. This practice transforms the Azure portal into a space that mirrors your understanding of your projects and solutions.

In your journey with Azure, as you define and create resource groups, you'll find that these logical containers become indispensable in managing your cloud resources. They provide structure, foster security, facilitate cost management, and simplify deployments. By embracing the practice of creating thoughtful and well-defined resource groups, you position yourself for a seamless and productive experience in the Azure ecosystem.

Embarking on the exploration of common Azure resources is akin to stepping into a vibrant marketplace, each stall offering a unique and essential service designed to augment your cloud experience. Azure provides a rich set of resources and services that cater to a variety of needs, spanning from computing and storage to networking and artificial intelligence. Let's delve into the heart of this bustling marketplace and explore some of the common resources that Azure has to offer.

Azure Virtual Machines (VMs) are one of the most familiar resources to those venturing into the cloud. Like powerful computers that you can rent, VMs allow you to run applications, host data, and scale your operations with ease. These versatile machines come in different shapes and sizes, tailored to suit specific workloads, ensuring that there's always a perfect fit for your needs.

Complementing VMs, Azure Blob Storage steps in as a reliable companion for storing vast amounts of unstructured data. Be it documents, images, or videos, Blob Storage offers a convenient and scalable solution to ensure that your data is safe and accessible. The flexibility it brings to the table allows for seamless integration with various applications and services.

Venturing further, Azure SQL Database introduces itself as a fully managed relational database service, offering a robust and scalable environment for your data storage needs. It simplifies the process of managing databases by taking care of backups, updates, and scaling, allowing you to focus on creating exceptional applications.

Azure App Service enters the scene as a platform for hosting web applications, mobile app backends, and RESTful APIs. With built-in infrastructure management, it ensures that deploying and scaling web applications is a breeze. It supports a variety of programming languages and integrates seamlessly with other Azure services.

The Azure Marketplace is brimming with more specialized resources, such as Azure Kubernetes Service (AKS), which offers a managed environment for deploying, managing, and scaling containerized applications. AKS simplifies the complex tasks associated with orchestrating containers, thus easing the journey of developers venturing into microservices architectures.

Azure Functions, a serverless compute service, introduces a paradigm where you can write, deploy, and run event-driven functions without worrying about infrastructure. This resource is all about focusing on the code while Azure takes care of the underlying platform, scaling, and maintenance.

In the realm of networking, Azure Virtual Network stands out as a critical resource, offering an isolated and highly secure environment to run virtual machines and applications. It empowers users to create their own private networks in Azure and connect them to on-premises data centers, crafting a cohesive and secure network experience.

Azure Active Directory, often encountered on this journey, is a comprehensive identity and access management solution.

It ensures secure access to applications and resources, enhancing security through multi-factor authentication and conditional access policies.

For those with an inclination towards artificial intelligence, Azure Cognitive Services extends a warm welcome. It provides a suite of APIs and services that bring AI within the reach of every developer, without requiring machine learning expertise. From vision and speech to language and decision-making, Cognitive Services has a treasure trove of capabilities.

Azure DevOps Services is another common resource that often catches the eye. It offers a set of development tools, services, and features that enable teams to plan, develop, test, and deliver software with speed and quality. This suite fosters collaboration and enhances the software development lifecycle.

As we stroll through this rich marketplace, we encounter Azure Logic Apps, which enables the creation of automated workflows between apps and services. Logic Apps simplifies the process of designing workflows, allowing you to automate tasks and processes seamlessly.

Azure Redis Cache is a delightful addition to the collection of resources, enhancing application performance by allowing you to retrieve data from a fast, managed, in-memory cache, rather than relying solely on slower disk-based databases. It offers a swift and efficient mechanism to enhance application responsiveness.

Azure's Content Delivery Network (CDN) is another resource designed to optimize the delivery of web content and applications to users. By caching content at strategic locations, it ensures that users experience minimal latency and receive data swiftly and efficiently.

The Azure Security Center is akin to a vigilant sentinel, providing advanced threat protection across all Azure services. It offers tools to monitor, manage, and ensure the security of resources, thereby fostering a secure and compliant cloud environment.

Azure Event Hubs emerges as a fully managed, real-time data ingestion service that allows you to stream millions of events per second. It caters to the needs of big data and real-time analytics, providing a unified platform to ingest and process massive streams of data.

Azure's API Management service is like a maestro orchestrating seamless interactions between various applications and services. It enables developers to create, manage, secure, and scale APIs, ensuring that applications can communicate and transact smoothly.

In the realm of analytics, Azure Synapse Analytics presents itself as an integrated analytics service that accelerates the process of extracting insights from data. It brings together big data and data warehousing, creating a seamless environment for analytics.

As we explore, we encounter Azure Monitor, which offers full-stack monitoring, advanced analytics, and intelligent insights to ensure the performance and availability of applications. It acts as a vigilant guardian, ensuring that your resources are always performing optimally.

While this journey through the Azure marketplace is brief, it offers a glimpse into the diversity and richness of resources available. Each resource, meticulously crafted, plays a unique role in solving distinct challenges. Together, they weave a tapestry of services and solutions that enable businesses and developers to build, deploy, and scale applications with unprecedented ease and flexibility. Embracing Azure is not just about adopting a cloud platform, but about stepping into a world replete with possibilities, innovation, and continuous evolution.

Chapter 6: Delving into Basic Azure Services

Azure Virtual Machines, or VMs, open up a realm of possibilities in the cloud, offering flexibility, scalability, and control in deploying applications and workloads. With Azure VMs, you have the convenience of choosing the operating system, configuring custom settings, and tailoring the environment to your specific needs. These virtual machines, running in Microsoft's Azure cloud, offer a wide array of options suited for different tasks, from hosting websites to running data-intensive applications.

Understanding the essence of a virtual machine is akin to appreciating the beauty of having a dedicated computer, right at your fingertips, but located remotely in a secure data center. Azure VMs are an emulation of physical computers, replicating the same environment and offering similar functionality. They come with processors, memory, storage, and networking resources, while allowing you to choose from a variety of hardware configurations and specifications.

When you create an Azure VM, it's like setting up a new computer tailored to your preferences. You select the operating system, be it Windows, Linux, or any other supported OS, and decide on the hardware specifications, such as the amount of memory and storage. The magic of Azure VMs lies in this personalization, allowing you to tailor the virtual environment to the specific needs of your applications.

One of the most compelling aspects of Azure VMs is their scalability. With Azure, you can easily scale your resources up or down based on your workload's demands. If your application experiences a sudden surge in traffic, you can quickly scale up your VMs to accommodate the increased load, ensuring smooth performance and a positive user experience.

The range of VM sizes and types in Azure caters to diverse workloads. From general-purpose VMs that offer a balance of compute, memory, and storage to compute-optimized VMs that are ideal for heavy computational tasks, Azure has you covered. There are also memory-optimized VMs suitable for applications that demand more memory, like databases and caching servers.

Security is a paramount concern, and Azure VMs come equipped with robust security features. Azure provides tools and services that help you secure your virtual machines and the data within them. Network security groups can be used to control inbound and outbound traffic to network interfaces, while Azure Identity and Access Management ensures secure and scoped access to your resources.

Moreover, Azure offers features such as Azure Backup and Azure Site Recovery to protect your data and applications from loss and outages. These services enable you to create backups and devise disaster recovery strategies to ensure your applications remain resilient in the face of unforeseen circumstances.

The ease of management is another hallmark of Azure VMs. Azure provides intuitive tools and interfaces such as the Azure Portal, Azure PowerShell, and Azure CLI that make managing VMs a straightforward task. With a few clicks or commands, you can create, start, stop, and delete VMs, allowing you to focus more on your applications and less on infrastructure management.

One of the exciting aspects of Azure VMs is their seamless integration with other Azure services. For instance, you can easily connect your VMs to Azure Blob Storage to store large amounts of unstructured data or use Azure SQL Database to handle your relational data needs. This integration ensures a cohesive and streamlined experience.

Azure VMs also provide cost savings over traditional physical hardware. With Azure's pay-as-you-go model, you only pay for what you use, eliminating the need for upfront capital expenditure on hardware. This model provides flexibility and allows businesses to adapt to changing needs without being weighed down by heavy investments.

The customization possibilities with Azure VMs extend beyond just choosing the operating system and hardware specifications. Azure VM extensions allow you to configure additional settings, install software, and run scripts on your VMs. These extensions enable you to automate post-deployment tasks and configurations, ensuring that your VMs are tailored to your exact requirements.

Azure also offers the possibility of using pre-configured VM images from the Azure Marketplace. These images come with pre-installed applications and configurations, making it easy to deploy specific software environments. From databases and developer tools to security solutions, the Azure Marketplace offers a variety of software that can be deployed on your VMs with just a few clicks.

Monitoring and maintaining the performance of your Azure VMs is facilitated by tools such as Azure Monitor and Azure Security Center. These tools provide insights into the operations, health, and performance of your VMs, offering actionable intelligence to ensure optimal functioning.

Understanding Azure VMs is a journey that unfolds the convenience of having a powerful, customizable, and secure computing environment at your disposal. Whether you are deploying a single website or orchestrating a complex set of microservices, Azure VMs stand ready to empower your endeavors.

By tapping into the potential of Azure VMs, businesses and developers are freed from the constraints of physical hardware, allowing them to innovate, experiment, and scale with unprecedented agility. The versatility, security, and ease of management that Azure VMs provide make them an indispensable tool in the modern cloud-centric world.

In essence, Azure Virtual Machines encapsulate the promise of the cloud: endless possibilities, boundless scalability, and the freedom to create and innovate. With each VM tailored to fit like a well-crafted suit, every workload finds its home, every application its playground, and every innovation its stage. Embracing Azure VMs is not just a technological choice but a strategic decision that propels organizations and individuals towards achieving more, all while being cradled in the secure, efficient, and ever-evolving ecosystem that is Microsoft Azure. Azure Web Apps and App Services are game changers in the world of web application development and deployment, offering a multitude of features designed to streamline the entire process. With Azure Web Apps, the task of setting up, deploying, and scaling web applications becomes incredibly straightforward, allowing developers to focus on coding and innovation while leaving the infrastructure management to Azure. These services provide a fully managed platform, enabling the creation of powerful cloud-based web applications that are both robust and scalable.

The ease of deploying a web application using Azure Web Apps is one of its most alluring features. Whether you're working with .NET, Java, Node.js, Python, or PHP, Azure Web Apps is designed to support a diverse range of programming languages and frameworks. This inclusivity ensures that developers can continue using their preferred tools and technologies while taking advantage of the benefits offered by Azure.

One of the first aspects that you'll notice with Azure Web Apps is the elimination of the need to manage server infrastructure. The underlying hardware, network, and operating system are all abstracted away, leaving you free to concentrate on your application's code and functionality. Azure takes care of all the routine maintenance tasks, such as patching, updates, and security, saving valuable time and resources.

Azure Web Apps is part of the larger suite of services known as Azure App Service, which is designed to aid developers in building, hosting, and scaling web applications and APIs. Azure App Service integrates various services and features that enhance the development experience. It includes built-in development operations, automated patching, staging environments, custom domain and SSL configuration, and scaling options that make the deployment of web applications seamless and efficient.

The auto-scaling feature in Azure App Service is particularly noteworthy. It allows your application to automatically adjust the number of VM instances that run your app, ensuring that the demand is met without over-provisioning resources. This not only optimizes cost but also ensures that your application can handle fluctuations in traffic gracefully.

Azure Web Apps and App Services are designed with continuous integration and continuous deployment (CI/CD) in mind. With support for popular platforms like GitHub, Bitbucket, and Azure DevOps, developers can set up a fully automated pipeline that takes their code from repository to production with minimal manual intervention. Every code push can trigger a build and deployment process, ensuring that your application is always up-to-date with the latest changes.

Integration with various Azure services further enhances the capabilities of your web applications. For instance, Azure

Web Apps can easily connect to Azure SQL Database, Azure Blob Storage, and Cosmos DB, thereby providing a wide array of data storage and retrieval options. Similarly, integration with Azure Cognitive Services can empower your applications with artificial intelligence capabilities, such as image recognition and natural language processing.

One often overlooked but incredibly beneficial feature is the ability to use custom domains and secure sockets layer (SSL) certificates with Azure Web Apps. This provides a professional touch to your web applications, ensuring that they are accessible via a custom domain and secured with industry-standard encryption.

Monitoring and diagnostics are vital for the health and performance of any application, and Azure Web Apps provides a rich set of tools for this purpose. Services such as Azure Monitor and Application Insights can be used to keep an eye on your application's performance and troubleshoot any issues that may arise. These tools provide insights into request execution times, error trends, server health, and more, all of which are crucial for maintaining a high-performing web application.

Developers looking to build and deploy mobile backends find a valuable ally in Azure App Service. With support for offline sync, push notifications, and seamless integration with mobile-specific data stores, Azure App Service simplifies the task of building mobile application backends.

Azure Web Apps also offer support for Docker containers, which means that you can package your application along with its dependencies into a container and deploy it on Azure. This containerization ensures that your application runs the same way, regardless of where it's deployed, and provides an additional layer of flexibility and portability.

Environment variables and application settings can be easily configured directly from the Azure Portal, allowing developers to customize the behavior of their applications without changing the code. These settings are securely stored and can be accessed by your application at runtime.

For those who wish to run background tasks alongside their web applications, Azure Web Jobs provide a convenient way to run scripts or programs as background services. These jobs can be triggered in various ways, including on a schedule, thereby providing additional functionality to your web applications.

Azure Web Apps and App Services aren't just about deploying code and forgetting about it. They are about creating a dynamic, flexible, and scalable environment where your web applications can thrive. From the smallest of startups to the largest enterprises, the ease of use, extensive feature set, and robustness of Azure Web Apps make it a preferred choice for web application hosting.

Exploring Azure Web Apps and App Services is akin to opening a treasure chest of capabilities and features designed to make a developer's life easier. These services represent a confluence of convenience, functionality, and innovation. By taking care of the mundane aspects of web hosting, they free up developers to focus on creating remarkable web applications that can scale and evolve with ease.

In the realm of cloud computing, where agility and speed are of the essence, Azure Web Apps and App Services stand out as invaluable tools. They encapsulate the spirit of what cloud computing aims to achieve: unburdening developers from infrastructure management, offering scalable and reliable hosting solutions, and providing a rich ecosystem of integrations and features. Embracing these services is a step towards efficient, modern, and agile web application development and deployment.

Chapter 7: Ensuring Security and Compliance: Azure Policies and Blueprints

The implementation of Azure Policies is a key step towards establishing effective governance across your cloud resources. Azure Policies are used to enforce organizational requirements and to ensure that your resources comply with certain standards and practices. By creating and applying policies, you can ensure consistency, improve security, and optimize costs across your Azure environment.

At the heart of Azure Policies is the concept of "policy definitions". These definitions describe the rules and effects that are applied to resources during the creation or update process. Each policy definition expresses what is allowed or disallowed under certain conditions. These definitions can then be assigned to different scopes, such as a management group, subscription, or resource group, providing flexibility in how policies are applied.

Creating an Azure Policy begins with defining the conditions under which it should be enforced and the effect that should take place when those conditions are met. For example, you could create a policy that prohibits the creation of public-facing storage accounts or one that ensures all virtual machines have a specific tag. These rules are expressed using a structured language, and Azure provides a variety of built-in policy definitions to get started.

When crafting a policy definition, you specify the parameters, rules, and the desired effect. Parameters allow you to reuse the same policy definition across different scenarios, providing you with the flexibility to tailor your policies to different requirements. Rules define the logical conditions that trigger the enforcement of the policy, while the effect dictates what action will be taken when the conditions are met, such as denying the request or auditing the resource.

Once a policy definition is created, it needs to be assigned to take effect. This is done through a "policy assignment", which specifies the scope and parameters for the policy. The scope could be an entire subscription or a specific resource group. This granularity ensures that you can enforce governance according to the specific needs of different departments, projects, or environments within your organization.

One of the benefits of Azure Policies is that they enable you to perform compliance assessments across your resources. By examining your resources against your policies, Azure can determine whether your environment adheres to your organization's standards and practices. The results of this assessment can be viewed through the Azure Policy Compliance blade, offering insights into the current state of your resources and any adjustments that may be necessary.

For organizations that have more complex governance needs, Azure Policy also allows the creation of initiatives. An initiative is a collection of policy definitions grouped together to achieve a larger governance goal. For example, an initiative could include policies to enforce naming conventions, apply certain tags, and restrict the locations where resources can be created. By grouping these policies together under a single initiative, you can streamline the assignment and management of policies.

Azure Policies also support the concept of exemptions. There are scenarios where certain resources or resource groups may need to be exempt from a policy or an initiative. Azure Policy allows you to create policy exemptions, which let you exclude a specific scope from the evaluation of policy assignments.

In the pursuit of automating governance, Azure Policies can be complemented by using Azure Blueprints. Azure Blueprints allow you to define a repeatable set of resources and configurations, including policies and role assignments, and then deploy these in a consistent manner across different subscriptions. By combining policies and blueprints, you can create an environment that is both compliant and easily replicable.

Implementing Azure Policies requires careful consideration and planning. It is important to evaluate the existing infrastructure, understand the compliance requirements, and engage stakeholders in the process. Often, it is advisable to start with a small set of policies and then gradually expand as you become more familiar with your governance needs.

Periodic review and adjustment of your policies is also essential. As your organization evolves, so too will your governance requirements. Regularly revisiting your policies ensures that they remain relevant and effective in maintaining the desired state of your resources.

Additionally, communication and education are crucial components of successful policy implementation. Ensuring that your team is aware of the policies in place and understands their purpose and impact can lead to smoother adoption and fewer instances of non-compliance.

Monitoring and auditing play an integral role in the governance process. Azure Policies provide logs and reports that can be analyzed to gain insights into compliance levels, policy effects, and potential areas of improvement. These insights can be invaluable in fine-tuning your policies and addressing any gaps in your governance strategy.

Azure Policies are not just a tool for enforcing rules; they are a mechanism for embedding best practices and compliance into the very fabric of your cloud environment. By strategically implementing Azure Policies, you elevate your governance efforts from being a reactive endeavor to a proactive strategy that ensures consistency, security, and optimal resource utilization.

In essence, Azure Policies empower organizations to manage their cloud resources effectively. By defining and enforcing specific criteria and rules, organizations can ensure that their Azure deployments are aligned with their governance, risk management, and compliance goals. In the ever-evolving landscape of cloud computing, having a robust and flexible tool like Azure Policies is instrumental in navigating the complexities of governance while reaping the benefits of the cloud.

Utilizing Azure Blueprints for compliance is akin to having a well-drawn map that guides you through the intricacies of setting up compliant environments. Azure Blueprints is a service that enables cloud architects and central information technology groups to define a repeatable set of Azure resources that adheres to organizational standards, patterns, and compliance requirements. Azure Blueprints make it easier to deploy fully governed subscriptions, ensuring that your environments are compliant with internal policies and external regulations from the start.

The beauty of Azure Blueprints lies in its ability to orchestrate the deployment of various resource templates and configurations in concert. It's like composing a symphony, where each musician plays their part at the right time to create a harmonious melody. In the context of Azure, this melody is a compliant and well-governed environment.

An Azure Blueprint is a declarative way of orchestrating the deployment of various services such as Azure Resource Manager templates, Azure Policy assignments, role-based access controls, and more. By packaging these components together, you can ensure that they are deployed in a consistent manner, effectively reducing the likelihood of errors or misconfigurations.

When you create an Azure Blueprint, you are essentially drafting a design that outlines the scaffolding of your environment. This design includes all the resources and configurations necessary to meet your specific compliance requirements. For instance, if you are setting up an environment that must adhere to a specific regulatory framework, you can design a blueprint that includes all the necessary policies, role assignments, and resource configurations required to meet those standards.

One of the standout features of Azure Blueprints is the ability to version your designs. Just as a cityscape may change and evolve over time, so too will your compliance requirements and best practices. Versioning allows you to keep pace with these changes without disrupting your existing environments. When you update a blueprint, the changes can be seamlessly rolled out across your subscriptions, ensuring that your environments evolve and adapt as necessary.

Assigning a blueprint to a subscription is like setting the wheels in motion. Once assigned, Azure Blueprints deploys and configures the resources as per the design you've crafted. This assignment process can also be parameterized, allowing you to tweak certain elements for different deployments while still adhering to the overall design and compliance requirements.

The ability to lock resources is another facet of Azure Blueprints that helps maintain compliance. Once a blueprint is assigned and the resources are deployed, you can apply a 'read-only' lock to prevent any modifications to those resources. This ensures that the environment remains in a compliant state and is immune to changes that might violate regulatory standards.

Tracking and monitoring compliance post-deployment is also a critical aspect of governance. Azure Blueprints facilitates this through detailed tracking and auditing features. Each assignment is logged and can be audited to ensure that it adheres to the prescribed blueprint. In cases where drift is detected, you can take corrective action to bring the environment back into compliance.

By providing a visual representation of your environment's architecture, Azure Blueprints helps demystify complex compliance requirements. For stakeholders who may not be deeply versed in the technical aspects of cloud governance, this visual approach can aid in understanding and ensuring that the desired compliance controls are in place.

Imagine the scenario where an organization needs to set up multiple environments that adhere to the same set of compliance requirements. Without Azure Blueprints, this could be a labor-intensive task, fraught with the risk of inconsistency and error. However, with Azure Blueprints, this process becomes streamlined and efficient. The blueprint serves as a template, ensuring uniformity and compliance across all deployments.

Azure Blueprints also enable organizations to maintain a repository of compliant solutions ready to be deployed as needed. This repository can be thought of as a library of blueprints, each tailored to meet a specific regulatory framework or organizational standard. When a new environment is needed, the right blueprint can be selected and deployed with confidence, knowing that it will meet the necessary criteria.

The seamless integration of Azure Blueprints with other Azure services enhances its effectiveness. For example, integration with Azure Policy ensures that policies are enforced at scale across multiple subscriptions. Similarly, integration with Azure Resource Manager templates ensures that resources are provisioned in a consistent and compliant manner.

In the journey towards achieving compliance in the cloud, Azure Blueprints acts as a reliable ally. It simplifies the complexities associated with deploying and managing compliant environments. By automating the deployment of resources and configurations, it ensures consistency and saves time, allowing you to focus on deriving value from your cloud investments.

Azure Blueprints are more than just a set of instructions; they represent a shift towards a more proactive and governance-focused approach to cloud management. By embedding compliance and governance into the very fabric of your cloud deployments, Azure Blueprints ensure that your journey in the cloud is secure, compliant, and aligned with your organizational goals.

In essence, Azure Blueprints allow you to craft a compliant foundation on which you can build your cloud experiences. This foundation ensures that regardless of the scale or complexity of your deployments, compliance is not an afterthought but an integral part of the process.

Chapter 8: Monitoring and Management Essentials

Embarking on a journey to explore the fundamentals of Azure Monitor and Alerts takes us into the realm of proactive and insightful management of applications, infrastructure, and network on the Microsoft Azure platform. Azure Monitor is a comprehensive service that provides advanced analytics and intelligent alerting, turning a flood of data into actionable insights. By capturing, analyzing, and acting on telemetry data from your Azure resources, Azure Monitor becomes the eyes and ears of your cloud environment.

Azure Monitor is adept at collecting data from a variety of sources, including application logs, operating system diagnostics, and network traffic. It becomes an invaluable tool in ensuring the performance and availability of your applications and infrastructure. It sifts through this sea of data to identify patterns, trends, and anomalies that could be indicative of underlying issues or opportunities for optimization.

The essence of Azure Monitor is its ability to create a unified view of an entire environment. It does this by aggregating data in a centralized space called Log Analytics workspace. Within this workspace, you can run complex queries, analyze data, and create visualizations that paint a clear picture of the state of your resources.

Azure Monitor doesn't just stop at capturing and visualizing data. It takes a step further by providing the ability to set up alerts, which serve as a mechanism to notify you when certain conditions are met. For example, you can set up an alert to notify you when CPU usage on a virtual machine crosses a certain threshold, or when the response time of a web application exceeds acceptable limits.

When an alert is triggered, it can initiate a variety of actions such as sending an email notification, triggering an Azure Function, or calling a webhook. This flexibility ensures that you can tailor your response mechanisms to the specific needs and workflows of your organization.

Understanding the relationship between metrics and logs in Azure Monitor is crucial. Metrics are numerical values that describe some aspect of a system at a particular point in time, whereas logs are different; they contain different kinds of data organized into records with different sets of properties for each type. Both are fundamental to the monitoring process, with metrics often used for alerting and fast detection of issues, while logs are used for detailed analysis and diagnostics.

Azure Monitor integrates seamlessly with Application Insights, providing detailed insights into your application's operations and aiding in the diagnosis of errors without affecting the user's experience. It enables you to inspect your application's distributed traces, allowing you to understand any anomalies or bottlenecks in your application's workflow.

Another key aspect of Azure Monitor is its ability to automate responses to alerts. This is accomplished using Action Groups, which define a collection of actions to execute when an alert is triggered. These actions could range from sending an email or SMS message to more complex tasks like running an Azure Function or Logic App.

Azure Monitor is designed to be extensible and integrates seamlessly with a wide array of tools and platforms. Whether you're using popular SIEM solutions like Splunk or using visualization tools like Grafana, Azure Monitor can feed data into these tools to enable more sophisticated analysis and reporting.

Leveraging Azure Monitor's capabilities, organizations can implement a robust and proactive monitoring strategy. By being alerted to issues before they affect users, and by having rich data at their fingertips, teams can troubleshoot issues faster, minimizing downtime and improving user satisfaction.

Azure Alerts, on the other hand, are conditions or thresholds set by the user, and when data surpasses these thresholds, an alert is triggered. These alerts act as an early warning system, helping you identify and rectify issues before they escalate.

One of the strengths of Azure Monitor and Alerts is its ability to offer granular control over your monitoring needs. You can create alerts for nearly any condition, and the service ensures that you're notified in real-time, allowing you to take corrective action promptly.

An important component to understand within Azure Monitor is Kusto Query Language (KQL), which is used to extract, analyze, and report data from your logs. By writing KQL queries, you can create custom monitoring scenarios tailored to your specific requirements.

The journey through Azure Monitor and Alerts reveals a landscape where data is transformed into insight, and insight leads to action. It offers peace of mind by providing the tools needed to ensure your applications and infrastructure are performing optimally.

In an era where downtime can lead to significant financial and reputational losses, having a tool like Azure Monitor becomes not just beneficial but essential. By continuously keeping an eye on your resources, analyzing the enormous amount of data generated, and alerting you at the first sign of trouble, Azure Monitor stands as a vigilant guardian of your cloud environment.

In summary, the exploration of Azure Monitor and Alerts brings to light the importance of proactive monitoring in a cloud environment. By understanding and leveraging the features and capabilities of Azure Monitor, organizations can ensure the health, performance, and compliance of their applications and infrastructure in Azure.

Navigating the world of cloud computing, it becomes evident that the proficient management of resources and diligent health checks are fundamental practices that underpin successful cloud operations. Efficient resource management in the cloud is akin to conducting a well-orchestrated symphony where each component, from virtual machines to databases, must play in harmony to create a seamless experience. It's about ensuring that your resources are not just available but are operating at their optimal capacity and are readily scalable to meet the demands of your applications and services.

When discussing resource management, the conversation naturally gravitates towards understanding how to allocate, deallocate, and monitor resources within your cloud environment. This entails a deep dive into resource provisioning, where you carefully select the type, size, and quantity of resources needed for your workloads. An integral part of this is being mindful of not over-provisioning, which can lead to unnecessary costs, or under-provisioning, which can result in performance bottlenecks.

In a cloud environment such as Microsoft Azure, resource management is facilitated through Azure Resource Manager (ARM), a robust management layer that allows users to create, update, and delete resources in their Azure account. ARM enables you to work with resources in your solution as a group, deploying, updating, and managing all resources cohesively and consistently.

Managing resources also involves understanding and managing dependencies, ensuring that resources that rely on each other are provisioned and managed in the correct sequence. For instance, a web application may depend on a database, and understanding this dependency is crucial for seamless operation.

Effective resource management is also about scaling, which could be either vertical, where you increase the capacity of your existing resources, or horizontal, where you add more resources to your pool. The cloud offers the flexibility to scale according to the changing demands, ensuring that the performance remains consistent while optimizing costs.

On the other hand, health checks are vital indicators of the well-being of your cloud resources. Regular health checks ensure that each component in your infrastructure is functioning correctly and efficiently. Just like a regular health checkup can detect and prevent potential medical issues, routine health checks in a cloud environment can help identify and rectify potential problems before they affect the performance or availability of your services.

Health checks often involve monitoring various metrics such as CPU usage, memory consumption, network latency, and more. For instance, an unexpected spike in CPU usage might indicate an underlying problem that needs to be addressed promptly.

In the context of web applications, health checks may involve sending requests to an endpoint and monitoring the response. If the application responds within the expected timeframe and with the correct data, it is considered healthy. On the contrary, if the application fails to respond or responds with an error, it may indicate an issue that warrants immediate attention.

Periodic health checks can be automated, and many cloud services provide tools and features to facilitate this. For example, Azure offers Azure Monitor, a service that provides full-stack monitoring, advanced analytics, and intelligent alerting for your cloud resources. It allows you to set up automated health checks and alerts, ensuring that you are immediately notified if any issues are detected.

Resource management and health checks are intertwined, as effective management of resources necessitates regular health checks. Similarly, the insights obtained from health checks can guide better resource management decisions, enabling optimal utilization and cost efficiency.

Understanding your resource utilization patterns can also lead to cost savings. For instance, if your health checks reveal that a certain resource is consistently underutilized, you may decide to downscale or even eliminate that resource to save costs.

In essence, mastering the basics of resource management and health checks sets the foundation for robust and resilient cloud operations. It allows organizations to deliver high-quality, reliable, and cost-effective services to their users.

An organization that gives due diligence to regular health checks and efficient resource management is like a well-oiled machine, ready to take on challenges and adapt to changes swiftly. By meticulously planning resources and regularly checking their health, organizations ensure not only the smooth functioning of their services but also long-term sustainability and growth.

While the landscape of cloud computing continues to evolve, the principles of vigilant resource management and health checks remain constant. They are the silent sentinels that ensure your cloud environment is not just surviving but thriving and evolving. Embracing these practices equips organizations with the foresight and agility needed to navigate the ever-changing cloud landscape.

In a world where the only constant is change, the ability to efficiently manage resources and ensure their health is not just a desirable skill but a necessity. By investing time and effort into understanding and implementing sound resource management and health check practices, organizations lay down a solid foundation upon which they can build and scale their cloud endeavors confidently.

Chapter 9: Cost Management and Billing

Azure's pricing and billing models may seem intricate at first, but once you grasp the basics, it becomes clear how they cater to different needs and workloads. Understanding the cost implications of deploying resources on Microsoft Azure is paramount to ensure that you're making the most out of your investments while optimizing expenses. The intricacies of Azure's pricing models are designed to offer flexibility and various options that can be tailored to suit the diverse requirements and budget constraints of organizations.

Diving into the realm of Azure pricing, one quickly realizes that the 'pay-as-you-go' model is at its core. This model is designed to ensure that users only pay for the resources they consume, avoiding any upfront costs or long-term commitments. This approach provides flexibility and makes it easier for businesses to adapt to changing needs without worrying about sunk costs.

Every resource within Azure has its pricing details meticulously laid out, with the costs often determined by factors such as the type, size, and location of the deployed resources. For instance, the cost of running a virtual machine will depend on factors like the VM's size, the operating system it runs, and the Azure region where it is deployed.

Azure offers a plethora of pricing calculators and tools designed to assist you in estimating the costs associated with various services. The Azure Pricing Calculator, for example, is a user-friendly tool that enables users to estimate the cost of Azure products based on their projected usage. By selecting and configuring services in this tool, one can get a clear picture of the potential expenditures.

Azure's pricing is also influenced by the chosen region where the resources are deployed. Different regions may have distinct pricing due to factors such as demand, local regulations, and infrastructure costs. By being mindful of the region selected for deploying resources, organizations can sometimes optimize costs.

Additionally, Azure provides options for reserved instances, allowing users to commit to one or three-year terms for specific resources. By making this commitment, users can avail significant discounts over the standard pay-as-you-go pricing model. Reserved instances can be a cost-effective choice for organizations that have predictable workloads and resource needs.

Yet another aspect of Azure's pricing model is the Azure Hybrid Benefit, which allows organizations with existing Microsoft licenses to utilize them on Azure, leading to cost savings. For organizations migrating from on-premises solutions to the cloud, this can represent substantial savings and ease the financial burden of the transition.

Azure Cost Management is a native Azure tool that provides insights into your cloud spending. It allows users to track cloud costs, optimize resources, and implement governance across their Azure resources. By using Azure Cost Management, organizations can identify underused resources that can be downscaled or eliminated, leading to potential cost reductions.

Billing in Azure is equally transparent, with invoices being generated that provide detailed insights into your consumption of Azure resources. The invoices categorize the costs by services, allowing you to analyze and understand where your budget is being allocated.

Understanding how Azure deals with data transfer costs is also essential. Typically, inbound data transfers, i.e., data moving into Azure data centers, are free, but outbound data transfers, i.e., data moving out of Azure data centers, are billed. Being aware of these data transfer costs is crucial for applications that require significant data exchange with external systems.

Azure also offers a wide array of support plans, each designed to meet different needs and budgets. These support plans range from basic plans that provide access to documentation and forums to more comprehensive and premium plans that include 24/7 access to Support Engineers.

Azure pricing and billing models also cater to developers and small enterprises by providing a set of free services every month as part of the Azure free account. These free services are a way for users to experiment and familiarize themselves with Azure without incurring costs.

Furthermore, Azure offers pricing for specific industries, ensuring compliance with industry-specific regulations while offering pricing that aligns with the industry's needs. For instance, Azure offers specific pricing and services for sectors like healthcare, education, and government.

Navigating Azure's pricing and billing intricacies can seem daunting, but with time, it becomes evident that the structure is designed to provide flexibility and cost optimization opportunities to organizations of all sizes. By understanding the different pricing options and models, organizations can strategically plan their cloud investments and make informed decisions that align with their budgetary constraints and operational needs.

Adopting cloud services is not merely about embracing technological advancement but also about understanding the financial implications and strategically planning the utilization of resources. Azure's transparent and flexible pricing and billing models ensure that organizations can tailor their cloud journey in alignment with their financial capacities.

Understanding Azure's pricing and billing models is akin to equipping oneself with a navigational compass that guides you through the cloud journey, ensuring that you are always in control of your expenditures and are making informed decisions. By strategically utilizing the array of tools, options, and models offered by Azure, organizations can turn their cloud endeavors into financially sound investments.

In the realm of cloud computing, where technological prowess must align with budgetary constraints, Azure's pricing and billing models stand as testaments to the platform's commitment to providing accessible and cost-effective solutions. It underscores the idea that the cloud is not just a technological leap but also a financially viable option for organizations eager to innovate and grow.

Embarking on a journey to effectively manage costs in any organization requires a strategic approach that is rooted in thoughtful planning, constant monitoring, and consistent optimization efforts. Regardless of the industry or size of the organization, having a comprehensive cost management strategy is imperative to ensure financial stability and long-term growth. Effective cost management is not about making indiscriminate cuts but about optimizing spending to achieve more with less.

To begin, understanding the nature of your costs is foundational to formulating an effective strategy. Costs can be broadly categorized as fixed, variable, or semi-variable. While fixed costs do not change with the volume of production, variable costs do, and semi-variable costs have elements of both. Gaining insights into how these costs behave allows organizations to make informed decisions and prioritize areas of focus.

A robust cost management strategy also involves setting clear and measurable objectives. Establishing what the organization aims to achieve in terms of cost reduction or optimization sets a direction for the initiatives. Aligning these objectives with the overall business goals ensures that cost management efforts contribute meaningfully to the organization's success.

Budgeting is a powerful tool in the realm of cost management. By creating detailed and realistic budgets, organizations can allocate resources judiciously and set benchmarks for performance. Budgets act as roadmaps that guide organizations through their financial landscape, ensuring that resources are allocated where they are needed most.

Visibility into costs is crucial for effective cost management. Implementing systems and technologies that provide real-time insights into spending can help organizations identify trends, detect anomalies, and make timely adjustments. Tools such as cloud-based financial software can be instrumental in providing this level of visibility and control.

Monitoring and controlling overhead costs is another important aspect of cost management. Overhead costs, which are not directly tied to production or service delivery, can sometimes escalate and need to be kept in check. Regularly reviewing these costs and identifying areas for potential savings can lead to substantial reductions over time.

Benchmarking against industry standards or competitors can provide valuable insights. By understanding how similar organizations manage their costs, you can identify areas where your organization might be overspending or underutilizing resources. Benchmarking can expose gaps in your strategy and open up opportunities for improvement.

Engaging employees in cost management efforts can also prove beneficial. Employees often have insights into inefficiencies and can suggest practical ways to reduce costs.

Fostering a culture of cost consciousness and encouraging employees to contribute ideas can lead to innovative solutions and foster a sense of ownership among the staff.

Evaluating and renegotiating contracts with suppliers and vendors is another strategy that can lead to cost savings. By seeking better terms or exploring alternative suppliers, organizations can often secure more favorable pricing and improve their cost structures.

Leveraging technology and automation can lead to significant cost reductions and efficiency gains. Automating repetitive tasks can not only reduce labor costs but also increase accuracy and free up employees to focus on more strategic activities. Investing in technology can sometimes require upfront costs but can lead to long-term savings and increased competitiveness.

Effective cost management also involves regular reviews and adjustments. The business environment is dynamic, and what worked yesterday may not be the most optimal solution today. Regularly reviewing your cost structures and being willing to adapt and change as necessary is crucial for maintaining an effective cost management strategy.

Additionally, it is important to consider the quality and value proposition of the products or services offered. Cost-cutting measures should not compromise the value delivered to the customers. Striking a balance between cost management and quality assurance is crucial to ensure customer satisfaction and loyalty.

Another strategy involves exploring opportunities for collaboration and partnerships. Sometimes, sharing resources or entering into strategic alliances can lead to cost reductions and create synergies that are beneficial for all parties involved.

A focus on process improvement methodologies, such as Lean or Six Sigma, can also contribute to effective cost management. These methodologies aim to reduce waste, improve efficiency, and enhance customer value, often leading to cost savings.

Emphasizing preventive measures, such as regular maintenance and quality checks, can also be a part of a cost-effective strategy. By preventing breakdowns or quality issues before they occur, organizations can avoid costly repairs and reputation damage.

It's also beneficial to adopt a long-term perspective in cost management strategies. While some cost-cutting measures may yield immediate savings, it is important to consider the long-term implications and sustainability of these measures.

When implementing cost management strategies, clear communication and transparency are key. Keeping stakeholders informed about why certain cost management measures are being implemented and how they align with the overall business goals can lead to better understanding and support.

Moreover, cost management is not a one-size-fits-all endeavor. Strategies need to be tailored to the unique needs, context, and goals of each organization. Customizing your approach and being open to learning and iterating are essential aspects of effective cost management.

In summary, effective cost management is an ongoing journey that requires a combination of strategic thinking, tactical implementation, and constant vigilance. By understanding the intricacies of costs, leveraging technology, fostering a culture of cost consciousness, and being adaptable to change, organizations can navigate their way to financial stability and success.

Chapter 10: Crafting Your Azure Journey

Embarking on the journey to master Microsoft Azure is akin to stepping into a world abundant with possibilities, where a plethora of tools and services are at your disposal to create, innovate, and solve problems. The path to Azure mastery is not a straight line but rather a winding road, filled with opportunities to deepen your understanding and enhance your skills. Let's explore how one can navigate this exciting path.

To start, understanding the foundational concepts of cloud computing is crucial. Familiarize yourself with the basics of Infrastructure as a Service (IaaS), Platform as a Service (PaaS), and Software as a Service (SaaS), along with key principles such as scalability, elasticity, and high availability. These concepts form the bedrock upon which your Azure knowledge will be built.

Once you've grasped the fundamentals of cloud computing, the next step is to dive into the core services offered by Azure. Explore Azure's computing services such as Virtual Machines, App Services, and Functions, which allow you to run applications in the cloud. Delve into storage solutions offered by Azure, such as Blob Storage and Azure SQL Database, and understand how they can cater to different data needs.

Networking is an essential aspect of cloud services, and gaining a good understanding of Azure's networking capabilities is imperative. Learn about Virtual Networks, VPN Gateways, and Azure Traffic Manager, and understand how these services ensure connectivity, reliability, and security.

Security and compliance are paramount in the cloud, and Azure provides a suite of tools to ensure your resources are protected. Explore Azure Active Directory, Network Security Groups, and Azure Policy to understand how to secure and govern your Azure resources.

As you become familiar with Azure's core services, it's time to explore more specialized services that cater to specific needs. Delve into Azure's AI and machine learning services, like Azure Machine Learning and Cognitive Services, which can enhance applications with intelligent features. Understand how Azure's Internet of Things (IoT) services, such as IoT Hub, can help you build solutions for connected devices.

Databases are central to many applications, and Azure offers a wide range of database services. Explore the differences and use cases for Azure SQL Database, Cosmos DB, and other database services to understand how to store and retrieve data effectively.

Developing applications to run in the cloud requires an understanding of DevOps practices and tools. Azure DevOps Services and GitHub provide a suite of tools to support continuous integration and continuous deployment (CI/CD). Learn how these tools can help streamline your development workflow and enhance collaboration.

Azure's analytics and big data services, such as Azure Synapse Analytics and Azure Databricks, are powerful tools for processing large volumes of data and gaining insights. Familiarize yourself with these services and understand how they can be used to drive data-driven decision-making.

As you delve deeper into Azure, it's essential to gain hands-on experience. Azure offers a free tier that allows you to experiment with services without incurring costs. Utilize this opportunity to create resources, experiment with configurations, and build sample projects.

While hands-on experience is crucial, theoretical knowledge is equally important. Microsoft offers a variety of certifications ranging from fundamentals to expert level. Preparing for these certifications can provide a structured learning path and validate your knowledge and skills.

Azure's versatility extends to supporting a wide range of programming languages. Whether you're comfortable with

.NET, Python, Java, or Node.js, Azure has tools and SDKs that cater to your preferred language. Familiarize yourself with the SDKs and tools available for your language of choice and understand how they can be used to interact with Azure services.

Staying updated with Azure's ever-evolving landscape is important. Microsoft regularly updates existing services and introduces new ones. Regularly check Azure updates, follow blogs, and participate in forums and communities to stay abreast of the latest developments.

Azure's documentation is a treasure trove of information. It provides detailed guides, tutorials, and best practices for using Azure services. Regularly consult the documentation to deepen your understanding and find solutions to problems.

Real-world problems often require the orchestration of multiple Azure services to create a solution. Challenge yourself by working on projects that require you to integrate several services and solve real-world problems.

Learning from others' experiences can be invaluable. Engage with the community, attend webinars, and participate in hackathons and meetups. Learning from use cases and experiences shared by others can provide insights that are hard to gain otherwise.

Teaching is a powerful tool for learning. Share your knowledge through blogs, videos, or social media. Explaining concepts to others can deepen your understanding and position you as a thought leader in the community.

Finally, remember that the path to Azure mastery is a continuous journey of learning and growing. The cloud landscape is dynamic, and there's always something new to learn. Embrace the journey with curiosity and enthusiasm, and you'll find that the path to Azure mastery is both rewarding and fulfilling.

Staying updated with Azure trends and updates is a crucial aspect of being an adept cloud professional. Microsoft Azure, being a dynamic cloud platform, evolves continually, with new services, features, and updates being rolled out frequently. Navigating this constant flow of information might seem overwhelming, but with the right approach, it can be an enriching experience. It's essential to understand that being conversant with the latest trends not only enhances your skills but also empowers you to leverage Azure's capabilities to the fullest.

One of the most straightforward ways to keep track of Azure updates is to regularly visit the Azure updates page. This dedicated page provides a comprehensive list of all the latest releases, updates, and announcements related to Azure services. It's a centralized hub that offers insights into what's new, what's been improved, and what's in the pipeline. Scanning through this page can be a quick way to stay abreast of the most recent developments.

Subscribing to Azure newsletters is another effective strategy. Newsletters, curated by both Microsoft and community enthusiasts, often bring together the most impactful updates, articles, and tutorials. They can serve as a convenient summary delivered straight to your inbox, saving you the time and effort to seek out information.

Engaging with the Azure blog is a beneficial practice as well. Microsoft's Azure blog is a rich source of detailed articles, where new features and services are often introduced and explained. These articles delve deeper, offering use cases, benefits, and sometimes even tutorials on how to get started with the new offerings.

Social media platforms can serve as invaluable tools for real-time updates. By following official Azure accounts on platforms such as Twitter, LinkedIn, and Facebook, you can receive instant notifications about the latest news and updates. Additionally, joining forums and discussion groups can provide a more interactive way to stay informed.

Listening to podcasts and watching webinars can be a convenient way to stay updated while multitasking. Several Azure-focused podcasts and webinar series regularly feature discussions, interviews, and news related to the platform. They can provide insights not only about the technical aspects but also about the industry trends and best practices.

Engaging with community-driven content is another enriching way to stay updated. Platforms like GitHub, Stack Overflow, and various blogs often host discussions, code samples, and solutions that revolve around the latest Azure features. These platforms allow you to see how other professionals and enthusiasts are leveraging new updates in real-world scenarios.

Participation in local or virtual meetups and user groups can also be quite beneficial. These gatherings are often platforms where experiences are shared, and the latest trends and updates are discussed. Attending conferences, whether physical or virtual, is another avenue where you can learn about Azure's newest offerings and hear from experts in the field.

Azure also provides a roadmap that outlines upcoming features and updates. By regularly checking the Azure roadmap, you can gain insights into what's on the horizon and plan accordingly. This forward-looking approach ensures that you are not just reacting to changes but are also strategically prepared for future developments.

Interactive platforms such as Microsoft Learn and various online forums provide learning paths and modules tailored to keep you updated with the latest features and best practices in Azure. These modules can be a structured and systematic way to absorb new information.

Monitoring online courses from educational platforms can also be beneficial. Platforms like Coursera, Udemy, and Pluralsight frequently update their course content to align with the latest Azure updates and trends. Enrolling in these courses can provide a more structured and detailed understanding of new features and services.

It's also worthwhile to develop a habit of experimentation. When a new feature or service is announced, take the initiative to explore it hands-on. Azure's free tier and sandbox environments provide a risk-free space to try out new services and understand their practical applications.

Additionally, cultivating a network of peers and mentors in the field is invaluable. Regular discussions with fellow professionals can lead to an exchange of information about the latest trends, best practices, and experiences with Azure services. Building such a network can be mutually beneficial and can often lead to collaborative learning.

Regularly revisiting your existing projects and assessing whether they can benefit from new features or updates is a proactive strategy. This practice not only keeps your projects optimized but also ensures that you are applying your knowledge practically.

Remember that staying updated is not a one-time effort but a continuous process. The field of cloud computing is one that is marked by constant change and evolution. Therefore, fostering a mindset of lifelong learning and curiosity is key.

In summary, the journey of staying updated with Azure trends and updates is multifaceted and requires an amalgamation of different strategies. By being proactive, engaging with a variety of resources, and fostering a community of learning and sharing, you can ensure that you are always at the forefront of Azure's ever-evolving landscape. This continual learning journey not only enhances your professional skills but also ensures that you are always ready to harness the full potential of what Azure has to offer.

BOOK 2
MASTERING IDENTITY & RESOURCE MANAGEMENT IN AZURE
A COMPREHENSIVE GUIDE TO AZ-104

ROB BOTWRIGHT

Chapter 1: The Pillars of Identity in Azure

Identity and Access Management (IAM) is a framework that involves the policies, processes, and technologies used to manage digital identities and specify how they are used to access resources. At its core, IAM is about ensuring that the right individuals have the right access to the right resources and at the right times. It is a crucial aspect of any organization's security strategy, ensuring that only authorized individuals can access certain systems or data.

The first component of IAM is the concept of identity. In the digital world, an identity can be associated with a person, a device, or even an application. When you log into an application using a username and password, you are essentially asserting your identity. Similarly, when a device connects to a network or a software application accesses a database, it, too, needs an identity.

Access management is the other side of the IAM coin. Once an identity is established, access management determines what resources that identity can interact with, and what actions it can perform. This is usually based on a set of policies or rules set by an administrator.

To manage these identities and access rights, IAM systems use several key technologies and processes. One such process is authentication, which verifies the identity of a user, device, or application. This often involves a username and password, but can also include more secure methods such as two-factor authentication or biometric data.

Once authenticated, the next step is authorization, which determines what actions the authenticated identity is allowed to perform. This could range from viewing a file to modifying data in a database. The specifics of what is allowed are usually determined by policies set by administrators or dynamically determined by the system.

IAM also often involves the principle of least privilege, which is the practice of granting only the minimal levels of access, or permissions, needed to accomplish a task. This reduces the risk of an accidental or deliberate breach.

Single sign-on (SSO) is another common IAM technology. SSO allows users to log in once and gain access to multiple applications without needing to log in again. This not only improves user experience but also centralizes the authentication process, making it easier to manage and monitor.

Identity federation is a form of SSO that extends the convenience of single sign-on across organizational boundaries. This enables a user to use a single identity, such as a username and password, to access resources in multiple organizations or cloud environments.

Another essential aspect of IAM is the lifecycle management of identities. This refers to the processes involved in creating, maintaining, and eventually retiring identities. Proper lifecycle management ensures that identities are kept up-to-date and that old or unnecessary access rights are revoked.

Auditing and reporting are crucial for keeping track of who is accessing what, when, and how. By regularly auditing access logs and reports, administrators can identify potentially malicious activity or find areas where access needs to be adjusted.

IAM solutions can be on-premises, but increasingly, they are moving to the cloud. Cloud-based IAM offers scalability, ease of management, and integration with a wide variety of applications and services.

The implementation of IAM is not without challenges. One such challenge is striking the right balance between security and convenience. Overly strict access controls can impede productivity, while too lax controls can expose sensitive data.

Another challenge is the constant evolution of technology and the increasing sophistication of cyber threats. IAM solutions must be continually updated and adapted to stay ahead of potential security breaches.

The growing trend of remote work and mobile device usage also brings its own set of IAM challenges. With users accessing resources from a variety of locations and devices, IAM solutions must be flexible enough to adapt to this changing landscape.

Despite these challenges, effective IAM is critical for the security and efficiency of modern organizations. It enables businesses to safeguard their data and systems while ensuring that employees and other stakeholders have the access they need to be productive.

In the context of cloud environments, like Microsoft Azure or Amazon AWS, IAM takes on additional layers of complexity and importance. These platforms provide their own IAM solutions, such as Azure Active Directory and AWS Identity and Access Management, which are designed to integrate seamlessly with their respective cloud services.

In such environments, IAM policies can be used to control access to cloud resources such as virtual machines, databases, and storage accounts. These policies can specify who can create, modify, or delete resources, and can even control access based on factors such as time of day or geographic location.

By understanding and implementing IAM effectively, organizations can create a secure and efficient environment that safeguards against unauthorized access and data breaches. It provides a framework that not only protects sensitive data but also enhances user experience and ensures that resources are used optimally.

In the ever-evolving landscape of digital transformation, grasping the nuances of IAM is imperative. It is not just a technical requirement but a strategic element that can determine the robustness of an organization's security posture.

So, as you delve deeper into the world of IAM, remember that it is a multifaceted discipline that intertwines technology, policy, and process. By aligning these facets effectively, organizations can ensure that they are not only protecting their digital assets but also paving the way for innovation and growth.

Azure Active Directory, commonly referred to as Azure AD, is a cloud-based identity and access management service provided by Microsoft. It is designed to help organizations securely manage and authenticate the identities of their users and devices, which access applications in a modern computing environment. Think of Azure AD as the cornerstone that supports the framework of an organization's online presence and ensures secure and seamless interactions.

At its essence, Azure AD is a comprehensive solution that offers a range of identity services, including single sign-on (SSO), multi-factor authentication (MFA), device management, and more. With Azure AD, organizations can ensure that the right people have the right access to the right resources, thereby establishing a solid foundation for their identity management strategy.

Let's delve into how Azure AD facilitates the provision of secure and seamless access. Single sign-on, one of the most appreciated features, allows users to sign in once and access multiple services and applications without needing to log in again. This not only enhances the user experience but also consolidates login data for administrators, simplifying monitoring and management.

Another essential feature is multi-factor authentication, which adds an additional layer of security by requiring users to provide two or more forms of identity verification. This could be something they know, like a password, something they have, like a mobile device, or something they are, like a fingerprint. By employing MFA, Azure AD ensures that a stolen password alone is not sufficient for a malicious actor to gain access.

Azure AD is also instrumental in facilitating collaboration across organizational boundaries. Through features such as B2B (Business to Business) and B2C (Business to Consumer) collaboration, organizations can securely share their applications and services with guest users and external partners. This flexibility is crucial in today's interconnected business landscape.

Furthermore, Azure AD provides robust lifecycle management capabilities. This involves the creation, updating, and eventual decommissioning of user identities and their access permissions. By automating these processes, organizations can ensure that users have the necessary access when they need it and that outdated access rights are promptly revoked.

Integration is another strong suit of Azure AD. It can be integrated seamlessly with a multitude of applications, both on-premises and in the cloud. This integration is not limited to Microsoft services alone but extends to a broad range of third-party applications and platforms. Through Azure AD, organizations can centralize their identity management strategy even in a highly heterogeneous IT environment.

Device management is an integral part of the modern workspace, and Azure AD addresses this need through its seamless integration with Microsoft Intune and other mobile device management solutions. This allows organizations to enforce security policies on devices that access their resources, ensuring that only compliant devices can access sensitive data.

Azure AD also equips administrators with tools for insightful reporting and monitoring. With these capabilities, organizations can keep an eye on usage patterns, identify potential security risks, and ensure compliance with industry regulations and standards. This level of oversight is invaluable in an era where data breaches can have significant ramifications.

By using conditional access policies, Azure AD can dynamically adapt authentication requirements based on the user's context, such as their location, device, and behavior. This intelligent approach ensures that security does not impede productivity and that user access is appropriately secured based on the level of risk.

Azure AD also supports the use of identity governance, which helps organizations to grant access rights more securely. By employing practices such as access reviews, privileged identity management, and entitlement management, organizations can ensure that access rights are granted judiciously and reviewed regularly.

Azure AD is not just a standalone service but is also a part of the larger Microsoft 365 ecosystem. By being deeply integrated with services such as Microsoft Teams, SharePoint, and Exchange Online, Azure AD ensures that identity and access management is consistent and secure across the entire suite of Microsoft 365 applications.

Organizations can also extend their on-premises directories to Azure AD using Azure AD Connect, creating a hybrid identity solution. This facilitates a smooth transition to the cloud while allowing organizations to leverage their existing infrastructure.

Moreover, Azure AD supports the use of open standards such as OAuth 2.0, OpenID Connect, and SAML, ensuring that it can be integrated seamlessly with a variety of applications and platforms. This commitment to open standards ensures that organizations are not locked into a single vendor and can use Azure AD in diverse IT environments.

The scalability of Azure AD is noteworthy. Whether an organization has a few dozen users or several million, Azure AD can scale to meet its needs. This scalability ensures that as an organization grows, its identity management solution can grow with it.

In understanding Azure AD, it's essential to appreciate its role as a foundational element in an organization's security strategy. In an era where cyber threats are continually evolving, having a robust and flexible identity and access management solution is not just an operational requirement but a strategic imperative.

Through its wide array of features, seamless integrations, and commitment to security and compliance, Azure AD stands as a pillar that supports the modern organization's identity needs. By providing tools that enable secure access, collaboration, and monitoring, Azure AD ensures that organizations can navigate the digital landscape with confidence.

So, as we explore the world of Azure AD, we see that it's not just an identity and access management service. It is a comprehensive solution that aligns with an organization's strategic goals, ensuring not only security and compliance but also fostering collaboration and innovation.

Chapter 2: Navigating Azure Active Directory (AAD)

Setting up and managing Azure AD tenants is a crucial task for organizations aiming to utilize Microsoft's cloud services effectively. An Azure AD tenant represents an organization's dedicated instance of Azure AD, and it is created automatically when an organization subscribes to a Microsoft cloud service such as Azure, Microsoft Intune, or Microsoft 365. In essence, a tenant serves as a container for your organization's identities, subscriptions, and resources within the Azure environment.

When initiating the setup of an Azure AD tenant, administrators start by signing up for an Azure subscription. During this process, they provide details about the organization, select a unique domain name, and configure initial settings. This domain name is crucial, as it forms the basis of the unique URL for your Azure AD instance and is used for user authentication.

Following the creation of the tenant, administrators can customize the settings to suit the specific needs and policies of the organization. For example, they can specify password policies, enable or disable features like multi-factor authentication, and configure conditional access rules that determine how users can access resources within the tenant.

To ensure the tenant aligns with the organization's structure, administrators can create and manage user accounts, groups, and organizational units within Azure AD. User accounts represent the individuals in the organization and can be manually created, imported from a CSV file, or synchronized from an on-premises Active Directory using Azure AD Connect.

Groups, on the other hand, allow administrators to bundle users together based on their roles, departments, or any other defining characteristic. By assigning permissions and access rights to a group rather than individual users, administrators can significantly simplify the task of managing access to resources.

Azure AD Connect plays a pivotal role for organizations that seek to create a seamless hybrid environment by extending their on-premises directories to Azure AD. By synchronizing user accounts, groups, and other data between the on-premises Active Directory and Azure AD, organizations can ensure a consistent identity experience for users, regardless of where the resources are hosted.

Management of devices is another aspect that administrators need to focus on within an Azure AD tenant. By registering and managing devices within the tenant, administrators can enforce security policies, ensure compliance, and facilitate features such as conditional access and single sign-on.

One remarkable feature that enhances the management of Azure AD tenants is the Azure AD Administrative Units. Administrative Units allow organizations to delegate administrative tasks and permissions within specific scopes, thus providing granular control over different parts of the organization. This is particularly useful for large organizations or those with complex structures.

The customization of branding within an Azure AD tenant allows organizations to create a familiar and consistent sign-in experience for users. Administrators can customize the sign-in pages with the organization's logo, color scheme, and other branding elements.

To foster collaboration and business partnerships, Azure AD tenants can be configured to allow guest access. Through Azure AD B2B, administrators can invite external users to access the organization's resources without the need to create new accounts for them. This ensures secure collaboration while keeping management overhead to a minimum.

Role-based access control (RBAC) within Azure AD allows administrators to assign permissions to users, groups, or applications based on predefined roles. By assigning roles judiciously, organizations can ensure that users have the minimum necessary access to perform their duties, aligning with the principle of least privilege.

Monitoring and auditing are crucial aspects of managing an Azure AD tenant. Administrators can utilize Azure AD logs and reporting features to keep track of sign-in activity, changes made within the tenant, and security-related events. This information is invaluable for troubleshooting, ensuring compliance, and enhancing security.

Azure AD tenants can also be integrated with a wide variety of third-party applications and services. Through the Azure AD App Gallery, administrators can enable single sign-on and user provisioning for thousands of software-as-a-service (SaaS) applications, thereby expanding the utility of their Azure AD tenant beyond just Microsoft services.

Automation and scripting using PowerShell or the Azure CLI can further simplify the management of Azure AD tenants. By leveraging these tools, administrators can automate repetitive tasks, perform bulk operations, and ensure consistency in their management practices.

Licensing plays a significant role in determining the features that are available within an Azure AD tenant. Azure AD comes in different editions, such as Free, Office 365 Apps, Premium P1, and Premium P2, each offering a different set of capabilities. Organizations must choose the appropriate licensing tier based on their needs, budget, and desired features.

The management of Azure AD tenants is not a one-time task but an ongoing responsibility. Organizations must continuously assess their needs, monitor the health and security of the tenant, and adapt to changes and updates introduced by Microsoft.

Ensuring the security and integrity of the Azure AD tenant is paramount. Regularly reviewing access rights, keeping abreast of the latest security recommendations, and promptly addressing vulnerabilities are all part of the routine activities that administrators must engage in.

Additionally, administrators must stay informed about updates and new features introduced to Azure AD. Microsoft regularly updates Azure AD with new capabilities, enhancements, and security features. By staying updated, organizations can leverage these improvements to optimize their Azure AD tenant management.

In summary, setting up and managing Azure AD tenants is a multifaceted task that involves understanding the organization's needs, configuring the tenant to meet those needs, and continuously monitoring and adapting to changes. By effectively managing Azure AD tenants, organizations can ensure a secure, efficient, and seamless identity and access management experience for their users.

User and Group Management in Azure Active Directory (AD) is central to effective identity and access management within an organization utilizing Microsoft's cloud services. By administering users and groups efficiently, organizations can ensure secure access to resources, maintain compliance, and facilitate seamless collaboration.

When it comes to user management in Azure AD, the first step often involves creating and configuring user accounts. These accounts represent individuals within the organization and can be manually added through the Azure portal. However, in scenarios where there are numerous users, bulk user creation might be more efficient, and this can be done by importing a CSV file containing user details.

User accounts in Azure AD contain information such as the user's name, username, password, and other attributes. These details are crucial for personalizing the user experience and enforcing security policies. Administrators can specify password policies that dictate the complexity and expiration of passwords to enhance security.

Another aspect of user management is dealing with lifecycle events, such as onboarding new employees, modifying user attributes when roles change, and deprovisioning accounts when an employee leaves the organization. Automating these lifecycle events can save time and reduce the risk of errors.

Azure AD Connect is a tool that plays a pivotal role in user management for organizations aiming to synchronize their on-premises Active Directory with Azure AD. It allows user attributes, credentials, and other data to be automatically synchronized, thereby creating a consistent identity experience across on-premises and cloud environments.

In scenarios where an organization wishes to provide temporary or limited access to external partners, vendors, or consultants, Azure AD offers the ability to create guest accounts. These accounts can be managed similarly to internal user accounts but have access restrictions that administrators can define and control.

Group management in Azure AD is centered around the principle of simplifying access management by grouping users with similar access needs. By creating a group, an administrator can collectively assign access rights to multiple users, thereby simplifying the permissions model.

Groups in Azure AD can be of different types, such as security groups or Microsoft 365 groups. While security groups are primarily for granting access permissions, Microsoft 365 groups also provide collaboration opportunities by creating a shared mailbox, calendar, and file library for group members.

Dynamic groups offer a significant advantage in automating group membership based on user attributes. For instance, a dynamic group could automatically include all users from a particular department or geographical location. This ensures that the group's membership stays up-to-date without manual intervention, even as users join, leave, or move within the organization.

To facilitate the management of large organizations with varied departments and roles, Azure AD introduces the concept of Administrative Units. With Administrative Units, administrators can create subsets of users and groups and delegate administrative responsibilities. This is particularly useful for delegating tasks such as resetting passwords or assigning licenses to specific departments without granting overarching permissions.

Azure AD provides a variety of predefined roles that can be assigned to users and groups to grant specific administrative privileges. Role-based access control (RBAC) ensures that users have the least privilege necessary to perform their tasks. For instance, a user assigned the role of User Administrator can manage user accounts, but not configure domain settings or security features.

Compliance and reporting are integral parts of user and group management. Azure AD provides detailed logs and reports that administrators can use to audit changes, track sign-in activity, and ensure compliance with organizational policies. Regularly reviewing these logs can help in identifying any anomalous activity or potential security threats.

To cater to a variety of applications and services, Azure AD allows administrators to integrate third-party applications with the directory. This integration enables single sign-on and user provisioning for a wide range of software-as-a-service (SaaS) applications, thereby simplifying the user experience and reducing administrative overhead.

Automation and scripting play a crucial role in efficient user and group management. By using PowerShell or Azure CLI scripts, administrators can automate repetitive tasks, such as creating user accounts, assigning licenses, and managing group memberships. Automation not only saves time but also ensures consistency and accuracy in management tasks.

Licenses in Azure AD determine the features that are available to users. Assigning and managing licenses is a task that administrators must perform to ensure users have access to the necessary tools and services. Proper license management also helps organizations optimize costs and stay within budget.

An important aspect of user and group management is ensuring data security and privacy. By configuring features such as multi-factor authentication (MFA) and conditional access policies, administrators can add layers of security that go beyond just usernames and passwords.

Periodically reviewing and updating user and group access rights is a good practice to ensure that the principle of least privilege is maintained. Regular audits can help in identifying excessive permissions and rectifying them promptly.

In the ever-evolving landscape of cloud services, staying informed about updates and new features introduced to Azure AD is essential. Microsoft continuously enhances Azure AD with new capabilities, and by staying updated, administrators can leverage these features to optimize user and group management.

In essence, effective user and group management in Azure AD is about striking the right balance between security, compliance, automation, and ease of use. By understanding the various features and tools available within Azure AD and applying best practices, administrators can create a secure and efficient environment that facilitates productivity and collaboration.

Chapter 3: Implementing Role-Based Access Control (RBAC)

Role-Based Access Control, commonly known as RBAC, is a crucial aspect of managing resources within Microsoft Azure, ensuring that the right individuals have the appropriate access and permissions. Grasping the fundamentals of RBAC in Azure can be pivotal in enhancing security and simplifying access management across a multitude of resources. It revolves around the principle of assigning specific roles to users, groups, or applications to define what actions they can perform on a given resource.

In Azure, RBAC operates with a set of predefined roles that encapsulate permissions meant to accomplish certain tasks. These roles include, but are not limited to, Owner, Contributor, and Reader. The Owner role, for instance, grants full access to resources, allowing individuals to manage and delegate permissions. The Contributor role also permits extensive rights but stops short of allowing access management. In contrast, the Reader role only provides read-only access, allowing users to view resource configurations but not make changes.

The granularity of RBAC extends beyond these basic roles, with Azure providing a plethora of built-in roles designed to cater to specific needs. For instance, there are roles specifically tailored for managing virtual machines, network configurations, databases, and more. Each of these roles has a carefully crafted set of permissions that align with best practices and the principle of least privilege.

Defining custom roles is an option available for organizations that need to fine-tune permissions beyond what's offered by the built-in roles. By creating a custom role, administrators can specify the exact actions, not-actions, data operations, and not-data operations that are permitted or denied, thereby creating a tailored security posture that aligns with their unique requirements.

The scope at which an RBAC role is assigned plays a significant role in determining the access a user, group, or application has. Azure enables the assignment of roles at different levels, such as management groups, subscriptions, resource groups, and individual resources. Assigning a role at a higher scope, like a subscription, inherently grants the same permissions to all underlying resources within that scope.

In practical terms, when an administrator assigns the Contributor role to a user at the subscription level, that user can create and manage resources like virtual machines, databases, and networks across the entire subscription. This cascading nature of permissions makes it essential to carefully plan role assignments to avoid inadvertently granting excessive permissions.

Azure RBAC leverages Azure AD as the identity provider, meaning that role assignments can be made to Azure AD user accounts, groups, service principals, and managed identities. Assigning roles to groups rather than individual users is a practice that simplifies management and ensures that access rights are easier to track and audit.

Implementing RBAC is not just about assigning roles; it is also about continuously monitoring and managing access to ensure compliance and security. Azure provides tools and features that aid administrators in auditing role assignments and access patterns. Azure Activity Log and Azure Policy can be employed to audit access and enforce organizational policies respectively.

Understanding the principle of least privilege is integral to effectively implementing RBAC in Azure. It suggests that users should be granted only the permissions necessary to complete their tasks, thereby minimizing the potential impact of a security breach. Regularly reviewing and revoking unnecessary permissions helps in maintaining a secure environment.

RBAC in Azure is dynamic and can be adapted to the evolving needs of an organization. As projects grow or teams restructure, role assignments can be modified to reflect these changes. Regular audits can help administrators identify and rectify redundant or excessive permissions, ensuring that access rights remain aligned with organizational needs and security policies.

Azure RBAC also allows for temporary access by utilizing role assignments that expire after a certain duration. This is particularly useful in scenarios where temporary elevated access is required, such as during troubleshooting or project migrations.

Deny assignments are another facet of Azure RBAC that can be employed to explicitly block certain actions, even if a user has been granted permissions through other role assignments. This can be a powerful tool for enforcing strict security policies and ensuring that certain actions are restricted regardless of other permissions.

Azure RBAC supports conditional access policies that can add an additional layer of security by defining conditions under which access is allowed or denied. For example, an organization might set up a policy that requires multi-factor authentication when accessing sensitive resources from an unfamiliar location.

Integration with Azure Monitor and Azure Security Center can provide administrators with insights and alerts related to RBAC changes and access patterns. By keeping an eye on these alerts and reports, administrators can ensure that they stay ahead of potential security risks and maintain a strong security posture.

While RBAC is a powerful tool for managing access, it's important to understand that it is just one piece of the larger security and governance puzzle in Azure. Complementing RBAC with other practices such as network security, data encryption, and monitoring ensures a comprehensive approach to security and compliance.

In the realm of cloud services, where resources are dynamic and can scale quickly, effective access management is paramount. By understanding and implementing RBAC effectively, organizations can ensure that their Azure resources are secure, compliant, and accessible to those who need them.

In summary, mastering the fundamentals of RBAC in Azure involves understanding predefined roles, custom roles, scopes, role assignments, and best practices related to access management. By combining these principles with continuous monitoring and regular audits, organizations can foster a secure and efficient environment within Azure.

Assigning roles and permissions effectively is an art and a science that combines the understanding of an organization's structure, the sensitivity of the resources involved, and the responsibilities of individuals or groups. When done correctly, this ensures that every member in an organization can access only what they need, thereby bolstering security and optimizing workflow. In the context of cloud services and platforms like Microsoft Azure, this process often starts by comprehending the complexity and diversity of available resources and their corresponding permissions.

One of the first steps in assigning roles and permissions effectively is conducting an assessment to understand the needs and responsibilities of different users and teams within an organization. By gathering information on what resources are required for various tasks and what level of access is necessary, administrators can craft a thoughtful and efficient access strategy. It is vital to establish clear criteria for access, such as job roles, projects, or departments, which can then be mapped to corresponding permissions.

With a clear understanding of user needs, administrators can begin to explore predefined roles that might be a good fit. In platforms like Azure, a plethora of built-in roles exist, which can be a time-saving boon for administrators. These roles, often descriptive in their naming conventions, bundle together permissions that are commonly used together, thereby streamlining the assignment process.

However, it's also common for organizations to have unique needs that don't perfectly align with predefined roles. In such instances, creating custom roles becomes necessary. Custom roles allow administrators to finely tune the permissions granted, ensuring that each user or group gets access that aligns closely with their responsibilities.

A crucial principle to adhere to during this process is the principle of least privilege (POLP). This principle suggests that users should be given the minimum level of access—or permissions—needed to accomplish their tasks. By doing so, the risk associated with accidental or intentional data breaches is minimized. This principle extends not only to user accounts but also to applications and services that may require access to resources.

Effective role and permission management also involves regularly revisiting and auditing assignments. Organizations evolve, and so do the roles and responsibilities of their members. Regular audits can help identify redundant permissions and ensure that access levels still align with users' current roles within the organization. By conducting these audits, administrators can revoke unnecessary permissions, thereby maintaining a cleaner and more secure environment.

The concept of inheritance and scope is another crucial aspect of assigning roles and permissions effectively. In hierarchical systems like Azure, permissions assigned at a higher level can cascade down to lower levels. Understanding this hierarchy is pivotal to avoid unintentional oversharing of access rights. For example, assigning a user Contributor role at a subscription level in Azure would grant them extensive permissions across all resources under that subscription.

Similarly, understanding and effectively utilizing group-based access is beneficial. Instead of assigning permissions to individual users, permissions can be assigned to a group, and users can be added or removed from that group as necessary. This approach simplifies management and ensures a more consistent and easier-to-audit access policy.

In some instances, temporary elevated access may be necessary for specific tasks, such as troubleshooting or performing a one-time operation. Platforms like Azure allow for temporary role assignments, ensuring that users have elevated access only for a limited period, thereby adhering to the principle of least privilege.

It's also beneficial to understand and use conditional access policies where applicable. These policies add an extra layer of security by defining conditions under which access is allowed. For instance, a policy could require multi-factor authentication when accessing sensitive resources from an unfamiliar location.

In the context of Azure and many other platforms, role and permission assignments are not limited to just users but also extend to applications and services. Service principals, which are essentially identities created for applications, can be assigned roles and permissions, allowing them to interact with other resources securely.

Monitoring and logging access and usage patterns is also part of effective role and permission management. Tools and services that provide insights into access patterns can help administrators identify potential security risks and ensure that assigned permissions are appropriate and being used correctly.

Effective role and permission management is an ongoing process that evolves with the organization and the landscape of threats and opportunities. By staying informed about best practices, emerging threats, and new features or tools, administrators can continuously optimize access to resources.

The seamless flow of work within an organization depends significantly on how effectively roles and permissions are managed. By ensuring that every individual and service has just the right level of access to resources, administrators can contribute to a secure, efficient, and harmonious working environment. Thus, understanding and mastering the art of assigning roles and permissions effectively is an invaluable skill in today's digital landscape.

Chapter 4: Azure Governance: Policies and Management Groups

Implementing Azure policies is a strategic approach to maintaining consistency, compliance, and control over the resources and services within an Azure environment. Azure policies act as a set of rules that govern the creation and management of resources, ensuring that all actions align with an organization's standards and requirements. When configured thoughtfully, Azure policies can be a powerful tool to establish and maintain uniformity across various resources and subscriptions.

Imagine a scenario where an organization has a strict naming convention for all virtual machines to adhere to, or perhaps a specific region where resources must be deployed due to data residency regulations. Azure policies can enforce these criteria, either blocking non-compliant actions or alerting administrators to deviations. This helps in ensuring that all deployments and configurations across the environment are harmonious and consistent with the organization's objectives and regulatory requirements.

Azure policies work by evaluating the properties of resources as they are created or modified. A policy definition expresses what to evaluate and what action to take. For instance, a policy could dictate that only certain types of virtual machines are allowed, or it could enforce that all resources have a specific tag attached to them. By evaluating resources in real-time, Azure policies ensure that resources stay compliant with the defined criteria.

To implement Azure policies effectively, it is crucial to understand the structure of a policy definition. A policy definition includes several components such as the 'if' condition, the 'then' effect, and parameters. The 'if' condition defines the criteria to evaluate, the 'then' effect determines the action to take when the 'if' condition is met, and parameters allow for customization of the policy to suit specific needs.

Creating a custom policy begins by identifying the requirement that the policy needs to enforce. It's important to be clear on what you're trying to achieve with the policy, whether it's compliance with a particular standard, enforcement of a best practice, or adherence to an organizational rule. Once the objective is clear, crafting the policy definition to meet this requirement becomes more straightforward.

When defining a policy, consider using parameters to make the policy more versatile. For example, if you're creating a policy to restrict the regions where resources can be deployed, using a parameter for the list of allowed regions makes the policy easily reusable and adaptable to different scenarios. This means the same policy can be applied to different scopes or subscriptions with varying parameters, thereby ensuring consistency with minimal duplication of effort.

After creating a policy definition, it must be assigned to take effect. Policy assignments determine where and how the policy will be enforced. An assignment includes the scope, which could be a management group, subscription, resource group, or a specific resource, and the parameters as needed. Being mindful of the scope is crucial, as a policy assigned at a higher scope, like a subscription, will cascade down and apply to all resources under that scope.

It's also important to test policies in a non-disruptive manner before widespread implementation. Azure allows for a policy effect called 'audit' which doesn't enforce the policy but logs compliance data. By using the 'audit' effect, administrators can gauge the impact of a policy without preventing resource creation or modifications. This step is crucial in understanding the implications of the policy and ensuring that it aligns with the intended objectives without causing unintended disruptions.

Additionally, leveraging Azure Policy's initiative definitions can be useful when dealing with multiple related policies. An initiative definition is a collection of policy definitions that are tailored to achieve a single, overarching goal. For instance, an initiative could include several policies related to security and compliance standards. By grouping these policies together, administrators can manage and assign them more efficiently.

To ensure consistent implementation, monitoring policy compliance is essential. Azure provides detailed compliance data, which helps in identifying non-compliant resources and taking corrective action as necessary. Regular reviews of compliance data can highlight potential gaps or areas where policies may need to be adjusted or expanded upon.

A practical aspect of implementing Azure policies is considering the potential for policy exemptions. There could be scenarios where a specific resource or set of resources needs to be exempted from a policy due to unique requirements. Azure allows for policy exemptions, which can be defined to bypass a policy for a particular scope while still maintaining overall consistency.

Effective communication within the organization is also a vital component of successful policy implementation. Keeping stakeholders informed about policies, their impact, and the reasons behind them can lead to smoother adoption and fewer conflicts. Training and documentation that explain the policies and the rationale behind them can be beneficial.

Continuous improvement is another aspect to consider. Regularly revisiting and evaluating the effectiveness and relevance of Azure policies can lead to a more refined and efficient environment. As organizational goals and technologies evolve, so should the policies that govern the Azure environment.

In summary, implementing Azure policies for consistency involves a thoughtful approach to defining, assigning, monitoring, and continuously improving policies. By utilizing Azure policies effectively, organizations can ensure that their cloud environments remain consistent, compliant, and aligned with their strategic objectives and regulatory requirements. Through careful planning, regular monitoring, and ongoing refinement, Azure policies can become a cornerstone in maintaining a secure and harmonious cloud environment.

Organizing resources efficiently within Azure can be a challenging task, especially when dealing with large-scale environments that span across multiple subscriptions and departments. Azure Management Groups provide a solution to this challenge by offering a layer of management that is above subscriptions. By using Management Groups, administrators can effectively manage access, policies, and compliance for numerous subscriptions, ensuring a cohesive and organized setup.

Azure Management Groups allow you to build a hierarchical structure that provides a way to manage access, policies, and compliance for an entire organization. When you consider the architecture of an Azure environment, individual resources like virtual machines or storage accounts reside within resource groups. These resource groups, in turn, belong to subscriptions. Management Groups take this hierarchy a step further by grouping subscriptions together, allowing you to apply governance conditions to a collection of subscriptions.

Let's delve into the benefits that come from using Azure Management Groups. One of the most prominent advantages is the ability to apply Azure Policy and Azure Role-Based Access Control (RBAC) settings at scale. When you have multiple subscriptions under a Management Group, any policy or role assignments applied to the Management Group are inherited by the underlying subscriptions and resources.

Imagine a scenario where an organization needs to ensure that all virtual machines across different departments and subscriptions are compliant with specific security standards. Instead of individually applying policies to each subscription, a policy can be applied once at the Management Group level, thereby ensuring consistent governance across all subscriptions and resources within that Management Group. Similarly, Azure Management Groups simplify role assignments for identity and access management. If certain individuals or teams need access to multiple subscriptions, assigning roles at the Management Group level can provide them with the required permissions across all subscriptions within the Management Group. This approach reduces administrative overhead and potential errors that could arise from managing permissions at each subscription level.

Designing a hierarchy with Azure Management Groups requires careful planning. The hierarchy can have up to six levels of Management Groups, not including the root level or the subscription level. Each directory is given a single top-level Management Group called the 'Root' Management Group. This 'Root' Management Group is built into the hierarchy to have all Management Groups and subscriptions fold up to it.

Understanding the organizational structure and requirements is crucial before setting up Management Groups. For example, you might design a hierarchy where

Management Groups represent different departments, like finance, human resources, and IT, each having their respective subscriptions and resources under them. Alternatively, Management Groups could be set up based on environments such as production, development, and testing. When setting up Management Groups, it is essential to establish clear naming conventions. Having a consistent and descriptive naming convention can make it easier to identify the purpose of each Management Group and the subscriptions it contains. A good practice is to include relevant information such as the department, environment, or region in the name, which can make management and navigation more intuitive.

Once the hierarchy is set up, moving subscriptions between Management Groups is a straightforward process. This flexibility allows organizations to restructure their Azure environment as their needs evolve without significant disruption. However, it is important to note that moving subscriptions might cause inherited policies and permissions to change, which should be taken into consideration to avoid unintended consequences.

Another aspect of Management Groups is that they do not incur any additional cost. This means organizations can leverage Management Groups to simplify governance and management without worrying about increasing their Azure expenditure. However, while Management Groups themselves are free, the resources and policies applied may have associated costs.

In addition to policies and permissions, Azure Management Groups can also help in applying consistent tagging practices across subscriptions. Tags are key-value pairs that can be applied to resources and are often used for organizing resources, tracking ownership, or managing costs. By enforcing tagging policies at the Management Group level, organizations can ensure that resources across multiple subscriptions adhere to consistent tagging practices.

Continuous monitoring and review of the Management Group hierarchy can lead to more efficient management of resources. Regularly assessing whether the hierarchy still aligns with organizational needs and making adjustments as necessary can lead to better governance and more streamlined operations.

In essence, Azure Management Groups offer a powerful and scalable way to manage governance and compliance across multiple subscriptions and resources. By taking the time to design a thoughtful hierarchy and leveraging the capabilities of Management Groups, organizations can create a robust and organized Azure environment. From applying policies and permissions to ensuring consistent tagging practices, Management Groups provide the tools needed to manage resources effectively. With proper planning and regular review, Management Groups can become a cornerstone of an efficient and well-governed Azure environment.

Chapter 5: Diving into Resource Management Strategies

Navigating the complexities of resource allocation requires a nuanced understanding of both the current demands on your system and the potential for future growth. Efficient resource allocation is a fundamental aspect of successful management, regardless of whether you're dealing with human resources, financial assets, or technological capabilities. It involves distributing available resources in a manner that optimizes productivity while minimizing waste and expenses.

Understanding the demand for resources is the first step in the process of resource allocation. By carefully analyzing the needs of various tasks or projects, you can ascertain what resources are necessary and how they should be distributed. This analysis should not only consider immediate needs but should also forecast future requirements and potential changes in the environment.

When dealing with technological resources such as computing power, storage, and network bandwidth, dynamic allocation can be a powerful strategy. Dynamic allocation allows resources to be adjusted on-the-fly, responding to changes in demand without manual intervention. For instance, a cloud computing platform might automatically allocate more processing power to an application experiencing a surge in user activity.

Balancing the needs of different tasks or departments is an integral part of resource allocation. Prioritizing resource distribution based on the criticality, urgency, and strategic importance of tasks ensures that the most vital operations have what they need to succeed. This prioritization can involve a delicate balancing act, as it may be necessary to redistribute resources when unexpected needs arise.

Efficient resource allocation is closely tied to effective cost management. By ensuring that resources are not being underutilized or wasted, organizations can often achieve significant cost savings. For instance, using cloud services that allow for scaling up or down based on demand ensures that you're only paying for the resources you're actively using.

Implementing monitoring tools can provide insights into how resources are being used and can help identify bottlenecks or areas of inefficiency. For instance, analytics that highlight underused servers or excessive bandwidth usage can guide adjustments to resource allocation strategies. Continuous monitoring allows for a proactive approach to resource management, enabling adjustments before problems escalate.

When considering human resources, the principles of efficient resource allocation can be applied to optimizing workloads and ensuring that employees are engaged in tasks that align with their skills and the organization's goals. This involves understanding the strengths and capabilities of your team and allocating work in a manner that leverages these strengths while ensuring fair and manageable workloads.

Diversifying resource investments can also be a useful strategy for efficient allocation. By not placing all your resources into a single project or asset, you safeguard against potential failures or unexpected changes in the market. This diversification can manifest as investing in multiple technologies, engaging in various projects, or ensuring a mix of skills within a team.

In the realm of project management, employing agile methodologies can contribute to efficient resource allocation. Agile frameworks encourage flexibility and responsiveness to change, allowing resources to be reallocated swiftly as project requirements evolve. This approach stands in contrast to more traditional, rigid project management styles, where resource allocation is fixed at the outset.

Effective communication and transparency within an organization can also enhance resource allocation strategies.

By ensuring that all stakeholders are aware of how resources are being allocated and why certain decisions are being made, you foster an environment of trust and collaboration. This open communication can lead to valuable feedback and insights, which can further refine resource allocation strategies.

It is also beneficial to consider the longevity and sustainability of resources during the allocation process. Opting for resources that are renewable or sustainable can often lead to long-term cost savings and is likely to be viewed favorably in terms of corporate responsibility. This principle can apply to everything from opting for renewable energy sources for your data centers to investing in ongoing training for your staff to ensure their skills remain relevant.

Utilizing automation and artificial intelligence can also enhance resource allocation strategies. Automated systems can analyze data, predict trends, and adjust resource allocation in real-time to meet demand. These systems can often identify patterns and make adjustments more swiftly and accurately than human operators.

Periodically reviewing and reassessing your resource allocation strategy is essential to ensure its continued effectiveness. The needs of an organization can change over time, and strategies that were once efficient may no longer be optimal. Regular reviews allow for adjustments and refinements to be made, ensuring that the resource allocation strategy evolves alongside the organization.

It's also worthwhile to consider the potential for external partnerships and collaborations as part of a resource allocation strategy. Sometimes, pooling resources with external partners or outsourcing certain tasks can lead to efficiencies that wouldn't be possible when working alone.

Educating and training those responsible for allocating resources is another key aspect of ensuring efficiency. By ensuring that your team is equipped with the latest knowledge and understands the tools at their disposal, you empower them to make informed and effective decisions regarding resource allocation.

Being mindful of potential risks and preparing contingency plans is a prudent aspect of resource allocation. By considering what might go wrong and having a plan in place to adjust resource allocation in response to unexpected events, you can ensure a level of resilience and adaptability in your strategy.

Cultivating a culture that values efficiency and is open to innovation can lead to organic improvements in resource allocation. When staff at all levels are encouraged to identify and suggest improvements, the collective intelligence of the organization can lead to optimized resource usage.

In summary, efficient resource allocation is a multifaceted challenge that requires ongoing attention and adaptability. By considering the needs and demands of your organization, employing technology effectively, fostering open communication, and regularly reassessing your strategies, you can ensure that your resources are used to their fullest potential, driving success and sustainability.

Effective resource management is a crucial aspect of navigating the cloud ecosystem, and Azure resource tagging is a powerful tool in this endeavor. Tagging resources in Azure involves assigning metadata to your resources, giving additional information that can be used to manage and organize them efficiently. Thoughtful tagging can make a world of difference when it comes to streamlining your operations and ensuring clarity in your cloud environment.

When you commence your tagging journey, it's essential to have a clear and consistent tagging strategy from the get-go. A well-defined strategy helps ensure uniformity and avoids confusion as your Azure environment scales. Establishing a set of standard tags that everyone in the organization adheres to promotes consistency across different projects and teams.

These tags can cover various aspects such as project names, cost centers, owners, and environments.

Ensuring that your tags are descriptive and meaningful enhances their utility manifold. Generic or ambiguous tags can lead to confusion, and the value of tagging is significantly diminished if the tags do not provide clear and useful information. Thus, opt for tags that succinctly describe the purpose, ownership, or other critical aspects of the resource.

The concept of granularity is also vital when discussing best practices for Azure resource tagging. Tagging should be granular enough to offer valuable insights but not so detailed that it becomes cumbersome to manage. Striking a balance between granularity and simplicity can ensure that your tags are both informative and manageable.

One aspect that is often overlooked is planning for changes and evolution in your tagging strategy. As your organization grows and evolves, your tagging needs may also change. Building in flexibility to your tagging strategy ensures that it can adapt and evolve to meet your changing needs without causing disruption or confusion.

Using tags for cost management is a smart and strategic approach. By tagging resources with information related to cost centers, budgets, or departments, you can leverage Azure Cost Management tools to gain insights into your spending. This allows for effective tracking and optimization of costs associated with various resources.

Security and compliance are paramount, and resource tagging can be employed effectively to ensure adherence to regulatory standards and security best practices. For example, resources that store sensitive data can be tagged accordingly, which can then be used to apply specific security policies or to ensure that they are included in compliance audits.

Automation and scripting can be employed to ensure that your tagging strategy is consistently applied across all resources. Utilizing automation can help enforce tagging standards, validate tag values, and ensure that no resources are left untagged. Azure Policy can be used to enforce specific tagging requirements, ensuring that resources are compliant with your organizational standards.

Periodic reviews and audits of your tagging strategy and its implementation are vital. Regularly reviewing your tags ensures that they remain relevant, accurate, and compliant with any changes in organizational strategy or external regulations. This review process can help identify and rectify any inconsistencies or errors in your tagging practices.

Being mindful of the limitations of Azure tagging is also important. There are limits to the number of tags you can apply to each resource and the total number of tags in a subscription. Being aware of these limits can help you plan your tagging strategy effectively and avoid running into issues as your environment grows.

Ensuring that your tagging strategy is well-documented is another best practice. A well-maintained documentation that outlines your tagging strategy, the purpose of each tag, and any specific guidelines for their use can be invaluable. This documentation can serve as a reference for your team, ensuring clarity and consistency in how tags are applied and used across your Azure environment.

Consideration for interoperability and integration with other tools is also essential. Your tagging strategy should be designed in a way that it works seamlessly with other tools and services you use, ensuring that your tags provide value not just within Azure, but across your entire technological ecosystem.

Resource tagging can also play a significant role in disaster recovery strategies. Resources can be tagged based on their criticality, allowing for prioritization in recovery efforts. By tagging resources according to their function or role in your applications, you can ensure that they are brought back online in the correct order to ensure smooth recovery.

Training and awareness among your team members about the importance of tagging and the best practices to be followed are critical. By ensuring that everyone understands the value and importance of tagging, you can foster a culture of responsibility and proactive management of resources.

When it comes to performance optimization and troubleshooting, resource tags can also prove to be beneficial. By tagging resources with information related to their intended performance or role within an application, you can quickly identify and rectify any issues that may arise.

In the context of collaboration and multi-team environments, resource tagging can be used to denote ownership or responsibility. Tags indicating a specific team or individual as the owner of a resource can simplify communication and responsibility tracking.

Using tags to mark the lifecycle stage of resources can help manage deployments and identify resources that may be due for updates or decommissioning. For instance, tags indicating whether a resource is in the development, staging, or production stage can help ensure that resources are managed and monitored appropriately based on their lifecycle stage.

To sum up, effective Azure resource tagging is an art that, when done right, can significantly enhance resource management, cost optimization, security, compliance, and overall operational efficiency. By adopting a thoughtful and consistent approach to tagging, you can ensure that your Azure environment is well-organized, easy to navigate, and aligned with your organizational goals.

Chapter 6: Advanced User and Group Management in AAD

Implementing fine-grained access management is a crucial undertaking to ensure that resources and data are safeguarded, while still being accessible to those who require it for their roles. Fine-grained access management refers to the practice of precisely defining and controlling user access to resources at a very detailed level. This approach ensures that access is tailored to the exact needs and responsibilities of each user, thereby minimizing potential security risks.

In a cloud environment like Azure, fine-grained access management can involve a multitude of services and features designed to tailor user access. Role-Based Access Control (RBAC) is one such service that allows administrators to assign permissions to users, groups, or applications at a very detailed level. By using RBAC, administrators can assign specific permissions, such as read, write, or delete, to specific resources or groups of resources.

Implementing fine-grained access management begins with a thorough understanding of your organization's requirements and an audit of the existing access control mechanisms. This involves identifying the various roles within your organization, understanding what access each role requires, and mapping out the resources that need to be secured. A meticulous audit can help uncover any overly permissive access rights or identify areas that require more stringent controls.

Once you have a clear understanding of your organization's needs, you can proceed to design your access policies. Here, the principle of least privilege, which involves granting only the minimum level of access necessary to perform a task, is paramount. By strictly adhering to this principle, you minimize the risk of unnecessary exposure of sensitive resources.

A well-defined access control strategy should also incorporate segregation of duties, ensuring that no single user has complete control over a resource or process. This practice helps mitigate the risk of malicious actions or errors causing significant impact on your systems. Segregation of duties involves dividing tasks and privileges among multiple users or teams to prevent conflicts of interest or fraud.

Fine-grained access management should also extend to the data level. Data-Level Security (DLS) can help restrict access to specific items of data based on user attributes or claims. Implementing DLS involves creating security policies that filter data based on user roles or attributes, thereby providing highly granular control over data access.

Audit trails and monitoring are essential components of fine-grained access management. Keeping detailed logs of access and changes to resources allows for accountability and aids in identifying and investigating any suspicious activities. Utilizing monitoring tools and setting up alerts for unusual access patterns or changes can help in quickly identifying and addressing potential security incidents.

In a cloud environment, it's also important to consider temporary access requirements. Sometimes, a user may need elevated access temporarily for a specific task. Implementing a Just-In-Time (JIT) access model ensures that such access is granted only for the required duration and is automatically revoked once the task is complete. This approach minimizes the window of opportunity for any potential misuse.

Another crucial aspect is the continuous evaluation and updating of access policies. As your organization evolves, so too will your access requirements. Regularly reviewing and updating your access control policies ensures that they remain aligned with your organization's needs and any changes in external regulations or threats.

Access management should also consider external users or third-party entities that might require access to your resources. By employing Identity Federation, you can allow users from external systems to access your resources securely, without having to create a separate identity for them in your system.

Implementing multi-factor authentication (MFA) is an additional layer that can strengthen your fine-grained access management strategy. MFA requires users to provide two or more verification factors to gain access to a resource, adding an extra layer of security.

Fine-grained access management should also be extended to applications. When dealing with application identities, Managed Service Identities (MSI) can be used to automatically manage credentials, ensuring that applications have the precise permissions they need.

It's also essential to be mindful of the user experience. While security is paramount, implementing fine-grained access management should not impede users' ability to perform their roles effectively. Striking a balance between security and user experience is critical.

Implementing fine-grained access management may also require training and awareness among staff. Educating users on the importance of security practices and the reasons behind access controls can foster a culture of responsibility and vigilance.

One must also consider scalability when implementing fine-grained access management. As your organization grows, your access control mechanisms should be able to adapt without becoming overly complex or difficult to manage.

When considering cloud resources, it's also wise to factor in geographic access restrictions. Geofencing or conditional access policies can restrict access to resources based on the geographic location of the user, adding an additional layer of control.

Consistency in your access management policies across different platforms and environments is crucial. Whether dealing with on-premises systems or cloud resources, having a uniform approach to access management ensures ease of administration and a cohesive security posture.

Incorporating automation in your fine-grained access management strategy can also streamline the process. Automated workflows for access requests, approvals, and revocations can ensure timely and accurate management of access rights.

In essence, implementing fine-grained access management is an ongoing process that requires a thoughtful approach, continuous monitoring, and regular updates to meet the evolving needs of your organization.

Managing users and groups in bulk can be a tremendous time-saver for administrators who oversee large organizations or complex systems. In environments where there are a multitude of users and groups, the task of creating, modifying, or deleting accounts individually can become a cumbersome and time-consuming affair. Fortunately, many modern systems and platforms, including cloud services like Azure, provide tools and features that make bulk management of users and groups an efficient and straightforward process.

For instance, administrators might need to create accounts for a large number of employees who are joining the company as part of a recruitment drive. Doing this manually for each user can be tedious. Instead, using bulk management techniques, an administrator can upload a single file containing the details of all the new users, and the system can process these details to create the accounts automatically.

Similarly, when it comes to group management, bulk operations can simplify tasks such as adding multiple users to a group or modifying the attributes of several groups at once. This can be especially useful in scenarios where project teams are frequently reorganized or when organizational restructuring necessitates changes to access permissions.

To begin managing users and groups in bulk, it's essential to gather all the necessary data accurately. Data such as usernames, email addresses, group names, and other relevant attributes should be collected and organized systematically. Typically, this data can be arranged in a CSV file, which is a widely supported format for bulk operations.

Using CSV files for bulk operations is beneficial because it allows administrators to lay out all the necessary information in a tabular format that is easy to understand and manipulate. Each row in the file can represent a user or a group, while the columns can represent attributes such as name, email, department, and so on.

Once the data is prepared, the next step is to use the tools provided by the platform to perform the bulk operations. In the context of Azure, the Azure Active Directory portal offers options for bulk user and group management. The portal allows administrators to upload a CSV file and then maps the columns in the file to the corresponding attributes in Azure AD.

Validation is an important step in this process. The system will often check the uploaded data for any inconsistencies or errors. This ensures that all user and group details are correct and adhere to the system's requirements before the bulk operation is executed.

When performing bulk operations, it's crucial to be aware of the permissions and access levels that are being assigned to users and groups. Administrators need to ensure that they are adhering to the principle of least privilege, granting only the access that is necessary for users and groups to perform their roles.

Additionally, administrators should be mindful of the potential need for rollback. Sometimes, a bulk operation might have unintended consequences, and it may be necessary to undo the changes. Having a backup of the original state and a clear understanding of how to revert changes is an essential safety measure.

Bulk management is not limited to just creation or deletion of users and groups. It can also be used for modifying attributes or permissions. For instance, if an organization undergoes a rebranding and email domains change, an administrator can update the email addresses of all users in bulk, ensuring consistency and minimizing disruption.

Scheduling is another aspect that can be considered when managing users and groups in bulk. Sometimes, changes need to be applied at a specific time, such as outside of business hours to minimize impact. Some systems allow administrators to schedule bulk operations to run at a predetermined time.

Automation can also play a significant role in bulk management. By utilizing scripts or automation tools, routine tasks such as account provisioning or group updates can be triggered by specific events or scheduled to run at regular intervals. This can ensure a dynamic and responsive system that adapts to changes efficiently.

Audit trails and logs are important in tracking the changes made during bulk operations. These records provide accountability and can be crucial for troubleshooting or investigating security incidents. A good practice is to review logs regularly to ensure that all changes were executed as intended.

It's also essential to communicate effectively with stakeholders and users when performing bulk operations. Informing users of any changes to their accounts, or notifying them of new group memberships, ensures transparency and helps in gaining user cooperation and understanding.

Bulk management can sometimes involve dealing with sensitive data. Therefore, administrators must ensure that data is handled securely, with due attention to privacy and compliance requirements. Encrypting data files, using secure channels for data transmission, and adhering to data protection regulations are all crucial aspects of secure bulk management.

Performance considerations also come into play when managing users and groups in bulk. Large-scale operations can sometimes be resource-intensive, and administrators should be mindful of the system load and potential impact on performance.

Moreover, organizations should provide training and resources to administrators to equip them with the skills needed for effective bulk management. This ensures that administrators are well-versed in best practices and are capable of utilizing the tools and features effectively.

In summary, managing users and groups in bulk is an invaluable capability that can save time, ensure consistency, and enhance the responsiveness of systems to organizational changes. By preparing data meticulously, utilizing available tools wisely, adhering to security and compliance standards, and paying attention to the nuances of the process, administrators can successfully streamline the management of users and groups in any environment.

Chapter 7: Securing Access with Multi-Factor Authentication (MFA)

Setting up and configuring Multi-Factor Authentication (MFA) in Azure Active Directory is an essential step in strengthening the security posture of an organization. By implementing MFA, organizations add an extra layer of protection to their user accounts, ensuring that even if a password is compromised, unauthorized access is still mitigated. MFA requires users to present at least two or more separate forms of identification before they are granted access to an account or system.

The first form of identification is usually something the user knows, such as a password. The second form is something the user has, such as a mobile device or a smart card, and sometimes, it can even be something the user is, such as a biometric feature like a fingerprint. By combining these different forms of identification, MFA makes it significantly more challenging for malicious actors to gain unauthorized access.

Azure Active Directory (Azure AD), Microsoft's cloud-based identity and access management service, provides robust capabilities for setting up MFA. The process of configuring MFA in Azure AD is designed to be user-friendly and efficient, making it accessible for administrators to enforce and for users to adopt.

To start configuring MFA in Azure AD, administrators first need to navigate to the Azure portal. Within the portal, they can find the Azure Active Directory service and then access the security features available. Here, administrators will find the option for MFA, which guides them through the process of enabling this feature for their organization.

When enabling MFA, administrators can choose to enforce this security measure for all users or select specific users or groups. This flexibility allows organizations to apply MFA where it is most needed, considering the risk profile and functional requirements of different user roles.

Administrators can also define trusted locations or IP address ranges where MFA requirements might be relaxed. For example, users accessing resources from within the company's physical premises might not be prompted for MFA, while access requests from unknown locations would trigger the additional authentication steps.

The next step in configuring MFA in Azure AD is to select the authentication methods that users can employ. Azure AD offers various options, such as authentication through a mobile app, a phone call, or a text message containing a verification code. Administrators can decide which methods are suitable for their organization and even allow users to choose their preferred method.

Configuring the Azure Authenticator app is a common choice for MFA. Users can download the app on their mobile devices and use it to receive notifications for approval or generate verification codes. This method is considered secure and provides a convenient user experience.

When configuring MFA, administrators should also consider setting up self-service password reset and account unlock capabilities. This ensures that users can recover their accounts quickly if they encounter any issues, thereby reducing the load on support teams.

It's crucial to educate users about the importance of MFA and guide them through the initial setup process. Communication about why MFA is being implemented and how it protects both the organization and the user's data can contribute to a smoother adoption.

Once MFA is configured and rolled out, monitoring and analyzing usage and authentication patterns is a good practice. Azure AD provides detailed reports and logs that administrators can use to track sign-in activities and identify any unusual patterns that could indicate a security concern.

One aspect to be mindful of when implementing MFA is user convenience. While security is paramount, it is also important to strike a balance so that users do not find the authentication process overly cumbersome. Tailoring the MFA prompts to the risk context, such as only requiring MFA for specific applications or data access, can enhance user experience without compromising security.

Testing the MFA setup before rolling it out organization-wide is also recommended. By conducting a pilot with a smaller group of users, administrators can gather feedback, identify potential issues, and make any necessary adjustments to the configuration or communication strategy.

In addition to the technical setup, organizations should also establish clear policies regarding MFA. These policies should outline when and how MFA is to be used, and detail any exceptions or alternative processes that are in place for scenarios where MFA may not be applicable.

Regularly reviewing and updating the MFA configuration is vital to ensure that it continues to align with the evolving security landscape and organizational needs. This includes staying abreast of new authentication methods and technologies that may enhance security and user experience.

Accessibility is another factor that administrators should consider when configuring MFA. Ensuring that all users, including those with disabilities, can successfully authenticate is important for both inclusivity and compliance with legal standards.

Implementing MFA is part of a broader approach to security known as Zero Trust, where trust is never assumed and verification is required at every step. By layering MFA with other security measures such as conditional access policies, data encryption, and regular security training for users, organizations can build a robust defense against unauthorized access and potential data breaches.

In the dynamic and often challenging landscape of cybersecurity, the importance of safeguarding access to resources cannot be overstated. By thoughtfully configuring and effectively implementing MFA in Azure AD, organizations can significantly enhance their security posture while still providing users with a seamless and productive experience.

Implementing Multi-Factor Authentication (MFA) is a strategic move for any organization aiming to enhance its security, but the efficacy of this measure is significantly amplified when coupled with well-designed policies and thorough user education. Crafting a comprehensive and efficient MFA policy involves a thoughtful blend of technology, human behavior, and organization-specific needs. The policy should outline clear guidelines on when and how MFA is required, detailing the authentication methods that are permissible and any circumstances under which exceptions can be made.

A well-articulated MFA policy should aim for a balance between stringent security and user convenience. Striking this equilibrium ensures that users are protected without feeling overwhelmed or stifled by the security protocols. For instance, organizations can adopt adaptive MFA policies, which assess the risk context of a login attempt and only trigger MFA when necessary, such as when a user attempts to access sensitive data or logs in from an unfamiliar location.

One best practice is to enable a variety of authentication methods, such as authentication apps, text messages, phone calls, or even biometrics, offering users the flexibility to choose the method most convenient to them. However, it is crucial to ensure that all options uphold the same high standard of security. The policy should also account for scenarios where users might not have access to their primary MFA method and provide alternatives or fallback options.

Organizations should also consider time-bound re-authentication, wherein users are prompted to verify their identity periodically or when transitioning between different sensitivity levels of data access. Periodic reviews of the MFA policy to ensure it aligns with emerging security trends, organizational changes, and technological advancements is also a best practice.

Once the MFA policy is established, user education comes to the fore as a critical aspect of successful implementation. Educating users about the why and how of MFA is just as vital as the technical setup. Users are more likely to adhere to security practices when they understand the rationale behind them and the potential risks of non-compliance.

Training sessions, webinars, and informative materials can be used to educate users about the importance of MFA and how it fits into the larger security landscape. Real-world examples of security breaches and how MFA could have prevented them can be effective in communicating the relevance of these protocols. Simultaneously, it is important to ensure that the education material is accessible, easy to understand, and free from jargon.

Step-by-step guides, video tutorials, and interactive sessions can assist users in setting up and using MFA. Organizations should also provide clear instructions on what to do if users encounter issues, such as being unable to receive a verification code or losing access to their authentication device. Having a responsive support system in place can mitigate frustration and ensure continuous adherence to MFA practices.

Regular communication about updates, changes, or enhancements to the MFA policy keeps users informed and engaged. Periodic reminders about the importance of security and tips for safeguarding their credentials can reinforce good practices.

In addition, organizations should foster a culture of security where users feel comfortable reporting suspicious activity or potential security incidents without fear of retribution. Creating a positive and proactive security culture encourages users to be vigilant and take ownership of their role in safeguarding the organization's digital assets.

It is also beneficial to simulate phishing attempts and other security threats to gauge user response and identify areas where further education might be needed. These simulated exercises can provide valuable insights into user behavior and help tailor education programs more effectively.

Furthermore, feedback from users can be invaluable in refining both MFA policies and education strategies. Understanding the user experience, any hurdles faced, and areas of confusion can help organizations make necessary adjustments to ensure smoother implementation and adherence.

Organizations should also ensure that their MFA education and policies are inclusive and accessible to all users, including those with disabilities. This might involve providing alternative authentication methods or additional support to ensure everyone can authenticate securely and efficiently.

By approaching MFA with a dual focus on robust policies and comprehensive user education, organizations can fortify their defenses against unauthorized access and potential breaches. The confluence of technology and human behavior in this context underscores the importance of not just implementing security measures, but also ensuring that users are equipped and motivated to use them effectively.

In the evolving landscape of cybersecurity, where threats are continually growing in sophistication, an organization's resilience is often determined by its weakest link. By ensuring that MFA policies are well-crafted, adaptive, and clearly communicated, and by investing in user education, organizations can transform potential vulnerabilities into strengths.

In the end, the goal is to create an environment where security is a seamless and integral part of the workflow, not a cumbersome add-on. Through thoughtful policy creation, continuous education, and fostering a culture of security awareness, organizations can navigate the complex digital landscape with confidence and resilience.

Chapter 8: Efficient Deployment and Management of Azure Resources

Navigating the world of cloud computing requires agility and the ability to adapt, deploy, and scale quickly, which is why automated deployment using Azure Resource Manager (ARM) templates is such a vital skill for professionals working with Azure. ARM templates offer a declarative syntax in JSON, allowing you to define what resources you need rather than writing complex scripts to create them. This simplifies the deployment and management of resources within Azure, allowing for consistency, repeatability, and resource orchestration.

Imagine having to manually create numerous virtual machines, databases, and networks every time you want to set up an environment. This process would be time-consuming, error-prone, and inconsistent. ARM templates mitigate these challenges by defining the infrastructure as code (IaC), allowing you to represent complex environments in a readable and maintainable manner.

When you use an ARM template for deployment, you submit the desired configuration to the Azure Resource Manager, which takes on the responsibility of orchestrating the creation of all the specified resources. This results in deployments that can be predictably repeated, which is vital for creating testing, staging, and production environments that are identical in configuration.

Let's explore the structure of an ARM template to understand how it facilitates automated deployment. An ARM template is divided into several sections, each serving a specific purpose in the deployment process. The 'parameters' section allows you to input values that customize your deployment, such as the name of a virtual machine or the size of a database. Parameters can be prompted during deployment or predefined, offering flexibility in tailoring the template for different scenarios.

The 'variables' section in an ARM template allows you to define values that are reused throughout the template. By using variables, you can simplify your template and make it easier to read and maintain. For instance, if you're creating a naming convention for resources, you can define it once in the variables section and reference it wherever needed.

In the 'resources' section, you define the Azure resources that you want to create and configure. Each resource is specified by its type, such as a virtual machine or a storage account, and is assigned properties that determine its configuration. Here, you can define dependencies between resources, ensuring that they are created in the correct order.

The 'outputs' section of an ARM template allows you to return values from the deployed resources. This can be useful for retrieving information such as IP addresses or connection strings that are generated during the deployment process.

When you deploy an ARM template, Azure Resource Manager processes the file and orchestrates the creation of the resources in the correct order and with the specified configuration. If an error occurs during deployment, Azure can automatically roll back changes, ensuring that you don't end up with partially deployed or misconfigured resources.

ARM templates also support incremental deployments, allowing you to modify an existing environment by adding or updating resources. This can be extremely beneficial for iterative development and continuous integration processes, ensuring that your infrastructure evolves alongside your application.

Given the benefits, you might wonder how to create an ARM template. There are several approaches. You can author a template from scratch using a JSON editor, or you can use visual tools provided by Azure, such as the Azure Portal, which allows you to create resources and then export the configuration as an ARM template. Additionally, there are repositories of pre-created templates that can be modified to suit your needs.

Testing your ARM templates before deploying them to production is a prudent practice. Tools like the ARM Template Toolkit (arm-ttk) or the 'What-If' operation in Azure PowerShell and Azure CLI can help you validate templates and preview changes before they are applied.

Version control is another important aspect of working with ARM templates. By storing your templates in a source control system like Git, you can track changes, maintain a history of deployments, and ensure that the correct versions of templates are used.

In larger organizations and complex projects, ARM templates can be combined with Azure DevOps, allowing for continuous integration and continuous deployment (CI/CD) of infrastructure alongside application code. This integration ensures that your infrastructure is always in sync with your application's requirements and can be updated or scaled as needed.

Automating deployments using ARM templates not only leads to time savings but also contributes to reducing errors that can occur during manual setup. By treating infrastructure as code, you align the disciplines of software development and operations, paving the way for more efficient and collaborative practices such as DevOps.

The learning curve for ARM templates can seem steep initially, but the investment in understanding their nuances pays off in the form of streamlined and reliable deployments. As cloud environments grow in complexity and scale, the ability to automate and manage resources efficiently becomes invaluable.

In essence, ARM templates embody the principle of working smarter, not harder. By automating repetitive tasks, you free up time and resources to focus on innovation and value creation. The ability to deploy, replicate, and manage complex environments at the click of a button, or the execution of a command, is a powerful capability afforded by Azure.

Effective management of resources and costs in a cloud environment such as Azure requires thoughtful planning, continuous monitoring, and proactive adjustments. One of the most appealing aspects of cloud computing is its flexibility and scalability, allowing organizations to adjust their infrastructure usage based on demand. However, without careful management, costs can quickly escalate, making optimization essential.

To start, it's crucial to assess the needs of your applications and services accurately. Overprovisioning leads to unnecessary costs, while underprovisioning can result in performance issues and unsatisfactory user experiences. Striking the right balance is the key to optimizing resource utilization without compromising on performance.

Understanding the pricing model of each Azure service is foundational for cost optimization. Azure offers a pay-as-you-go model, where you pay for what you use, but it also provides reserved instances which can be more cost-effective for long-term usage. Reserved instances allow organizations to commit to a specific service for one or three years at a lower rate compared to the pay-as-you-go model.

Regularly analyzing and monitoring your cloud expenditure is vital. Tools such as Azure Cost Management and Azure Advisor provide insights into your spending patterns and offer recommendations to optimize costs. Azure Cost Management allows you to track resource usage and manage costs across all your Azure subscriptions, while Azure Advisor offers personalized best practices guidance.

Implementing cost allocation tagging is a smart strategy for managing and attributing costs accurately. By tagging resources with information such as department, project, or environment, you can track usage and costs more precisely. This granular visibility into your expenditures can reveal opportunities for cost savings and facilitate more accurate budgeting and forecasting.

Azure's Auto Scaling capabilities can be leveraged to adjust resources dynamically based on demand. With Auto Scaling, you can set rules that automatically scale your applications out or in, aligning resource utilization with actual demand and avoiding overprovisioning. For instance, you can scale virtual machine instances or database throughput units up when demand is high and scale them down when demand subsides.

For organizations with predictable workloads, scheduling the start and stop of resources can contribute to significant cost savings. For instance, development and testing environments are typically only needed during business hours and can be shut down overnight and on weekends, reducing costs.

Optimizing storage is another area where costs can be trimmed. Azure offers different types of storage, each with its pricing model. By evaluating the performance requirements and access frequencies of your data, you can choose the most cost-effective storage option. For example, infrequently accessed data can be moved to Azure Blob Storage's Cool or Archive tiers, which are cheaper than the Hot tier but come with different retrieval times and costs.

Similarly, optimizing data transfer can result in savings. Transferring data into Azure is usually free, but outbound data transfer can incur costs. By understanding data transfer patterns and optimizing them, for example, by caching or using Content Delivery Networks (CDNs), you can reduce outbound data transfer costs.

Identifying and deallocating unused or underused resources is akin to decluttering your cloud environment. Over time, it's common for resources to become redundant, forgotten, or barely used. Regular audits can help identify these resources, allowing you to stop or delete them, thereby eliminating unnecessary costs.

Optimizing your application's architecture can also lead to more efficient resource utilization. Refactoring applications to take full advantage of cloud-native features, such as serverless computing with Azure Functions or containerization with Azure Kubernetes Service (AKS), can lead to more efficient resource usage and lower costs.

Leveraging Azure's hybrid benefits and licensing optimizations can also contribute to cost savings. For example, if you already have on-premises Windows Server or SQL Server licenses, you can often use these licenses in Azure with the Azure Hybrid Benefit, reducing costs compared to pay-as-you-go pricing.

Implementing budget alerts and cost thresholds ensures that you are promptly notified when your spending exceeds predefined limits. By setting up alerts, you can take proactive measures before costs escalate unexpectedly.

Evaluating and opting for cost-effective regions for your resources can also contribute to savings. Sometimes, deploying resources in a different Azure region can be more cost-effective due to variations in pricing across regions.

Engaging in a continuous learning process to stay updated with Azure's pricing and services ensures that you can take advantage of new features, pricing options, or services that could offer better performance at a lower cost. Microsoft frequently updates its offerings, and staying informed is part of an effective cost optimization strategy.

In essence, optimizing resource utilization and costs in Azure is a continuous and multifaceted task. It involves a deep understanding of both your applications' needs and Azure's offerings, combined with proactive monitoring, management, and adjustments. By adopting a proactive and informed approach, you can ensure that you are getting the most value from Azure while keeping costs in check.

Chapter 9: Monitoring and Auditing: Ensuring Compliance

Embarking on the journey to ensure compliance within your cloud environment can be both an essential and intricate endeavor. Azure Monitor and Azure Security Center stand as two robust pillars that facilitate this pursuit by providing comprehensive monitoring, security, and compliance solutions tailored for the ever-evolving digital landscape. Grasping the nuances of configuring these services is fundamental to establishing a secure and compliant cloud environment.

Azure Monitor is a versatile tool that collects, analyzes, and acts on telemetry data from your Azure resources. It offers you full-stack visibility, advanced analytics, and intelligent insights to help ensure the performance and availability of your applications. On the other hand, Azure Security Center is a unified infrastructure security management system that strengthens the security posture of your data centers and provides advanced threat protection.

Let's delve into the configuration of Azure Monitor first. By weaving a tapestry of logs and metrics, Azure Monitor provides a real-time and historical view of your resources. It gathers data from a multitude of sources, including application logs, operating system logs, and resource logs. To kickstart this process, you need to set up diagnostic settings on your Azure resources. These settings allow you to specify the categories of data that you wish to collect and route this information to the appropriate destination, such as Log Analytics workspaces, Event Hubs, or storage accounts.

A pivotal component of Azure Monitor is Log Analytics, which allows you to run advanced queries on the data collected, thereby enabling you to derive insights and facilitate compliance. Setting up a Log Analytics workspace and directing your logs to this workspace is a primary step. Once configured, you can create and run queries using the Kusto Query Language (KQL) to explore and analyze your data.

Application Insights, a feature of Azure Monitor, focuses on the application layer and assists in identifying performance anomalies, diagnosing errors, and understanding how to improve the overall user experience. To employ Application Insights, you need to integrate it into your application code, enabling the collection of telemetry data that offers insight into your application's operations and associated user interactions.

Alerting and action groups in Azure Monitor are essential in ensuring compliance. By creating alert rules, you can define conditions based on your metrics and logs, and trigger actions when these conditions are met. Actions could range from sending an email notification to invoking Azure Functions or Logic Apps to take corrective automated actions.

Shifting focus to Azure Security Center, it's important to comprehend how it fortifies your resources against threats and helps you align with compliance standards. The first step in utilizing Azure Security Center is to enable the standard tier, which provides advanced threat detection capabilities compared to the free tier.

Azure Security Center continually assesses your resources, networks, and configurations for security vulnerabilities and deviations from compliance standards. It then presents these findings in the form of security recommendations. By reviewing and implementing these recommendations, you can bolster your security posture and enhance compliance.

Policy and compliance assessments are integral aspects of Azure Security Center. You can configure security policies for your Azure subscriptions and resource groups, defining your desired configuration baseline. Azure Security Center uses these policies to evaluate and report on the compliance status of your resources.

Azure Security Center also provides Just-In-Time (JIT) VM access, which reduces your exposure to network vulnerabilities by enabling access to VMs only when needed. By configuring JIT, you ensure that your virtual machines are not left open to potential threats, thus aligning with compliance requirements.

Another noteworthy feature is Adaptive Application Controls, which helps in identifying and allowing only known good applications to run on your VMs, creating a whitelist approach and reducing the attack surface. This aligns well with the principle of least privilege, a fundamental compliance and security tenet.

Azure Security Center's regulatory compliance dashboard provides insights into your compliance stance against industry standards such as ISO 27001, PCI DSS, and others. By configuring the dashboard to reflect the standards relevant to your organization, you gain a comprehensive view of your compliance status, enabling you to take targeted actions.

Integration of Azure Monitor and Azure Security Center can provide synergistic benefits. For instance, security alerts generated by Azure Security Center can be sent to Azure Monitor logs. This allows you to combine data from various sources, craft complex queries, and create comprehensive dashboards that give you a holistic view of your environment's health and compliance.

Both Azure Monitor and Azure Security Center offer robust APIs, allowing you to integrate their capabilities into custom solutions or third-party tools. By doing so, you can tailor your monitoring, alerting, and compliance reporting to your organization's specific needs.

Data retention and privacy are crucial aspects of compliance. Both Azure Monitor and Azure Security Center allow you to configure data retention policies, ensuring that your data is stored for the necessary period to meet compliance requirements while respecting privacy constraints.

In essence, configuring Azure Monitor and Azure Security Center for compliance involves a thoughtful approach to data collection, analysis, alerting, and remediation. By meticulously crafting your configurations to align with your organization's needs and industry standards, you lay down a resilient foundation that not only safeguards your environment but also ensures adherence to compliance norms.

Navigating the realm of cloud governance, auditing, and reporting is a vital task that organizations undertake to ensure adherence to their compliance and operational standards. Azure Policy, a service within the Microsoft Azure ecosystem, plays an indispensable role in this journey by allowing organizations to create, assign, and manage policies. These policies enforce different rules and effects over your resources, so those resources stay compliant with your corporate standards and service level agreements.

Azure Policy evaluates your resources for non-compliance with assigned policies. For example, you can have a policy to allow only a certain SKU of virtual machines in your environment or restrict the creation of certain resources in a specific region. All of these policies ensure that your resources adhere to your organization's standards, regulatory requirements, and cost constraints.

Understanding how auditing and reporting work with Azure Policy begins with recognizing the lifecycle of a policy. When you define a policy in Azure, you specify the conditions under which it is enforced and the effect that takes place when those conditions are met. Once a policy is defined, it needs to be assigned to a specific scope of resources such as a subscription, resource group, or a management group.

When a policy is assigned, Azure Policy will evaluate your resources against the conditions in the policy. It's here that the auditing aspect comes into play. Azure Policy will mark resources as compliant or non-compliant based on the evaluation, and this data is made available for you to review.

Diving deeper into auditing, one can explore the Compliance blade in the Azure Policy service. This blade gives you an overview of the compliance state of your resources. It's an aggregated view where you can see the number of resources that are compliant and non-compliant against the policies that have been assigned.

Beyond just viewing this data in the Azure portal, you can take auditing a step further by leveraging Azure Policy's ability to export this data. Data regarding policy evaluations, compliance state, and more can be streamed to other services such as Azure Event Hubs, Azure Monitor logs, or even external SIEM systems. This is where the aspect of reporting gains prominence.

Crafting meaningful reports is essential to understand the compliance landscape of your Azure environment. By exporting your compliance data to Azure Monitor logs, you can create powerful queries and visualizations using Kusto Query Language (KQL). These visualizations can be pinned to a dashboard providing a real-time, interactive reporting experience.

For instance, you could create a report that showcases the compliance state of resources over time, giving you insights into how well your organization is adhering to your policies and where you might need to take corrective action.

Similarly, a report can be generated to highlight the most common non-compliance issues, aiding you in understanding areas that may require more attention or clearer communication with your teams.

Azure Policy also integrates seamlessly with Azure Security Center, enhancing the auditing and reporting capabilities. Policies recommended by Azure Security Center can be used to fortify your environment, and the compliance data can be visualized directly within Azure Security Center's dashboard.

Another powerful feature of Azure Policy is the ability to use remediation tasks. When a policy is found to be non-compliant, a remediation task can be triggered to rectify the situation. This ensures that your resources are not just audited for compliance but are also automatically brought back into compliance, thus minimizing any potential risks or violations.

Reporting is not just about visualizing data but also about understanding and interpreting that data to make informed decisions. By analyzing the reports generated from the compliance data, organizations can pinpoint areas that need improvement, understand trends, and make adjustments to their policies or resource configurations accordingly.

Creating custom policies is another layer that enhances auditing. Azure Policy comes with a set of built-in policies, but you might have unique requirements specific to your organization. By creating custom policies, you can tailor the auditing process to precisely match your needs, thereby ensuring that the reports generated are both relevant and insightful.

The use of initiatives in Azure Policy further streamlines auditing and reporting. An initiative definition is a set or group of policy definitions to help track your compliance state for a larger goal. By grouping related policies together, you can ensure that related resources are audited in a coordinated manner, and reporting can provide insights into a broader aspect of your environment.

In practice, auditing and reporting with Azure Policy is an iterative and continuous process. Policies may evolve as your organization grows, and your auditing and reporting mechanisms must adapt accordingly. Regularly reviewing your reports, adjusting your policies, and ensuring that your auditing mechanisms are correctly configured is crucial.

Furthermore, communication and education within your organization play a vital role. By ensuring that your teams are aware of the policies in place, understand the reasons behind them, and know how to interpret and act upon the reports generated, you can foster a culture of compliance and proactive management.

In essence, Azure Policy stands as a lighthouse guiding organizations in the sea of governance, compliance, and management. By effectively utilizing its auditing and reporting capabilities, organizations can not only ensure that their resources are in adherence to their standards but also gain insights that drive continuous improvement and informed decision-making.

Chapter 10: Troubleshooting Identity and Resource Management Issues

Navigating the realm of identity management can often present a labyrinth of challenges, intricacies, and considerations that organizations must deftly navigate. From ensuring secure access to resources to managing a myriad of user identities, the road to streamlined identity management is often fraught with obstacles. One of the primary challenges faced by many organizations is the proliferation of user identities and credentials across different systems, applications, and platforms.

In an era where digital transformation is omnipresent, organizations often find themselves grappling with disparate systems, each requiring its own set of credentials. This fragmented landscape can lead to what is often termed as 'identity sprawl'. Users, in an attempt to access various services, might end up juggling multiple usernames and passwords. This not only hampers productivity but also poses significant security risks, as users may resort to using weak or identical passwords across systems.

Another challenge that surfaces in the domain of identity management is ensuring the principle of least privilege. This principle dictates that a user should have the minimal level of access—or permissions—to perform their job functions. Striking the right balance can be tough as administrators have to ensure that employees have enough access to perform their tasks without compromising security by granting excessive permissions.

Authentication challenges also take center stage as organizations strive to strike a balance between security and user convenience. Single-factor authentication, often in the form of passwords, has proven to be vulnerable to attacks and breaches. However, introducing additional authentication mechanisms, such as multi-factor authentication (MFA), may sometimes meet resistance from users due to perceived inconvenience.

In the modern landscape where remote work is increasingly common, the challenge of securely managing identities extends beyond the boundaries of the traditional office environment. Remote workers access corporate resources from various locations and devices, which may not always adhere to the security standards upheld by the organization. This challenge of managing identities and ensuring secure access in a perimeter-less environment is often termed as the problem of the 'dissolving perimeter'.

Further, the rise of cloud computing has introduced a new set of complexities. Traditional identity management solutions that were designed for on-premises environments may not seamlessly translate to the cloud. Organizations often find themselves in hybrid environments where some resources are in the cloud while others are still on-premises. Managing identities consistently across this hybrid landscape becomes a formidable challenge.

With businesses often engaging with partners, vendors, and contractors, there arises a need for managing external identities. Providing secure and controlled access to external users while ensuring that the organization's resources are not put at risk is a common challenge. The concept of identity federation, where identities are shared across trusted domains, comes into play, but it brings with it the challenges of interoperability and standardization.

In the context of consumer-facing applications, organizations must handle the challenge of scaling their identity management solutions to accommodate potentially millions of users. Ensuring a seamless and secure user experience while managing such a large scale of identities necessitates robust and scalable identity management solutions.

Moreover, the regulatory landscape adds another layer of complexity to identity management. Organizations are often bound by legal and compliance requirements that dictate how user data and identities should be managed and protected. Navigating these regulatory requirements, which may vary by region and industry, requires a nuanced understanding and careful implementation of identity management practices.

The challenge of keeping up with the constantly evolving threat landscape is another significant aspect. Cyber adversaries are continually devising new ways to compromise identities and gain unauthorized access to systems. Organizations need to ensure that their identity management strategies evolve in tandem with these emerging threats.

Identity lifecycle management, which involves the processes of creating, managing, and eventually de-provisioning identities, is another area where challenges abound. Ensuring that identities are granted promptly when needed, managed effectively during their lifecycle, and revoked when no longer necessary, is a continuous task that requires coordination and vigilance.

The increasing adoption of Internet of Things (IoT) devices introduces yet another dimension to the challenge. With myriad devices requiring access to networks and resources, managing and securing these device identities alongside human identities is a task that organizations are still learning to navigate.

To address these challenges, organizations often turn to identity and access management (IAM) solutions that provide a comprehensive set of tools and capabilities to manage identities effectively. By employing practices such as single sign-on (SSO), MFA, and identity federation, organizations can begin to build a cohesive approach to identity management.

In the pursuit of streamlined and secure identity management, organizations are also recognizing the value of adopting a Zero Trust approach. This approach, which dictates that trust is never assumed and verification is required from anyone trying to access resources in your network, aligns well with the challenges of modern identity management.

Understanding user behavior is also emerging as a strategy to enhance identity management. By employing user and entity behavior analytics (UEBA), organizations can detect anomalies in user behavior that may indicate a potential security threat.

At the end of the day, addressing the challenges in identity management is not just about implementing technologies but also about fostering a culture of security awareness and continuous improvement. By staying abreast of emerging trends, understanding the evolving threat landscape, and adopting best practices, organizations can navigate the complexities of identity management and ensure that they are well-positioned to protect their resources and users.

In the intricate world of IT and cloud computing, resource conflicts are akin to puzzling mysteries that administrators must solve to ensure the seamless functioning of systems and applications. These conflicts can arise from a variety of circumstances, such as when multiple applications vie for the same resource or when configurations are misaligned. Grasping effective strategies for diagnosing and resolving these conflicts is crucial to maintain uninterrupted services and operations.

When faced with a resource conflict, the first step is to accurately identify the symptoms and signs of the issue. For instance, an application might be displaying unexpected behavior, systems may be running sluggishly, or there could be unexplained errors cropping up in logs. The discerning eye of an administrator should be able to pick up on these anomalies and recognize them as potential indicators of an underlying resource conflict.

Once the symptoms are observed, the process of diagnosis begins, which involves delving into logs, monitoring tools, and system metrics to uncover clues about the conflict. System logs can be invaluable in this process, often providing detailed information about errors, failed requests, or resource allocation issues. By combing through these logs, administrators can piece together the sequence of events leading up to the conflict.

Understanding the architecture and dependencies of the applications and systems in question is another key aspect of the diagnostic process. Knowing how components interact with each other, what resources they depend on, and how they are configured can provide vital context when attempting to identify the root cause of a conflict.

Once the root cause is identified, the next step is to formulate a strategy for resolution. This could involve making adjustments to resource allocations, reconfiguring applications, or tweaking system settings to ensure harmonious coexistence of all components. In some cases, it may be necessary to update or patch software to rectify compatibility issues that could be leading to conflicts.

Virtualization and containerization are powerful tools in the arsenal of strategies for resolving resource conflicts. By isolating applications and their dependencies in virtual machines or containers, administrators can prevent conflicts from arising due to overlapping requirements. This encapsulation ensures that each application operates in its own environment, oblivious to the potential conflicts that may exist outside its encapsulated space.

Another strategy involves employing load balancers and resource schedulers to judiciously distribute resources among competing applications and processes. Load balancers can evenly distribute network traffic across multiple servers, ensuring that no single server is overwhelmed and becomes a bottleneck. Similarly, resource schedulers can allocate CPU, memory, and other resources dynamically based on demand and priority, mitigating conflicts and ensuring optimal utilization.

In cloud environments, taking advantage of autoscaling features can also be a potent strategy for preventing and resolving resource conflicts. Autoscaling allows systems to dynamically adjust the number of running instances based on demand, thus preventing resource exhaustion and ensuring that applications have access to the resources they need.

Sometimes, resource conflicts can be preemptively avoided by implementing rigorous change management practices. By meticulously tracking, documenting, and testing changes to systems and configurations, administrators can catch potential conflicts before they manifest in a live environment. Utilizing staging or testing environments that mirror the production setup can be beneficial in spotting issues before they escalate.

In situations where resources are shared among multiple tenants or departments, implementing quotas and resource limits can be an effective strategy. By clearly defining and enforcing boundaries for resource usage, administrators can prevent scenarios where a single tenant or application hoards resources, leading to conflicts and degraded performance for others.

Having a robust monitoring and alerting system in place is also essential. Real-time monitoring can provide immediate insights into resource usage patterns, allowing administrators to detect and address conflicts proactively. By setting up alerts for specific conditions, such as CPU usage exceeding a certain threshold or memory running low, administrators can be notified instantly when potential conflicts are on the horizon.

Automation plays a significant role in both diagnosing and resolving conflicts. Scripted diagnostics and automated resolution workflows can expedite the process of identifying and fixing issues, reducing downtime and manual intervention. Infrastructure as code (IaC) tools can be employed to maintain consistent configurations and prevent drift, thereby reducing the likelihood of conflicts arising from misconfigurations.

When it comes to databases, conflicts can arise due to concurrent transactions, deadlocks, or schema discrepancies. Strategies for resolving these conflicts might include implementing transaction controls, optimizing queries, and ensuring that database schemas are aligned across different instances and environments.

Furthermore, fostering a culture of collaboration and communication among different teams and stakeholders can contribute to effective conflict resolution. Often, resource conflicts arise due to siloed operations and lack of visibility into the actions and requirements of different teams. By encouraging open communication, administrators can ensure that potential conflicts are flagged early and can be addressed before they escalate.

In certain cases, it might be beneficial to consult with vendors, support communities, or external experts who might have encountered similar conflicts and can provide insights or solutions. Tapping into collective knowledge can often lead to quicker resolution and can also provide new perspectives on tackling the problem.

Education and continuous learning are also essential strategies for administrators. Staying abreast of new technologies, best practices, and emerging trends can equip administrators with the knowledge and skills needed to diagnose and resolve conflicts effectively.

In the quest to diagnose and resolve resource conflicts, it's crucial to approach the task with a methodical mindset, combining technical acumen with strategic thinking. By leveraging tools, technologies, and best practices, administrators can ensure that resource conflicts are swiftly identified and resolved, ensuring smooth operations and optimal resource utilization. Ultimately, the goal is to create resilient, adaptable, and conflict-free environments that support the organization's objectives and deliver value seamlessly.

BOOK 3
AZURE NETWORKING AND STORAGE MASTERY ADVANCED
TECHNIQUES FOR AZ-104 ADMINISTRATORS

ROB BOTWRIGHT

Chapter 1: Deep Dive into Azure Networking Concepts

Diving into the world of Azure's network infrastructure is akin to exploring the intricate web of highways that keep a bustling city functioning smoothly. Azure's networking capabilities form the backbone that allows data to flow seamlessly between applications, data centers, and users. It is crucial to understand the components and nuances of Azure's network infrastructure to optimize connectivity, performance, and security.

Azure Virtual Network, often abbreviated as VNet, is a fundamental piece of this infrastructure, allowing you to create isolated, private cloud environments within Azure. By setting up a VNet, you can define your own private IP address space, segment the network into subnets, and control traffic flow with network security groups. These VNets facilitate secure communication between Azure resources, on-premises data centers, and even different regions.

Subnets within a VNet help in segmenting the network, similar to how neighborhoods in a city have distinct boundaries. By dividing your VNet into subnets, you can group related resources together and apply security or routing policies at a granular level. This segmentation not only helps in organizing resources but also plays a crucial role in enhancing security and simplifying management.

Network Security Groups (NSGs) in Azure act like vigilant traffic cops, controlling the inbound and outbound traffic to network interfaces, VMs, and subnets. By defining rules within NSGs, you can allow or deny traffic based on factors like source and destination IP addresses, ports, and protocols. This ensures that only legitimate traffic is allowed, thereby bolstering security.

Azure Route Tables, on the other hand, are like the signposts guiding data packets on their journey through the network. By customizing route tables, you can control the flow of data and ensure that it takes the most efficient path to its destination. This is particularly useful for creating complex networking setups with specific routing requirements.

Azure Load Balancer is another critical component, serving as a traffic director that ensures high availability and reliability by distributing incoming network traffic across multiple servers. Think of it as a skilled traffic manager, ensuring that no single server bears too much load, thereby maintaining a smooth and responsive user experience.

For scenarios that demand seamless connectivity between on-premises data centers and Azure, Azure VPN Gateway comes into play. It provides a secure and robust way to create a virtual private network, ensuring encrypted connections over the public Internet. This is much like building a secure, private tunnel through the bustling traffic of a public highway.

Azure ExpressRoute takes connectivity a step further by providing a dedicated, private connection to Azure. This is akin to having a private express lane on a highway that ensures consistent performance and lower latency, bypassing the public internet altogether.

Azure Application Gateway is a dedicated layer 7 load balancer, adept at managing web traffic. It comes with features like SSL termination, cookie-based session affinity, and URL-based routing. Imagine it as a sophisticated traffic director that understands the context and content of the requests and can make intelligent routing decisions.

Azure Traffic Manager, on the other hand, operates at the DNS level and directs client requests to the most appropriate endpoint based on factors like health, priority, and geographic proximity. This global load balancer ensures optimal distribution of user traffic to enhance availability and responsiveness.

For safeguarding the network infrastructure, Azure provides tools like Azure Firewall, a managed, cloud-native network security service that protects your Azure Virtual Network resources. It is like a vigilant guard, meticulously scrutinizing incoming and outgoing traffic based on rules defined by you.

Network Performance Monitor and Azure Network Watcher are tools that help in monitoring and diagnosing network issues. They can be compared to surveillance cameras and diagnostic tools that keep an eye on traffic, ensuring everything flows smoothly and anomalies are quickly detected and rectified.

Azure DNS, a hosting service for DNS domains, ensures that domain names are translated into IP addresses, facilitating smooth navigation on the internet. It acts like the directory assistance of the internet, directing users to the correct locations based on friendly, human-readable domain names.

Understanding connectivity within and across data centers is also crucial. Azure offers options like VNet Peering, which allows seamless connectivity across Azure Virtual Networks, enabling resources in different VNets to communicate as if they were on the same network. This is much like creating direct, no-stop routes between different neighborhoods in a city.

For scenarios demanding content delivery with high bandwidth and low latency, Azure Content Delivery Network (CDN) comes into play. By strategically placing cached content closer to the users, it ensures swift delivery of multimedia, graphics, and scripts, improving user experience and reducing load times.

In understanding Azure's network infrastructure, it is also essential to consider the importance of compliance and data residency. Azure offers a plethora of regions and availability zones, ensuring that you can host your applications close to your user base while adhering to legal and compliance requirements.

Azure also offers tools for network analytics and visualization. Azure Monitor and Azure Network Watcher provide insights and diagnostics to understand network performance and health. These tools can be likened to analytics and reporting systems that scrutinize traffic patterns and provide insights for optimization.

When dealing with hybrid cloud scenarios, Azure Arc extends Azure's management capabilities to other environments, creating a unified and seamless experience. It is like extending the jurisdiction of traffic management to roads beyond city limits, ensuring smooth traffic flow regardless of the boundaries.

The beauty of Azure's network infrastructure lies in its flexibility, scalability, and range of options catering to diverse needs. By understanding and leveraging these components effectively, one can architect robust, efficient, and secure network solutions that seamlessly integrate with various applications and services.

Navigating through Azure's network infrastructure might seem daunting initially, but with a keen understanding of each component and their interactions, it becomes a coherent and manageable task. Whether it's optimizing data flow, ensuring security, or guaranteeing high availability, Azure's networking services provide the tools and capabilities to meet and excel in these requirements.

Chapter 2: Mastering Virtual Networks and Subnetting

Embarking on a journey to explore network interfaces and IP addresses is like stepping into the bustling heart of a city where every building has a unique address and every doorway is an entry point. In the digital landscape, network interfaces serve as these entry points, while IP addresses act as the distinct addresses that allow data packets to find their way across the vast interconnected network. Understanding the intricate relationship between network interfaces and IP addresses is essential for anyone keen on deciphering the mechanics of network communication.

A network interface, whether it's a network adapter, a network connection, or a virtual interface, acts as a bridge between a computer or device and a network. It is through these interfaces that a device sends or receives data, making them akin to the doorways or gates through which information enters or exits a building. These interfaces could be physical, such as Ethernet ports on a computer, or virtual, as seen in cloud environments and virtual machines.

IP addresses, on the other hand, are unique identifiers assigned to each device or interface on a network. Much like the address of a house, an IP address allows data packets to find their way to a specific destination among a multitude of networked devices. There are two versions of IP addresses in use today: IPv4, which uses a 32-bit address scheme, and IPv6, which uses a 128-bit scheme.

IPv4 addresses are typically represented as four sets of numbers separated by periods, such as 192.168.1.1. Given the exponential growth of internet-connected devices, IPv4 addresses are becoming scarce, leading to the adoption of IPv6, which offers a significantly larger pool of addresses. An IPv6 address, being longer, appears as a series of hexadecimal numbers separated by colons, such as 1200:0000:AB00:1234:0000:2552:7777:1313.

Dynamic Host Configuration Protocol (DHCP) is a vital protocol that dynamically assigns IP addresses to devices on a network. Imagine a scenario where a guest enters a hotel and is assigned a room; DHCP works in a similar fashion. When a device connects to a network, DHCP assigns it an IP address from a pool of available addresses, ensuring that each device has a unique identifier while minimizing the administrative overhead of manual assignment.

In contrast, static IP addressing is like a reserved parking spot, where the address does not change. A device with a static IP address retains the same address every time it connects to the network, ensuring consistent and predictable communication, especially important for servers and network equipment.

Network interfaces and IP addresses work together to facilitate communication within and across networks. For instance, in cloud environments such as Microsoft Azure or Amazon Web Services, virtual network interfaces, often referred to as network interface cards (NICs), can be attached to virtual machines or other cloud resources. These NICs are then assigned IP addresses, either dynamically through DHCP or statically, ensuring that the cloud resources are reachable and can communicate with other devices.

Subnet masks and CIDR notation are additional concepts that help in understanding how IP addresses are used within networks. A subnet mask divides the IP address into network and host addresses, thereby determining which part of the IP address identifies the network and which part identifies the device. CIDR notation, on the other hand, appends a slash followed by a number to an IP address, such as 192.168.1.0/24, to indicate the subnet mask.

Address Resolution Protocol (ARP) is another crucial piece of the puzzle. ARP helps in mapping a 32-bit IP address to a physical address on the local network, known as a MAC address. This ensures that data packets reach the correct device on a local network.

Understanding the concept of private and public IP addresses is also crucial. Private IP addresses are used within a network and are not routable on the internet, while public IP addresses are unique across the entire internet. Network Address Translation (NAT) is a technique used to allow devices with private IP addresses to communicate over the internet by translating their addresses to a public IP address.

In cloud environments, it's common to assign a public IP address to a resource that needs to be accessible from the internet, such as a web server, while keeping other resources with only private IP addresses for security. Elastic IPs in AWS or Reserved IP addresses in Azure are examples of public IP addresses that can be dynamically associated with any resource, offering flexibility and ease of management.

When configuring network interfaces and IP addresses, it's also important to consider security implications. Firewalls, Security Groups, Network Security Groups, or Access Control Lists can be configured to control the traffic that is allowed to reach or leave a network interface.

Additionally, considering redundancy and failover strategies is essential. Multiple network interfaces can be attached to a single device to provide redundancy and load balancing. In the event of a failure, traffic can be seamlessly redirected to an alternate interface, ensuring continuous availability.

Quality of Service (QoS) is another aspect that can be configured at the network interface level. By prioritizing certain types of traffic, QoS ensures that critical applications receive the necessary bandwidth and latency requirements even in congested networks.

In the realm of IoT and edge computing, understanding network interfaces and IP addresses takes on additional importance. With myriad devices connecting to the network, efficiently managing IP addresses and ensuring seamless communication becomes pivotal.

Exploring network interfaces and IP addresses is akin to understanding the language and pathways of digital communication. By grasping these concepts, one can navigate, design, and optimize networks with confidence and precision, ensuring that data flows seamlessly like a well-directed symphony of digital signals.

Designing effective subnetting strategies is akin to planning the layout of a vast city, where the careful division and allocation of spaces ensure efficient traffic flow and connectivity among different regions. When crafting a subnetting strategy, it's crucial to understand that subnetting is the practice of dividing an IP network into sub-networks, each known as a subnet. By doing this, you can create logical divisions within your network, ensuring that data packets are routed efficiently, and the network remains scalable and manageable.

The process of subnetting starts by assessing the requirements of your network. This involves estimating the number of hosts you need to accommodate in each subnet, as well as considering the potential for future growth. By accurately gauging the present and future needs of your network, you can allocate IP addresses judiciously, preventing wastage and avoiding potential bottlenecks.

One of the key aspects to consider while subnetting is the IP address class you are working with. In the early days of the internet, IP addresses were categorized into classes A, B, and

C, each offering a different range of addresses suitable for various network sizes. However, as the internet grew, the need for more flexibility in IP address allocation led to the introduction of Classless Inter-Domain Routing (CIDR), which allows for more granular control over IP address assignment. CIDR notation facilitates the process of subnetting by allowing you to specify the subnet mask as a prefix length. For instance, an IP address written as 192.168.1.0/24 indicates that the first 24 bits are used for network identification, leaving the remaining 8 bits for host addresses. By altering the prefix length, you can create subnets of varying sizes tailored to your specific needs.

When designing a subnetting strategy, it's also important to think about the hierarchical structure of your network. Subnets can be created to mirror the physical or logical topology of your network, allowing you to group related devices together. For example, you might create separate subnets for different departments in an organization, ensuring that related devices are grouped together for ease of management and improved security.

Efficient subnetting also helps in minimizing network congestion. By segregating traffic into distinct subnets, you can ensure that broadcast traffic, which is sent to all devices in a subnet, is limited to a smaller number of devices. This not only reduces the load on the network but also enhances security by limiting the scope of broadcast traffic.

Another significant aspect to consider while subnetting is route summarization. Route summarization, also known as route aggregation, is the practice of representing a series of network addresses in a single summary address. By designing your subnets thoughtfully, you can ensure that routing tables remain concise and that routers can make quicker routing decisions, improving overall network performance.

When implementing a subnetting strategy, you should also consider the use of Variable Length Subnet Masking (VLSM). VLSM allows you to allocate IP addresses in a way that doesn't adhere strictly to the fixed lengths dictated by traditional IP address classes. This means you can create subnets of varying sizes, ensuring efficient utilization of IP addresses.

Consideration of network services and applications is also essential while designing your subnets. Certain applications may require specific network configurations or have particular bandwidth and latency requirements. By understanding these needs, you can create subnets that are optimized for these applications, ensuring smooth operation and improved user experience.

It's also beneficial to factor in redundancy and high availability when crafting your subnetting strategy. By creating subnets that can provide failover options and backup paths for data, you can build a network that is resilient and capable of maintaining functionality even when faced with hardware failures or other issues.

Additionally, paying attention to security and compliance requirements is crucial when designing your subnets. Certain data or applications may need to be isolated from the broader network to ensure privacy and compliance with regulatory standards. By strategically placing such data and applications in separate subnets, you can enforce stricter access controls and monitoring.

Network administrators should also be mindful of the potential challenges that can arise from overly complex subnetting strategies. Over-segmentation can lead to a cumbersome network that is difficult to manage and troubleshoot. Striking a balance between granularity and simplicity is key to crafting a subnetting strategy that is both efficient and manageable.

Moreover, embracing automation and network management tools can significantly simplify the process of implementing and managing your subnetting strategy. Tools that allow for IP address management, network monitoring, and automated configuration can be invaluable allies in ensuring that your subnetting strategy is effectively realized and maintained.

As organizations increasingly move towards hybrid and multi-cloud environments, understanding how to effectively subnet across these diverse landscapes becomes paramount. Crafting a subnetting strategy that is adaptable to both on-premises and cloud environments ensures consistency and eases the management burden.

In the age of Internet of Things (IoT), subnetting also plays a crucial role in managing the myriad devices that may be connected to the network. By creating dedicated subnets for IoT devices, network administrators can ensure better security and manageability.

Ultimately, designing an effective subnetting strategy is about foresight, understanding your network's needs, and ensuring that your approach is adaptable to future growth and change. Through careful planning and thoughtful implementation, you can create a network that is efficient, secure, and primed for success in the fast-evolving digital landscape.

Chapter 3: Advanced Network Traffic Management

Implementing load balancing and traffic manager solutions is akin to artfully orchestrating a symphony, where each component must work in harmony to deliver a seamless, responsive, and high-performing experience. Let's delve into the world of load balancing and traffic management to understand how these solutions ensure that applications and services run efficiently, and users are served without delay. Load balancing is the process of distributing network or application traffic across multiple servers to ensure that no single server bears too much demand. By doing this, it ensures that all servers share the load, optimizing resource use, maximizing throughput, minimizing response time, and ensuring fault tolerance and redundancy.

Load balancers can be categorized based on their layer of operation in the OSI model. Layer 4 load balancers operate at the transport layer and make decisions based on information like the source and destination IP addresses and ports. Layer 7 load balancers, on the other hand, operate at the application layer and can make more complex decisions based on content, such as HTTP headers, cookies, or application messages.

In the context of Azure, a variety of load balancing solutions cater to different needs. The Azure Load Balancer is a Layer 4 load balancer that provides high availability by distributing incoming network traffic across multiple virtual machines. It is a reliable and low-latency solution that scales up to millions of flows for all TCP and UDP applications.

Azure Application Gateway is another offering, operating at Layer 7, which provides application-level routing and load balancing services. It allows for more sophisticated routing rules based on URL paths, and can also offer SSL termination, which offloads the SSL handshake workload from the backend servers.

Azure Traffic Manager, meanwhile, is a DNS-based traffic load balancer that distributes traffic optimally to services across global Azure regions while ensuring high availability and responsiveness. It directs client requests to the nearest endpoint using DNS responses, ensuring users connect to the nearest or healthiest service endpoint.

When implementing load balancing solutions, it's important to consider the architecture of your application and the patterns of your traffic. Stateless applications, where each request is independent, are often easier to balance as any server can handle any request. Stateful applications, which maintain information across multiple requests, can require more thoughtful planning to ensure consistency and reliability.

Another consideration is session persistence, also known as sticky sessions. Some applications may require that a user's session is always directed to the same backend server. Load balancers can be configured to ensure such session affinity based on criteria like IP addresses or cookies.

In scenarios where services are deployed across different geographical locations, DNS-based solutions like Azure Traffic Manager become invaluable. It uses DNS to direct client requests to the appropriate service endpoint based on a traffic-routing method and the health of the endpoints. Traffic Manager is not a proxy or a gateway, and client connections are made directly to the selected endpoint.

One of the interesting features of Azure Traffic Manager is its ability to use a variety of routing methods to determine the best endpoint for each user request. It can route traffic based on priority, geographic location, performance, and even a weighted round-robin method.

In addition to the classic methods of load balancing, Azure also provides solutions for content delivery optimization via Azure Content Delivery Network (CDN). By caching content at strategic locations, CDNs reduce load on the primary servers and bring content geographically closer to users, thus minimizing latency.

Health probes are another vital aspect of load balancing and traffic management solutions. Load balancers and traffic managers use health probes to determine the status of the servers or endpoints in their configuration. If a server fails a health check, it can be automatically removed from the pool, ensuring that users are not directed to a faulty server.

Implementing load balancing and traffic manager solutions also requires attention to security. Secure Socket Layer (SSL) or Transport Layer Security (TLS) termination at the load balancer can offload cryptographic workload from the backend servers. However, it's important to consider end-to-end encryption requirements to ensure data privacy.

Azure's load balancing and traffic management solutions also offer detailed diagnostics and logging capabilities. Monitoring and logging can provide insights into application performance, user behavior, and potential security issues. Metrics and diagnostics data can be sent to Azure Monitor logs, allowing for comprehensive analytics and alerting.

In environments where microservices architectures are deployed, services like Azure Service Fabric or Kubernetes can also play a role in load balancing and traffic management. Kubernetes, for instance, provides its own load balancing capabilities that can work in conjunction with Azure's load balancing solutions.

When planning for disaster recovery, load balancing and traffic management solutions can also be configured for failover scenarios. Traffic can be rerouted to backup sites or regions in the event of a failure, ensuring continuity of service.

By understanding the nuances of each load balancing and traffic management solution, and aligning them with the needs of your application, you can craft a resilient, high-performing, and scalable environment. Whether you're optimizing for performance, geography, or simply ensuring high availability, Azure offers a suite of tools and services to fit the bill.

Implementing load balancing and traffic management is an ongoing task, requiring regular assessment and adjustment to meet changing demands and to adapt to evolving technologies. Through careful planning, vigilant monitoring, and judicious use of the tools at your disposal, you can ensure that your applications remain robust, responsive, and ready to meet the needs of your users, wherever they may be.

Customizing routing in a network environment provides the flexibility and control needed to direct traffic in ways that optimize performance, enhance security, and enable specialized configurations. This task becomes even more crucial in cloud environments, such as Microsoft Azure, where resources are dynamically provisioned and may span across multiple regions. Let's explore the concepts of route tables and IP forwarding as mechanisms to customize routing in network environments.

In a network, a route table contains rules, known as routes, that determine where network traffic from a subnet or a Virtual Network Interface (vNIC) should be directed. These tables act like a set of instructions for packet forwarding, allowing network administrators to control the flow of traffic. The destination of a packet is determined by consulting the route table, finding the route that matches the packet's destination, and then forwarding it accordingly.

In Microsoft Azure, route tables are crucial for efficiently navigating the network within your Virtual Network (VNet). A default route table is automatically created with every VNet, containing built-in routes that handle common traffic patterns. However, to address more specific needs, you can create custom route tables with user-defined routes to override or augment the default routes.

For instance, you may have scenarios where you want to route traffic between subnets through a Network Virtual Appliance (NVA), which could be a firewall, a WAN optimizer, or other network function delivered as a virtual machine. In such cases, customizing the route table is necessary.

When creating a user-defined route, you must specify a destination, the next hop type, and a next-hop address. The destination is the IP address range you're targeting, the next hop type defines the kind of Azure hop the packet should be forwarded to, and the next-hop address specifies the IP address packets will be forwarded to.

IP forwarding is another significant aspect of routing customization. When a virtual machine receives traffic not intended for one of its own IP addresses, it would typically drop the packets. However, by enabling IP forwarding on a virtual machine's network interface, you instruct Azure to allow the virtual machine to act as a router, forwarding traffic to other IP addresses.

This capability is crucial when you are deploying virtual appliances such as firewalls or load balancers, which need to handle traffic not destined for their own IP address. For example, a virtual machine acting as a router or a firewall will need IP forwarding enabled to correctly process and forward the packets to the intended destinations.

Combining route tables and IP forwarding allows for sophisticated scenarios. Imagine a situation where you have multiple subnets within an Azure VNet and you wish to control and inspect the traffic between them. You could deploy a Network Virtual Appliance and use custom route tables to direct traffic between the subnets through this NVA. With IP forwarding enabled on the NVA, it can analyze or modify the packets as needed before sending them on to their final destination.

In scenarios where you have hybrid connectivity, such as a site-to-site VPN or ExpressRoute connection from on-premises to Azure, understanding and customizing routing becomes even more important. You may want to ensure that traffic between your on-premises data center and your Azure resources takes an optimal path, or that certain types of traffic are inspected by network security appliances.

Azure also provides a feature known as Border Gateway Protocol (BGP) route propagation for VPN and ExpressRoute connections. BGP is a dynamic routing protocol that enables automatic updates of route tables based on the network's topology. By using BGP, you can ensure that your Azure route tables are automatically kept in sync with the routing configurations of your on-premises network.

While customizing routing allows for granular control, it's essential to consider the implications on security and performance. Misconfigurations can lead to unintended traffic patterns, creating security vulnerabilities or performance bottlenecks. Thorough planning, careful implementation, and continuous monitoring are key to successful network customization.

Another aspect to consider is the resilience and high availability of your NVAs or routing devices. Azure provides capabilities such as Availability Sets and Availability Zones to ensure that your virtual appliances are not single points of failure in your network architecture.

Moreover, Azure offers tools to troubleshoot and verify your routing configurations. Features such as Effective Routes in the Azure portal allow you to see the cumulative set of routes that a network interface applies, letting you confirm that your custom routing configurations are working as intended.

In the realm of cloud and hybrid networking, technologies and requirements are continuously evolving. Concepts like service endpoints and private endpoints in Azure offer new ways to control routing and access to Azure services. Network Watcher is a service in Azure that provides tools to monitor, diagnose, and gain insights into your network in Azure.

By leveraging the capabilities of route tables and IP forwarding in Azure, network administrators can tailor the network traffic flow to meet specific needs and requirements. Whether it's optimizing for performance, ensuring security compliance, or crafting complex hybrid network architectures, Azure provides the flexibility and control to customize routing effectively.

Understanding and mastering these tools and principles open up possibilities for designing and managing networks that are efficient, secure, and aligned with your organizational goals. With thoughtful design and diligent management, customized routing can become a powerful asset in your network architecture toolkit.

Chapter 4: Azure Storage Solutions: Beyond the Basics

Diving into the various storage services offered by Microsoft Azure can be an enriching experience, unveiling a world of possibilities for data management and application development. Azure's storage services, namely Blob, File, Table, and Queue Storage, provide a robust and versatile platform to store vast amounts of data in the cloud, catering to different needs and scenarios. Let's explore each of these services in detail to gain a comprehensive understanding of their functionalities and best use cases.

Azure Blob Storage is designed to store large amounts of unstructured data, such as text, images, videos, and binary data, making it a perfect fit for applications that deal with media and documents. The term "Blob" stands for Binary Large Object, and Blob Storage allows you to create containers, akin to directories, within which you can store an almost limitless number of blobs. This service is highly scalable and offers different access tiers, allowing you to optimize storage costs by choosing between frequent, infrequent, or archival access patterns.

Azure Blob Storage supports various data types, such as Block Blobs, which are optimized for streaming, and Append Blobs, which are ideal for scenarios where data needs to be added continuously, such as logging. With features such as automatic data tiering and lifecycle management, Azure Blob Storage can be a cost-effective solution for storing large amounts of unstructured data that might need to be accessed or modified regularly.

Next, let's explore Azure File Storage, which provides fully managed file shares accessible via the Server Message Block (SMB) protocol. This service facilitates the migration of legacy applications to the cloud by providing a shared file system that can be accessed concurrently by multiple application instances. Azure File Storage simplifies the process of sharing application data, configurations, and diagnostic logs across distributed cloud resources.

One of the compelling aspects of Azure File Storage is its seamless integration with on-premises deployments, enabling hybrid cloud scenarios. Businesses can replace or supplement their on-premises file servers and Network-Attached Storage (NAS) devices with Azure File Storage without having to alter their existing applications or workflows significantly.

Shifting the focus to structured data, Azure Table Storage offers a highly available, massively scalable storage solution that enables applications to store and retrieve structured data using a key/attribute store. With Table Storage, data is stored in tables that are similar to tables in a relational database, but more flexible. Each entity in a table has a primary key composed of a Partition Key and a Row Key, which together uniquely identify each entity.

Azure Table Storage is a NoSQL data store, making it suitable for applications that require a flexible schema design. It is ideal for storing large volumes of non-relational data, and its schema-less nature allows developers to integrate it rapidly with applications that need scalable and adaptable storage.

Last but not least, Azure Queue Storage offers a reliable messaging solution for asynchronous communication between application components. It acts as a mediator between different parts of an application, ensuring that they can communicate effectively without being directly connected. Azure Queue Storage supports decoupling components, making applications scalable, resilient, and easy to manage.

Queue Storage enables you to build flexible and scalable applications by allowing components to process messages asynchronously. For instance, a web application can enqueue tasks for background processing, ensuring quick response times for users, while background services can process the tasks as resources become available.

Each storage service in Azure is designed with specific scenarios in mind. Azure Blob Storage is suitable for applications that need to store large amounts of unstructured data. Azure File Storage is an excellent choice for shared file systems and migrating on-premises applications that rely on file shares. Azure Table Storage caters to applications that need to store large amounts of structured, non-relational data, and Azure Queue Storage is perfect for creating scalable applications through asynchronous message processing.

Security and data protection are inherent in all Azure storage services. Features like Shared Access Signatures (SAS), Azure Role-Based Access Control (RBAC), and encryption at rest and in transit ensure that your data is secure, regardless of the storage solution you choose.

Furthermore, Azure offers tools and services to optimize your storage usage and costs. Services like Azure Cost Management and Azure Storage Account Management help you monitor and control your expenditures and manage your resources efficiently.

In terms of performance, Azure Storage services provide options like premium tiers for high-throughput scenarios and geo-redundant storage for durability and high availability. With geo-replication, your data is stored in multiple geographical locations, ensuring that it is accessible even in the case of regional outages.

Integration capabilities of Azure Storage services are vast, with support for various programming languages and frameworks. Developers can use SDKs for languages such as .NET, Java, Python, and Node.js to interact with these services, making it easy to integrate Azure Storage into various application architectures.

In essence, Azure offers a diverse array of storage solutions, each tailored for different needs, allowing developers and businesses to select and customize their storage infrastructure based on their requirements. By understanding and strategically implementing Azure Blob, File, Table, and Queue Storage, one can build robust, scalable, and cost-efficient applications in the cloud.

Embarking on a journey through the realm of advanced storage configurations and data lakes opens up avenues for handling data in ways that bring forth the nuances of big data management and analytics. In this digital age, organizations are flooded with vast amounts of data, ranging from structured datasets to unstructured content like text, images, and videos. Taming this data deluge requires solutions that can store, manage, and analyze these diverse datasets efficiently and cost-effectively. Advanced storage configurations and data lakes serve as critical components in this data management puzzle, providing organizations with the tools to harness their data effectively.

Data lakes are designed to store vast volumes of data in their raw form, offering a centralized repository that can hold structured, semi-structured, and unstructured data. Unlike traditional databases or data warehouses, data lakes allow data to be stored at any scale and in any format. This versatile nature makes them suitable for businesses looking to gain insights from diverse datasets without being hindered by rigid schemas or storage limitations.

The concept of a data lake is closely associated with big data and analytics, as it provides a unified platform where organizations can perform sophisticated analytics and machine learning on their accumulated data. This includes data mining, predictive analytics, and real-time analytics, enabling businesses to derive actionable insights and make informed decisions.

In the context of advanced storage configurations, data lakes can be complemented with various features and technologies that enhance performance, security, and ease of use. One such technology is data tiering, which allows data to be automatically moved between different storage classes or tiers based on usage patterns. This ensures that frequently accessed data is readily available, while less frequently used data is moved to more cost-effective storage.

Storage solutions such as Azure Data Lake Storage (ADLS) exemplify the integration of advanced storage configurations with data lakes. ADLS is designed to support massively parallel processing, allowing data to be analyzed at scale and facilitating efficient querying of large datasets. It incorporates features like hierarchical namespace, which enables objects(files and directories) in the data lake to be organized into a hierarchy, similar to a file system.

ADLS also integrates seamlessly with various data analytics services and engines such as Azure Databricks, Azure HDInsight, and Apache Spark, providing organizations with powerful tools to analyze their data. By employing these tools, businesses can create sophisticated data pipelines and analytics workflows that can process and analyze data in real-time or in batches.

Data lakes often form a part of a larger data estate strategy that may include data warehouses, databases, and other storage solutions. Integration capabilities play a crucial role here, as organizations need to ensure that data can flow seamlessly between different storage and processing components. By leveraging connectors, APIs, and data integration services, businesses can build a cohesive and agile data infrastructure.

Security and data governance are critical aspects of advanced storage configurations and data lakes. Organizations must ensure that their data is protected from unauthorized access and that compliance requirements are met. Features such as encryption, access control, auditing, and data masking can be implemented to safeguard data and maintain privacy.

One challenge that organizations may face while working with data lakes is the potential for data sprawl and management complexities. Proper metadata management, data cataloging, and implementing a well-thought-out data governance strategy can mitigate these challenges. By tagging and classifying data effectively, organizations can ensure that data is easily discoverable, understandable, and usable.

Data lakes also play a pivotal role in enabling machine learning and artificial intelligence applications. They provide a vast and varied repository from which machine learning algorithms can learn and draw patterns. By facilitating the storage and analysis of large datasets, data lakes allow data scientists and machine learning engineers to build and train more accurate and sophisticated models.

Moreover, organizations can leverage technologies such as data deduplication and compression to optimize storage costs and enhance performance. These advanced storage configurations ensure that data is stored efficiently, without unnecessary redundancy, and can be retrieved quickly when needed.

As businesses continue to generate and accumulate more data, the need for scalable and flexible storage solutions becomes paramount. Data lakes, combined with advanced storage configurations, provide organizations with a powerful toolkit to handle their data needs.

In the era of cloud computing, data lakes are often complemented by additional cloud services that enhance their capabilities. For instance, services like Azure Purview can be used to automate the discovery and classification of data, ensuring that data governance policies are consistently applied across the data lake.

The ability to scale storage infrastructure elastically based on demand is another advantage offered by cloud-based data lakes. This ensures that organizations only pay for the storage they use, allowing them to optimize costs while having the flexibility to scale up as their data needs grow.

In a world that is increasingly data-driven, the strategic use of data lakes and advanced storage configurations can provide organizations with a competitive edge. By efficiently managing and analyzing their data, businesses can uncover insights, drive innovation, and create value for their customers and stakeholders.

In essence, data lakes and advanced storage configurations form a symbiotic relationship, with each enhancing the capabilities of the other. By understanding the intricacies of these technologies and strategically implementing them, organizations can build a robust and flexible data infrastructure that is capable of meeting the challenges of the modern data landscape.

Chapter 5: Optimizing and Securing Azure Storage Accounts

Navigating the expansive landscape of storage solutions requires a keen understanding of how to optimize performance to ensure data is accessible, retrievable, and usable in the most efficient manner. Storage performance optimization is a multi-faceted endeavor that encompasses various practices, tools, and techniques to enhance the speed, efficiency, and reliability of data storage systems. By focusing on best practices, organizations can ensure that their storage infrastructure meets the demands of their applications, users, and workflows.

One of the primary considerations for optimizing storage performance is selecting the right storage solution tailored to the specific needs and workloads of an organization. This means understanding the characteristics of different storage types, such as block storage, file storage, and object storage, and aligning them with the requirements of applications and services. For instance, block storage may be suitable for high-performance applications such as databases, while object storage could be ideal for large-scale data archiving.

Understanding the input/output operations per second (IOPS), throughput, and latency requirements of your applications is essential in making an informed decision about the storage solution. By assessing these metrics, organizations can gauge the performance needs of their applications and choose a storage solution that can meet or exceed those demands.

The placement of data plays a pivotal role in storage performance optimization. Strategies such as data tiering or hierarchical storage management can be employed to ensure that frequently accessed data is stored on faster, albeit more expensive, storage mediums, while less frequently accessed data is moved to slower, cost-effective storage. This intelligent allocation of resources ensures optimal utilization of storage capacities.

Caching is another powerful technique to enhance storage performance. By storing frequently accessed data in a cache memory, which is typically faster to access than the primary storage, applications can retrieve data more swiftly. Caching can be implemented at various levels, including the application layer, operating system, or storage device, to improve data retrieval times.

Leveraging storage protocols that are optimized for performance is also crucial. For example, choosing between protocols such as iSCSI, Fibre Channel, or NVMe over Fabrics can have a significant impact on the speed and efficiency of data transfers. Being well-acquainted with the nuances of these protocols allows organizations to align their storage infrastructure with the needs of their applications.

Optimizing the storage network is equally vital in ensuring that data can flow seamlessly and quickly between storage devices and applications. Implementing technologies such as high-speed Ethernet or Fibre Channel, and ensuring proper network configuration and redundancy can significantly enhance storage performance.

In the context of databases and applications, optimizing queries and implementing proper indexing can lead to more efficient data retrieval and better overall performance. Well-structured queries and appropriately indexed databases reduce the time and resources required to fetch data, thereby optimizing storage performance.

For organizations leveraging cloud storage solutions, understanding and selecting the appropriate storage classes and services offered by cloud providers can lead to performance gains. Cloud providers offer a variety of storage solutions tailored to different use cases, each with its performance characteristics and cost implications. By aligning cloud storage solutions with workload requirements, organizations can achieve a balance between cost and performance.

Another best practice involves regularly monitoring and analyzing storage performance metrics. By keeping a close eye on metrics such as IOPS, latency, throughput, and capacity utilization, organizations can proactively identify and address potential bottlenecks and performance issues. Utilizing tools and services that provide insights into storage performance can be invaluable in this regard.

Load balancing across multiple storage devices or paths can also enhance storage performance. This involves distributing data access requests evenly across several storage devices or network paths, preventing any single device or path from becoming a bottleneck. Load balancing ensures that storage resources are used efficiently and can handle high volumes of data requests without performance degradation.

Data compression and deduplication are techniques that can optimize storage usage and potentially improve performance. By reducing the size of stored data through compression and eliminating duplicate copies of data through deduplication, organizations can make more efficient use of their storage capacity. However, it's essential to consider the computational overhead associated with these techniques and weigh the benefits against any potential performance impact.

Implementing redundancy and failover mechanisms, such as RAID configurations, can also contribute to storage performance optimization. By strategically distributing data across multiple disks, RAID configurations can enhance data availability and improve read and write speeds. Choosing the right RAID level based on the desired balance between performance, redundancy, and capacity is a critical consideration.

Optimizing file systems and choosing the appropriate block sizes can also lead to improved storage performance. Different file systems have different characteristics and are optimized for various types of workloads. By selecting a file system that aligns well with the application's needs and configuring it appropriately, organizations can achieve more efficient data storage and retrieval.

For organizations leveraging virtualization, aligning virtual hard disks (VHDs) and ensuring proper configuration of the storage stack in virtual environments can enhance performance. Paying attention to details such as the alignment of partitions and optimizing the storage stack for virtualized workloads can lead to significant performance gains.

Implementing robust security and access controls for storage accounts is pivotal to safeguarding data and ensuring that only authorized individuals have access to sensitive information. In the modern digital age, where data is an invaluable asset, organizations must take a meticulous approach to secure their storage accounts. By understanding the different layers of security and the various tools and techniques available, organizations can establish a comprehensive strategy to protect their storage accounts.

One of the fundamental steps in securing storage accounts involves the implementation of identity and access management (IAM) policies. These policies define who has access to a particular storage account and delineate the actions they are permitted to perform. By assigning roles and permissions carefully, organizations can control access to their data while maintaining operational efficiency.

Authentication is the process of verifying the identity of a user or system attempting to access a storage account.

Implementing strong authentication mechanisms, such as multi-factor authentication (MFA), ensures that access is granted only to authenticated entities. By combining something the user knows, such as a password, with something the user has, like a mobile device or a smart card, MFA adds an extra layer of security that can thwart unauthorized access. Authorization, on the other hand, determines what actions an authenticated user or system is allowed to perform. By defining granular permissions, organizations can ensure that users have the least privileges necessary to perform their tasks, thereby reducing the risk of data exposure. Leveraging role-based access control (RBAC) enables organizations to assign permissions based on roles, making it easier to manage and audit access controls.

Data encryption is another crucial aspect of securing storage accounts. Encryption can be applied both in transit and at rest to protect data from unauthorized access and eavesdropping. By employing protocols such as Transport Layer Security (TLS) for data in transit and utilizing strong encryption algorithms for data at rest, organizations can ensure the confidentiality and integrity of their data.

Network security is an integral part of safeguarding storage accounts. By employing techniques such as Virtual Network (VNet) service endpoints and private endpoints, organizations can restrict access to their storage accounts to specific virtual networks and IP address ranges. Implementing firewalls and network security groups (NSGs) further enhances the ability to control the flow of traffic to and from storage accounts.

Securing the management plane is also crucial to ensure that only authorized personnel can perform administrative actions on storage accounts. By employing tools such as Azure Policy, organizations can enforce governance and compliance standards across their storage accounts, ensuring that configurations adhere to security best practices.

Storage accounts may contain sensitive data that necessitates compliance with regulatory standards such as the General Data Protection Regulation (GDPR), Health Insurance Portability and Accountability Act (HIPAA), or Payment Card Industry Data Security Standard (PCI DSS). By understanding and implementing security controls that align with these regulatory requirements, organizations can ensure compliance while securing their data.

Auditing and monitoring are indispensable practices in securing storage accounts. By keeping a close eye on access logs, usage patterns, and anomaly detection, organizations can identify and respond to potential security incidents promptly. Implementing tools and services that provide insights into storage account activity, such as Azure Monitor and Azure Security Center, enables organizations to proactively detect and mitigate security threats.

Data integrity checks are essential to ensure that the data stored in storage accounts has not been tampered with or altered in an unauthorized manner. By implementing mechanisms such as checksums and hash functions, organizations can verify the integrity of their data and identify discrepancies that may indicate a security breach.

Storage accounts may also benefit from advanced threat protection services that leverage artificial intelligence and machine learning to identify and mitigate threats. By continuously analyzing data access patterns and identifying unusual behavior, these services can provide early warning signs of potential security incidents.

Data residency and sovereignty considerations may also play a role in securing storage accounts. Organizations may need to ensure that their data is stored in specific geographic regions to comply with legal and regulatory requirements. By selecting the appropriate data centers and regions for their storage accounts, organizations can ensure compliance with data residency and sovereignty laws.

Access keys and shared access signatures (SAS) are common mechanisms for providing access to storage accounts. By managing and rotating access keys regularly and using SAS tokens judiciously, organizations can ensure that access credentials are not compromised. Implementing policies for key rotation and expiration of SAS tokens can enhance the security of storage accounts.

Data classification and labeling are practices that involve categorizing data based on its sensitivity and applying appropriate labels and protection accordingly. By classifying data and implementing controls based on data sensitivity, organizations can apply a tailored approach to securing different types of data within their storage accounts.

Additionally, organizations should consider implementing data recovery and backup strategies to safeguard against data loss due to accidental deletion or malicious attacks such as ransomware. By regularly backing up data and ensuring that recovery mechanisms are in place, organizations can enhance the resiliency of their storage accounts.

Periodic security assessments and penetration testing are valuable practices that can help organizations identify vulnerabilities and weaknesses in their storage account security posture. By proactively identifying and addressing potential security gaps, organizations can enhance the robustness of their storage account security.

Chapter 6: Exploring Azure Load Balancers and Traffic Managers

Achieving high availability in the cloud is a goal that many organizations strive for, and Azure Load Balancers play a significant role in making this a reality. By distributing incoming network traffic across multiple servers, a load balancer ensures that no single server bears too much demand, thereby providing redundancy and ensuring continuity of service even if one or more servers fail. Configuring Azure Load Balancers effectively is an art that combines a solid understanding of your application's requirements with the plethora of features offered by Azure.

Azure provides both Basic and Standard Load Balancers, each catering to different needs and scenarios. The Basic Load Balancer is suitable for smaller-scale applications and dev-test workloads, while the Standard Load Balancer is designed to deliver high scalability, robust performance, and greater flexibility for production workloads. When considering high availability, the Standard Load Balancer is often the preferred choice due to its enhanced capabilities and features.

To begin with, understanding the architecture of your application is crucial in configuring an Azure Load Balancer. Identifying the components that require load balancing, such as web servers or application servers, and mapping out the traffic flow are foundational steps in this process. Additionally, understanding the difference between public and internal load balancing is necessary. A public load balancer is used to distribute incoming internet traffic to resources that are publicly accessible, while an internal load balancer is used for traffic within a Virtual Network (VNet).

Once the groundwork is laid, the next step is to create an Azure Load Balancer instance. During the creation, specifying details such as subscription, resource group, name, region, and type (public or internal) are essential. It's important to note that for high availability, the Load Balancer and the resources it will distribute traffic to should be in the same region.

Configuring front-end IP configurations is a key step that involves specifying the IP addresses that the Load Balancer will use to listen for incoming traffic. For a public Load Balancer, this would be a public IP address, while for an internal Load Balancer, it would be a private IP address within the VNet.

Backend pool configuration is another crucial aspect of ensuring high availability. The backend pool is a set of servers to which the Load Balancer will distribute traffic. Adding Virtual Machines (VMs) or other resources to the backend pool ensures that there are multiple instances ready to handle incoming requests. Ensuring that these instances are identical and stateless is critical to provide a seamless user experience.

Health probes are mechanisms that the Azure Load Balancer uses to determine the health and availability of the backend instances. Configuring health probes correctly ensures that if a server is experiencing issues, the Load Balancer can detect this and route traffic to healthy servers instead. The health probe can be set up to check for HTTP responses, TCP responses, or other custom indicators of health.

Load balancing rules are central to determining how the traffic will be distributed among the backend instances. Configuring rules involves specifying details such as the protocol, frontend and backend port, backend pool, health probe, and session persistence. Session persistence can be configured to ensure that a user's session is directed to the same server for the duration of their interaction, which can be crucial for certain applications.

In the quest for high availability, it's essential to ensure that the Azure Load Balancer is configured to work seamlessly with the Azure Availability Zones or Availability Sets. By distributing the backend instances across different Availability Zones or placing them in an Availability Set, organizations can safeguard against localized failures affecting their application's availability.

Azure Load Balancer also offers features such as outbound rules, which control how responses are handled on their way back to the client. Configuring outbound rules correctly ensures that return traffic is managed effectively, providing a complete and well-rounded traffic management solution.

In scenarios where applications are deployed across regions, Azure Load Balancer can be complemented with Azure Traffic Manager to provide global load balancing. This ensures that users are directed to the nearest or most responsive instance of an application, thereby enhancing availability and reducing latency.

Monitoring and diagnostics are integral parts of maintaining high availability. Utilizing Azure Monitor and Azure Log Analytics, organizations can keep a close eye on the health and performance of their Load Balancer and backend instances. By setting up alerts and diagnostics, organizations can proactively identify and mitigate issues before they impact availability.

Scaling is a consideration that goes hand-in-hand with high availability. Azure Load Balancer is designed to handle millions of flows, ensuring that as the demand on an application grows, the Load Balancer can handle the increase in traffic. Planning for scale and understanding how the Load Balancer will behave under different loads is essential in ensuring uninterrupted service.

Fine-tuning the Azure Load Balancer for optimal performance involves tweaking settings such as idle timeout values and TCP reset settings. By understanding the nuances of these settings and configuring them to align with the application's needs, organizations can ensure a smooth and responsive user experience.

Security is another facet that cannot be overlooked when configuring Azure Load Balancer for high availability. Implementing Network Security Groups (NSGs) to control traffic to and from the Load Balancer and backend instances adds an additional layer of protection. Ensuring that security settings do not interfere with the Load Balancer's operation is crucial.

Disaster recovery and backup strategies are also important to consider. Having a well-documented and tested plan for recovering from failures ensures that even in the face of unexpected issues, the application can continue to provide service with minimal disruption.

In the world of cloud computing, achieving high availability is often a moving target. Technologies evolve, user expectations grow, and organizations must continuously adapt and optimize their configurations to meet these demands. By meticulously configuring Azure Load Balancers and staying abreast of best practices and new features, organizations can build resilient and highly available applications that stand the test of time.

Continuous learning and staying updated with advancements in Azure and cloud load balancing technologies ensure that organizations can leverage new features and improvements. Regularly revisiting and reassessing the Load Balancer configuration to align with the evolving needs of the application and the organization is a practice that can yield long-term benefits.

In essence, configuring Azure Load Balancers for high availability is a multifaceted endeavor that involves a deep understanding of the application's architecture, careful planning, and meticulous implementation of features and settings. By taking a holistic approach and considering factors such as scalability, security, monitoring, and continuous improvement, organizations can ensure that their applications are not just highly available, but also resilient and ready to meet the demands of the modern digital landscape.

The art of efficiently routing internet traffic is one of the subtle yet critical elements that can significantly enhance user experience and application performance. In the Microsoft

Azure ecosystem, Traffic Manager serves as an intelligent DNS-based traffic load balancer, ensuring optimal traffic distribution across various globally distributed endpoints. Leveraging the capabilities of Traffic Manager, organizations can ensure high availability, responsiveness, and resilience in their applications by directing traffic in a manner that aligns with predefined rules and policies.

At its core, Traffic Manager doesn't handle traffic per se; instead, it directs DNS queries to the most suitable endpoint based on the rules set by administrators. These endpoints can be Azure services, external websites, or other cloud services. The essence of Traffic Manager's operation is to improve application performance and ensure business continuity in case of endpoint failures.

To understand how Traffic Manager enhances user experience, it's important to delve into its routing methods. The first and perhaps most commonly used routing method is the Performance method. By directing user requests to the closest or most responsive endpoint in terms of network latency, the Performance method ensures that users experience minimal lag and optimal responsiveness while accessing an application.

Another routing method offered by Traffic Manager is Priority, which functions akin to a failover mechanism. In this method, Traffic Manager routes all traffic to the primary endpoint unless it's unavailable, in which case the traffic is routed to secondary endpoints in a predefined order. This method is particularly useful for scenarios where one wants to have standby services ready to take over if the primary service faces any disruptions.

Weighted routing is another method that gives administrators the flexibility to distribute traffic unevenly among multiple endpoints. This method is useful when, for example, you are testing a new feature and want to expose it to only a portion of your user base. By assigning different weights to endpoints, administrators can control the proportion of traffic each endpoint receives.

The Geographic routing method enables traffic routing based on the geographic location from which the DNS queries originate. This can be valuable in scenarios where there are data sovereignty requirements or when content needs to be customized based on geographic regions.

Subnet traffic routing allows administrators to define explicit mappings between sets of end-user IP address ranges, represented as CIDR notation subnets, and specific endpoints. This can be helpful when certain user communities need to be directed to specific endpoints.

A Multivalue routing method provides multiple healthy endpoints in response to DNS queries without making any decisions or assumptions regarding the health or responsiveness of the endpoints. This method is used when client-side logic determines the most appropriate endpoint.

Traffic Manager's capabilities extend beyond these routing methods, adding layers of intelligence to traffic routing. Endpoint monitoring is an intrinsic feature of Traffic Manager, ensuring that it continually assesses the health of endpoints and routes traffic away from endpoints that are deemed unhealthy.

By creating custom DNS names for the services, Traffic Manager also provides seamless domain name resolution, abstracting the complexities of service locations and making it easier for users to access services. This seamless name resolution becomes especially crucial when services are moved or scaled across regions.

When diving deeper into how Traffic Manager is configured, it's important to recognize that the DNS Time-To-Live (TTL) setting plays a significant role. The TTL determines how long a DNS resolution result is cached, and fine-tuning this parameter can influence how quickly changes in endpoint status are reflected on the client side.

Traffic Manager profiles are containers for your DNS routing configuration, and each profile contains a set of rules that define how traffic is routed. Understanding and configuring these profiles is fundamental in ensuring that Traffic Manager operates as per the desired traffic distribution strategy.

Given the distributed nature of applications today, having a tool like Traffic Manager that provides DNS-level traffic routing becomes indispensable. For instance, consider an e-commerce application that's deployed in multiple Azure regions to provide low-latency access to users across the globe. In this scenario, Traffic Manager can be configured to use the Performance routing method to ensure users are always directed to the nearest instance of the application.

But what happens if one of these instances faces an unexpected issue? Traffic Manager's automatic endpoint health checks and failover capabilities ensure that users are seamlessly redirected to a healthy instance, thereby ensuring business continuity and a consistent user experience.

In scenarios where there are regulatory compliance requirements, such as data residency stipulations, Traffic Manager's Geographic routing method can ensure that data processing and storage occur only in specific geographic regions. This capability ensures compliance with legal mandates while still optimizing for performance.

In cases where precise control over traffic distribution is required, for example during A/B testing or phased rollouts of new features, the Weighted routing method can be a powerful tool. By adjusting the weights assigned to different endpoints, organizations can control exposure and gather valuable data on feature reception and performance.

Traffic Manager also shines in hybrid and multi-cloud environments. Its ability to include external, non-Azure endpoints means that organizations can have a unified traffic routing mechanism even if their services are spread across multiple cloud providers and on-premises data centers.

Ensuring security and privacy in DNS queries is also a noteworthy feature of Traffic Manager. By supporting DNS

Security Extensions (DNSSEC), Traffic Manager provides a secure and trusted routing option, thereby enhancing overall application security.

Optimal traffic distribution isn't just about routing users to the nearest endpoint; it's a delicate balance that takes into account availability, responsiveness, compliance, and user experience. Azure Traffic Manager, with its array of routing methods and configurations, empowers organizations to strike this balance effectively.

When implementing Traffic Manager, it's beneficial to periodically review and adjust the configurations as the application evolves and user traffic patterns change. Regularly analyzing Traffic Manager logs and metrics can provide insights into the effectiveness of the current routing strategy and highlight areas for improvement.

In essence, ensuring optimal traffic distribution with Azure Traffic Manager is a continuous process of assessment, configuration, and optimization. By understanding the nuances of different routing methods and strategically leveraging Traffic Manager's capabilities, organizations can ensure that their applications are not just available and responsive, but also capable of delivering a tailored and seamless user experience.

Chapter 7: VPNs and Azure ExpressRoute: Building Secure Connections

Establishing a secure and reliable connection between disparate networks is a critical requirement for businesses operating in today's digital landscape. In the realm of Microsoft Azure, Site-to-Site Virtual Private Networks (VPNs) emerge as a robust solution to this challenge, facilitating secure communication between an on-premises network and an Azure virtual network. This connectivity ensures that data traversing the internet is secure, encapsulated, and accessible only to authorized entities.

Understanding the underlying mechanics of Site-to-Site VPNs starts with grasping the role of a VPN gateway. In the context of Azure, a VPN gateway is a specific type of virtual network gateway that is designed to send encrypted traffic across a public network, such as the internet. By leveraging industry-standard protocols such as IPsec and IKE, the VPN gateway ensures that the data being transmitted is not only secure but also efficiently routed.

Before diving into the process of setting up a Site-to-Site VPN, it is vital to comprehend the architecture of Azure networking and the components involved. An Azure virtual network is akin to a traditional network but exists in the cloud. When establishing a Site-to-Site VPN, the VPN gateway sits at the edge of the Azure virtual network and connects it to the on-premises VPN device, creating a secure pathway for data to flow.

The process of establishing a Site-to-Site VPN in Azure commences with the creation and configuration of a virtual network. During this stage, parameters such as address space, subnets, and regions are defined. Careful planning at this juncture ensures that the Azure virtual network is congruent with the broader network architecture of the organization.

Next, the focus shifts to the creation of the VPN gateway. This step involves specifying the Gateway subnet, which is crucial for hosting the VPN gateway and ensuring it has the necessary resources for operation. It's essential to recognize that the Gateway subnet is different from the other subnets in the virtual network and is reserved exclusively for Azure's gateway services.

Once the Gateway subnet is in place, the actual creation of the VPN gateway ensues. During this phase, details such as the Gateway type, VPN type, SKU, and generation need to be selected. The choices made here will depend on factors like required performance, routing type, and budget considerations.

Parallel to the creation of the VPN gateway, attention must also be directed towards preparing the on-premises network for connectivity. This involves configuring an on-premises VPN device with details such as IP address, shared keys, and routing specifications. The on-premises VPN device can be a dedicated hardware appliance or a software solution, depending on the organization's preferences and requirements.

With the VPN gateway and the on-premises VPN device configured, the next step is to create a connection between them. This connection is defined in Azure and includes details such as the public IP address of the on-premises VPN device, the shared key used for authentication, and the connection type, which in this case would be Site-to-Site.

Ensuring the correct configuration of routing is another critical aspect of establishing a Site-to-Site VPN. Azure supports both route-based and policy-based VPNs, and the choice between the two would depend on the organization's specific use case and the capabilities of the on-premises VPN device.

Once the connection is established and configured, it is essential to monitor and manage the VPN to ensure its optimal functioning. Azure provides various tools and services, such as Azure Monitor and Azure Network Watcher, that enable administrators to gain insights into the health and performance of the Site-to-Site VPN.

Periodic testing and validation of the VPN connection are recommended to ensure that the setup is functioning as expected. Conducting tests such as initiating connections from both ends, checking data encryption, and validating the latency and throughput can provide assurances regarding the reliability and security of the Site-to-Site VPN.

Beyond the technicalities of setting up the Site-to-Site VPN, considerations regarding compliance, data sovereignty, and cost are also paramount. Organizations must ensure that the data transmitted over the VPN adheres to legal and regulatory requirements. Additionally, keeping an eye on the cost associated with the VPN gateway, especially in terms of data transfer and required performance, is crucial for maintaining budgetary control.

Optimizing the performance of the Site-to-Site VPN is an ongoing task that involves tweaking configurations, updating route tables, and scaling resources as necessary. Regularly revisiting the setup and making adjustments based on evolving requirements can ensure that the VPN remains a robust and efficient bridge between the on-premises network and the Azure virtual network.

In scenarios where redundancy and high availability are of utmost importance, organizations can consider implementing multiple Site-to-Site VPN connections, effectively creating a VPN redundancy setup. This approach ensures that even if one connection faces an issue, the traffic can seamlessly failover to the other connection, thereby ensuring uninterrupted communication.

Understanding the nuances of connectivity is paramount when working with cloud services, and Microsoft Azure offers a plethora of options to ensure seamless and secure communication between your on-premises infrastructure and the cloud. Among these options, Azure ExpressRoute stands out as a dedicated, private connectivity solution that facilitates a direct connection to Azure and other Microsoft services. When it comes to transmitting sensitive data or managing large workloads, this level of direct connectivity is often preferred over internet-based connections.

Azure ExpressRoute is designed to extend your on-premises networks into the Microsoft cloud over a dedicated private connection facilitated by a connectivity provider. With ExpressRoute, you can establish connections to Microsoft cloud services, such as Azure, Office 365, and Dynamics 365. This bypassing of the public internet ensures better reliability, faster speeds, lower latencies, and higher security than typical internet connections.

One of the striking aspects of Azure ExpressRoute is the consistency it brings to network performance. Unlike public internet connections, which can be plagued by fluctuations in bandwidth and latency, ExpressRoute provides known, predictable, high-throughput network connectivity. This consistency is a boon for organizations that require precise control over their network performance.

ExpressRoute connections do not go over the public internet, thus providing higher security and reliability with reduced network latency. This is especially crucial for organizations that transfer sensitive data between the cloud and on-premises data centers or those with strict compliance and data protection requirements.

The setup of Azure ExpressRoute involves partnering with an ExpressRoute connectivity provider. These partners can offer either Layer 2 or Layer 3 connections to Azure, and the choice between these would depend on your organization's specific needs and existing infrastructure. It's important to select a partner and a peering location that align with your organizational goals and technical requirements.

Once the physical connection is established through the connectivity provider, the next step is to link this connection to your Azure virtual network. This involves creating and configuring an ExpressRoute circuit, which is a logical construct that represents the connection between your on-premises infrastructure and Azure.

ExpressRoute provides flexibility in terms of the bandwidth options it offers, allowing organizations to choose a speed that aligns with their needs. By enabling organizations to dynamically adjust the bandwidth of the circuit as per their requirements, ExpressRoute ensures that businesses can scale their network capabilities in line with their growth.

Redundancy is another critical factor to consider when discussing Azure ExpressRoute. Microsoft recommends configuring ExpressRoute circuits in a redundant configuration to ensure high availability. By having multiple circuits, you ensure that there is no single point of failure, thereby maintaining a resilient network connection.

ExpressRoute also enables multiple routing domains or peerings over the same physical connection. These peerings can be segregated into Azure public, Azure private, and Microsoft peering, each serving a distinct purpose. Azure public peering allows access to Azure services with public IP addresses, while Azure private peering facilitates communication with your Azure virtual network resources. Microsoft peering, on the other hand, provides access to Microsoft SaaS services such as Office 365.

Given that data transfer costs can be a significant consideration, the billing model for ExpressRoute is designed to be predictable. The billing for ExpressRoute involves a fixed monthly charge for the circuit and additional charges based on data transfer, providing clarity and predictability in costs.

ExpressRoute also provides the capability to integrate seamlessly with Azure services like Azure Virtual Network, Azure VMs, and Azure Blob Storage, thereby ensuring that your applications run smoothly with the best possible connectivity. Moreover, by using ExpressRoute Direct, you can connect directly to Microsoft's global network at peering locations strategically distributed across the globe.

Security and compliance are paramount for organizations, and ExpressRoute ensures that data in transit complies with industry standards and regulations. By bypassing the public internet, ExpressRoute offers a more secure and controlled environment for data transmission.

For organizations that need a hybrid cloud environment, Azure ExpressRoute becomes an essential component, ensuring seamless and secure communication between on-premises data centers and the Azure cloud. Whether it's a matter of migrating large datasets to the cloud, running high-performance applications, or ensuring data privacy and regulatory compliance, ExpressRoute provides a connectivity solution that meets these needs head-on.

It's also noteworthy that ExpressRoute provides support for Global Reach, which allows your on-premises sites to communicate with each other via the Microsoft network. This extends the benefits of a dedicated, reliable network beyond just your connection to Azure, enhancing the overall connectivity landscape of your organization.

In scenarios where organizations require real-time data replication or are engaged in activities such as big data analytics, the consistent low latencies provided by ExpressRoute prove to be invaluable. By ensuring that data can be transferred quickly and reliably, ExpressRoute enables businesses to make timely and informed decisions.

Understanding the intricacies of Azure ExpressRoute involves appreciating its potential in fostering a secure, reliable, and high-performing hybrid cloud environment. By strategically implementing ExpressRoute, organizations can harness the power of the cloud while maintaining the levels of performance and security that their operations demand.

In essence, Azure ExpressRoute stands as a testament to the flexibility and advanced capabilities of Azure's networking services. By providing dedicated, private connectivity that bypasses the unpredictability of the public internet, ExpressRoute ensures that businesses can confidently and securely extend their on-premises infrastructure into the cloud. This level of connectivity paves the way for a myriad of possibilities, unlocking new avenues for innovation and growth.

Chapter 8: Implementing Network Security Groups and Firewalls

Navigating the complex landscape of network security is an essential aspect of cloud management, and Azure Network Security Groups (NSGs) play a pivotal role in ensuring that your network resources are adequately protected. NSGs provide a way to control inbound and outbound traffic to network interfaces, effectively acting as a firewall for your Azure resources. By understanding and utilizing NSGs, you can create a more secure and efficient network architecture in Azure.

Azure Network Security Groups are used to filter network traffic to and from Azure resources in an Azure Virtual Network. NSGs can be associated with either subnets or individual network interfaces attached to virtual machines. This flexibility allows for precise application of security rules, enabling you to customize the network traffic flow within your Azure environment.

An NSG contains a list of security rules that allow or deny network traffic based on source and destination IP addresses, port numbers, and the protocol used. These rules are processed in priority order, with the lower-numbered rules being processed before the higher-numbered ones. By crafting specific rules and assigning them appropriate priorities, you can create a robust network security posture tailored to your needs.

Each security rule in an NSG specifies whether to allow or deny traffic, the source and destination IP address ranges, the source and destination port ranges, and the protocol. By default, NSGs include a set of default rules which are designed to allow communication within a Virtual Network while blocking communication from the internet.

For instance, you can create an NSG rule that allows HTTP traffic on port 80 from any source to any destination. Conversely, you could create a rule that denies all traffic from a specific malicious IP address. By strategically creating such rules, you ensure that your network remains secure and functions optimally.

Understanding the direction of the traffic is crucial when working with NSGs. Inbound security rules control the traffic entering a network interface, and outbound security rules control the traffic leaving the network interface. By segregating rules based on the direction of traffic, NSGs provide granular control over the flow of data.

NSGs are essential when designing a multi-tier application in Azure. For instance, in a three-tier architecture consisting of a web tier, an application tier, and a data tier, NSGs can be used to restrict traffic between the tiers. The web tier may be allowed to communicate only with the application tier and not directly with the data tier, thereby enforcing a strict security boundary.

It's essential to note that when an NSG is associated with a subnet, the rules apply to all resources connected to the subnet. Conversely, when an NSG is associated with a network interface, the rules apply only to the specific virtual machine that the network interface is attached to. This distinction allows for layered security where subnet-level NSGs provide a baseline security posture, and network interface-level NSGs offer further customization.

Monitoring and logging are integral aspects of network security, and NSGs are integrated with Azure's monitoring and diagnostics capabilities. By leveraging Azure Monitor and Azure Security Center, you can gain insights into the traffic that is being allowed or denied by your NSGs. This visibility not only aids in troubleshooting but also helps in identifying potential security threats.

Azure NSGs are also fully integrated with Azure Resource Manager, allowing you to use templates to create, configure, and manage your network security groups. By using templates, you can ensure consistency and repeatability in your security deployments, making your network more robust and easier to manage.

In a scenario where you are migrating an on-premises application to Azure, NSGs can be crucial in replicating your existing network security policies. By carefully analyzing your current rules and replicating them in NSGs, you can create a seamless and secure transition to the cloud.

Optimal utilization of NSGs involves regularly reviewing and updating your security rules to align with the evolving needs of your applications and to respond to emerging security threats. Regular audits of your NSG rules can help identify redundant or overly permissive rules that could potentially expose your network to vulnerabilities.

By strategically combining NSGs with other Azure networking and security features such as Azure Firewall, Virtual Network Peering, and Azure Bastion, you can create a comprehensive network security strategy. This multi-faceted approach ensures that your Azure resources are protected from threats while still maintaining optimal performance and accessibility.

In scenarios where organizations are deploying microservices, NSGs can be instrumental in enforcing a zero-trust security model. By crafting NSG rules that strictly define the communication pathways between different services, you can ensure that any unnecessary access is swiftly curtailed.

A practical approach to using NSGs involves starting with a restrictive stance, denying all traffic, and then carefully allowing only the necessary communication paths. This approach, often referred to as a 'deny by default' stance, ensures that only the minimal necessary access is granted, thereby enhancing security.

While NSGs provide a robust mechanism for controlling traffic to network interfaces, they are but one piece of the puzzle in securing your Azure environment. Integrating NSGs with other security practices, such as regular patching of virtual machines, using secure coding practices, and monitoring for anomalous activity, is essential.

Navigating the intricate aspects of network security within a cloud environment like Azure requires a good understanding of the tools and services at your disposal, such as Azure Firewall and Application Gateway. These services, when used judiciously, can significantly enhance the protective layer around your cloud resources, ensuring that data flow remains both efficient and secure. Azure Firewall and Application Gateway serve distinct yet complementary roles in maintaining a robust defensive perimeter.

Azure Firewall is a fully stateful firewall-as-a-service offering that allows you to control and monitor outbound and inbound traffic across Azure Virtual Networks (VNet). It delivers high availability and cloud scalability, ensuring that your network is guarded against malicious threats. Azure Firewall works seamlessly with Azure Monitor for logging and analytics, providing you with a detailed insight into network activities and potential threats.

One of the strengths of Azure Firewall is its ability to identify and filter traffic based on specified rules. It utilizes application and network-level filtering rules, allowing you to define access policies based on IP addresses, port, and protocol. This granular level of control ensures that you can tailor your firewall to the specific needs of your applications and workloads.

Furthermore, Azure Firewall is designed to integrate smoothly with your existing security infrastructure. By employing features like Threat Intelligence filtering, Azure Firewall can alert and deny traffic from or to known malicious IP addresses and domains, adding an additional layer of protection.

On the other hand, Azure Application Gateway is a dedicated application delivery controller (ADC) as a service, providing application-level routing for your web traffic. It is particularly beneficial for optimizing and managing web traffic, ensuring that your applications are both responsive and resilient to failure. Application Gateway includes features such as Web Application Firewall (WAF), cookie-based session affinity, and SSL termination, thereby facilitating secure and optimized web application management.

Azure Application Gateway's Web Application Firewall provides centralized, inbound protection against common exploits and vulnerabilities in your web applications. By filtering traffic at the application layer, it safeguards your applications from a variety of threats such as SQL injection, cross-site scripting, and session hijacks. This ensures that your web applications remain secure, without compromising on performance.

In an environment where a variety of applications and services coexist, ensuring smooth and secure communication between them can be challenging. However, by strategically using Azure Firewall and Application Gateway together, you can create a protective shield that is both robust and adaptive.

For instance, you could deploy Azure Firewall to safeguard your entire virtual network, applying broad rules and filters to control and monitor the overall network traffic. Concurrently, Azure Application Gateway could be employed to manage traffic to specific web applications, utilizing its WAF capabilities to protect against targeted attacks.

In scenarios where your organization relies heavily on web applications, the combination of Azure Firewall and Application Gateway can be particularly potent. Application Gateway can be configured to balance the load, ensuring that incoming web traffic is distributed evenly across multiple servers, thereby enhancing application responsiveness. Meanwhile, Azure Firewall can scrutinize and filter the broader network traffic, ensuring that only legitimate requests reach the Application Gateway.

Security is often about layering, and these Azure services allow you to create a multi-layered defense strategy. While Azure Firewall operates at the network layer, protecting the entirety of your Azure Virtual Network, Application Gateway functions at the application layer, providing more granular control over your web traffic.

Regularly monitoring and updating the rules and policies governing these services is essential. Security is a dynamic field, and what suffices today may not be adequate tomorrow. Therefore, staying vigilant and ensuring that your protective mechanisms evolve with the threat landscape is crucial.

Azure provides comprehensive logging and monitoring capabilities through Azure Monitor, Azure Security Center, and Azure Sentinel. By integrating these tools with Azure Firewall and Application Gateway, you can gain real-time insights into your network traffic and rapidly respond to potential threats.

Consider a scenario where your organization hosts multiple web applications, each catering to different user segments. Azure Application Gateway can be utilized to route traffic efficiently to the respective applications, while its WAF capabilities shield the applications from web-based attacks. Simultaneously, Azure Firewall can scrutinize the broader network traffic, blocking malicious actors and safeguarding your entire Azure environment.

Automation and scalability are other aspects where these Azure services shine. Both Azure Firewall and Application Gateway can be automatically scaled to meet your organization's demands, ensuring that you neither underutilize nor overprovision resources. This dynamism is a testament to the flexibility offered by cloud-native solutions.

Moreover, in hybrid cloud scenarios, where some resources reside on-premises while others are hosted in the cloud, Azure Firewall can be pivotal in ensuring secure communication between the environments. It can work hand in hand with VPNs and Azure ExpressRoute to create a seamless and secure network topology.

Implementing a Zero Trust security model is becoming increasingly important, and Azure Firewall and Application Gateway are tools that can help you achieve that. By meticulously crafting rules and policies that ensure only legitimate traffic is allowed, and by continuously monitoring and adapting to new threats, you can build a network that is inherently skeptical of all traffic, regardless of its origin.

In summary, protecting your cloud resources is a multifaceted endeavor that requires both vigilance and the strategic use of available tools. Azure Firewall and Application Gateway are potent weapons in your security arsenal, and when deployed judiciously, they can substantially enhance your cloud security posture. By understanding their capabilities and regularly updating your security strategies, you can ensure that your Azure environment remains both secure and efficient.

Chapter 9: Data Replication and Disaster Recovery Techniques

Navigating through the various options available for data storage replication in Microsoft Azure can sometimes be akin to steering through a maze. Yet, with a deep understanding of the choices at your disposal, you can ensure that your data remains resilient, accessible, and safeguarded against losses. Azure offers a range of storage replication options designed to cater to different needs for availability, durability, and costs.

Azure Storage provides the bedrock upon which many Azure services are built. Whether you're dealing with blobs, files, queues, or tables, understanding how your data is replicated and safeguarded is crucial. These replication options are designed to ensure that your data is stored redundantly across multiple physical locations, protecting against hardware failures, updates, and other transient issues.

The first replication option that Azure offers is Locally Redundant Storage (LRS). This is the most cost-effective option, and it replicates your data three times within a single data center. LRS is suitable for scenarios where you want to safeguard your data against hardware failures within a single facility but are willing to risk data loss if a more significant incident, such as a data center outage, occurs.

Next up is Geo-Redundant Storage (GRS), which significantly ups the ante in terms of data durability. GRS replicates your data six times across two data centers located in separate regions. This ensures that even if an entire data center or region experiences an outage, your data remains accessible and intact.

The third option, Zone-Redundant Storage (ZRS), provides a middle ground between LRS and GRS. ZRS replicates your data three times, but it does so across multiple availability zones within a single region. This means your data is more resilient than with LRS but doesn't have the geographical dispersion that GRS offers.

Then there is Geo-Zone-Redundant Storage (GZRS), which combines the benefits of GRS and ZRS by replicating your data across availability zones and geographically dispersed regions. This option ensures the highest level of durability and availability, protecting your data against local and regional outages.

Another variant, Read-Access Geo-Redundant Storage (RA-GRS), extends the capabilities of GRS by providing read-only access to your data at the secondary location. This can be particularly useful in scenarios where you need to ensure high availability for read access, even in the case of a regional outage.

Choosing between these replication options involves carefully considering your organization's needs in terms of data durability, availability, and cost. For instance, if you're dealing with non-critical, easily reproducible data, LRS might be a suitable choice. However, if your data is critical and must remain available even in the face of significant outages, GZRS or RA-GRS might be more appropriate.

Understanding the trade-offs between these options is essential. While LRS is the most cost-effective, it offers the least protection against data loss. Conversely, GZRS and RA-GRS offer the highest durability and availability but come at a higher cost.

When considering these replication options, it's also important to factor in your organization's compliance and regulatory requirements. Certain industries or data types may require geographical redundancy, making options like GRS or GZRS mandatory.

Additionally, the nature of your application can also influence the choice of replication. For instance, if you have a read-heavy application that requires consistent, low-latency access to data, utilizing RA-GRS might be beneficial as it allows you to load balance read operations across two regions.

In scenarios where you need to ensure business continuity and disaster recovery, the choice of replication strategy becomes even more crucial. GRS, GZRS, and RA-GRS can serve as key components of a comprehensive disaster recovery plan, ensuring that your data remains available and intact even in the face of significant disruptions.

It's also worthwhile to consider how these replication options interact with other Azure services. For instance, Azure Backup and Azure Site Recovery can be used in conjunction with specific replication options to create a robust data backup and recovery strategy.

When implementing any replication strategy, monitoring and management are key. Azure provides tools like Azure Monitor and Azure Storage metrics that allow you to keep a close eye on your storage accounts and ensure that your replication strategy is working as intended.

In the realm of data storage, one size rarely fits all, and Azure's variety of replication options is a testament to that fact. By carefully evaluating your needs and understanding the nuances of each option, you can craft a storage strategy that is resilient, cost-effective, and perfectly tailored to your needs.

Consider a scenario where an organization is migrating a critical application to Azure, one that requires high availability and handles sensitive data. In such a case, opting for GZRS or RA-GRS might be prudent as these options offer geographical redundancy and ensure that the application remains functional even if one region experiences an outage.

Business continuity is the lifeline that keeps an organization afloat in times of disruptions, and in the era of cloud computing, Azure Site Recovery plays a pivotal role in ensuring that operations remain uninterrupted. With its robust set of features, Azure Site Recovery empowers businesses to keep their applications and data available during planned and unplanned outages. Implementing this tool in your business continuity strategy can mean the difference between seamless recovery and prolonged downtime.

Azure Site Recovery is Microsoft's premier service for orchestrating disaster recovery for Azure VMs, on-premises VMs, and physical servers. It's an intelligent tool that not only ensures data is backed up, but also guarantees that entire workflows and applications can be brought back online in an alternate location with minimal effort. This migration capability ensures that services remain available to end-users even if the primary site is compromised.

Imagine a scenario where a data center hosting critical applications experiences an unexpected power outage. In such cases, businesses could face significant losses due to downtime. However, with Azure Site Recovery in place, the applications can be automatically and seamlessly transferred to another data center or to the Azure cloud, ensuring continuity.

Understanding the nuances of Azure Site Recovery begins with comprehending its workflow. The service works by continuously replicating data, systems, and applications to a secondary site, which can be another on-premises data center or an Azure environment. The replication process is designed to be flexible, allowing for both synchronous and asynchronous data transfers depending on the required

Recovery Point Objective (RPO) and Recovery Time Objective (RTO).

Customizing the replication process is vital for aligning it with business goals. Some applications might require near-instantaneous recovery, while others can afford a slightly more leisurely pace. Azure Site Recovery offers the flexibility to tailor the replication strategy according to these diverse needs.

When implementing Azure Site Recovery, it's important to start by conducting a comprehensive assessment of the applications, data, and workloads that need to be protected. Identifying dependencies among applications can ensure that when a failover occurs, services come back online in the correct order, avoiding potential conflicts or errors.

The next step involves configuring the replication settings to meet your business requirements. Azure Site Recovery offers several options, including Hyper-V Replica, Azure replication, and VMware/physical server replication using the Azure Site Recovery Provider and Recovery Services agent. Each option has its own benefits, and choosing the right one hinges on your existing infrastructure and desired outcomes.

The process doesn't end with setting up replication. Regular testing is paramount to ensure that, in the event of an actual disaster, the failover process works seamlessly. Azure Site Recovery provides a non-disruptive testing mechanism that allows organizations to validate their disaster recovery plans without impacting the production environment.

Security and compliance are also key considerations when implementing Azure Site Recovery. Ensuring that data remains secure during transit and at rest is essential. With Azure Site Recovery, data is encrypted both in transit and at the recovery site, providing peace of mind and compliance with industry regulations.

Beyond the technical implementation, successful deployment of Azure Site Recovery also requires aligning stakeholders within the organization. Educating teams about the new recovery processes, and ensuring that everyone knows their role in case of a failover, is essential for smooth operation during an actual disaster.

Cost management is another important aspect to consider. While ensuring business continuity is vital, it should be achieved in a cost-effective manner. Azure Site Recovery allows for a pay-as-you-go model, ensuring that you only pay for the resources you use. This can be a boon for organizations looking to balance cost and reliability.

Azure Site Recovery also integrates seamlessly with other Azure services, thereby enabling a cohesive and comprehensive business continuity strategy. For instance, Azure Backup can be used alongside Azure Site Recovery to ensure that, apart from replicating applications for quick failover, data is also backed up and can be restored at a granular level if needed.

Flexibility in terms of supported operating systems and configurations ensures that Azure Site Recovery can be a good fit for diverse IT environments. It supports replication for Windows and Linux-based VMs and physical servers, ensuring that a variety of workloads can be safeguarded.

Scalability is also one of the strengths of Azure Site Recovery. Whether you're protecting a few critical applications or an entire data center, the service scales to meet your needs. This scalability ensures that as your business grows, your business continuity strategy can grow along with it without necessitating a major overhaul.

Implementing Azure Site Recovery is not a set-and-forget task. Continuous monitoring and periodic reviews of the recovery plans are necessary to ensure that the system is always ready to swing into action when needed. Azure provides tools and logs that make monitoring the health of your disaster recovery setup straightforward.

In times of crisis, communication is key. Azure Site Recovery can be integrated with Azure Automation to create runbooks that can automate failover processes and also notify stakeholders via email or other communication channels in case of a disaster recovery event.

Considering different geographical locations for the secondary site is also crucial. Strategically choosing a location that is unlikely to be affected by the same regional outages can add an extra layer of resiliency.

In essence, Azure Site Recovery is akin to having an insurance policy for your applications and data. It ensures that no matter what disruptions come your way, your business can continue to operate with minimal interruption. By understanding its features, aligning it with your business needs, and implementing it effectively, Azure Site Recovery can become a cornerstone of your business continuity plan. Through meticulous planning and regular testing, you ensure that your organization is resilient and prepared for whatever challenges the future may bring.

Chapter 10: Troubleshooting and Optimizing Azure Networking and Storage

Navigating through the complexities of cloud networking can sometimes feel like embarking on a challenging voyage, especially when faced with the task of diagnosing common networking issues. Azure, with its extensive toolset and capabilities, offers a diverse range of features designed to simplify this journey. Being familiar with these features can help you troubleshoot and resolve networking issues swiftly, ensuring smooth operations in your Azure environment.

One common issue that may arise is related to connectivity, where you might find that resources such as virtual machines (VMs) are unable to communicate with each other or with external networks. Diagnosing this issue starts by verifying the network security group (NSG) rules and ensuring that the appropriate ports are open for communication. Azure Portal, Azure CLI, or PowerShell can be used to inspect and modify NSG rules to rectify any discrepancies.

Sometimes, the issue might not be with the NSG rules but with the routing tables. Azure automatically creates system routes that enable communication within a virtual network and to the internet. If you observe that resources in a virtual network are unable to communicate as expected, it's worth inspecting the route tables to ensure that there are no custom routes that might be inadvertently blocking traffic.

Azure provides several tools to assist in diagnosing these connectivity issues. Azure Network Watcher is a suite of tools designed to monitor, diagnose, and gain insights into network performance. One of its features, IP flow verify, allows you to test if a packet is allowed or denied based on the configured NSG rules.

Another valuable tool in Network Watcher is Next Hop, which determines the next hop type and IP address for a packet originating from a VM. This can be especially useful in diagnosing routing-related issues, as it shows the path that a packet takes through the Azure network fabric.

Sometimes, the issue might be related to Domain Name System (DNS) resolution. Azure provides both Azure-provided DNS and Azure DNS for resolving domain names. If you find that your VMs are unable to resolve domain names, it's prudent to check the DNS settings in the virtual network configuration and ensure that they are set up correctly.

Connectivity issues may also extend to hybrid networks, where on-premises resources are connected to Azure resources. In such cases, it's important to verify the configuration of the VPN or ExpressRoute connection. Azure provides detailed logging and diagnostics for these services, which can be accessed through the Azure Portal.

In some instances, you may face issues related to performance degradation in the network. To diagnose such issues, you can leverage Azure Monitor and Azure Network Watcher's Performance Monitor and Traffic Analytics features. These tools provide insights into your network's performance and can help identify bottlenecks.

Bandwidth constraints can also lead to network performance issues. Azure offers different types and sizes of VMs optimized for various workloads. Ensuring that the VM size aligns with the network bandwidth requirements of your application is crucial. Examining metrics such as Network In and Network Out through Azure Monitor can provide clues about whether your VM is facing bandwidth bottlenecks.

Load balancing is another area where issues might surface. Azure offers multiple load balancing solutions, including Azure Load Balancer, Application Gateway, and Traffic Manager. Ensuring that these resources are configured correctly, with proper health probes and routing rules, is essential for diagnosing issues related to traffic distribution.

Security concerns might also lead to networking issues. For instance, if a virtual network is peered with another virtual network, and the traffic between these networks needs to traverse through a network virtual appliance or firewall, it's important to ensure that the appropriate rules are set up to allow this traffic.

When dealing with applications that require data synchronization across multiple regions, latency can be a concern. Azure's Traffic Manager can be useful in such cases as it directs user traffic to the closest or most responsive endpoint in a global distribution of endpoints. Ensuring that Traffic Manager profiles are correctly set up can help in diagnosing latency-related issues.

Monitoring is an essential aspect of diagnosing networking issues. Setting up proper alerts using Azure Monitor, and logging using Azure Log Analytics, can be instrumental in quickly identifying and diagnosing issues as they arise. These tools can provide real-time data and historical trends about the network health.

Azure also provides specialized tools such as Azure Advisor, which gives personalized best practices recommendations. By following these recommendations, you can proactively improve the health, performance, and availability of your resources and avoid potential issues. In some cases, issues might not be with the network itself but with the application. Diagnosing such issues can involve looking at application logs, ensuring that the application is properly configured to work in a cloud environment, and checking if the application's dependencies are correctly set up and reachable over the network. Moreover, understanding the nature of your application and its interaction with other services is pivotal. For instance, an application that heavily relies on Azure Blob Storage might face issues if there are disruptions in the storage service. Azure Service Health can be checked to diagnose if there are any ongoing issues with Azure services that might be affecting your application.

In the realm of cloud networking, diagnosing issues can be a multifaceted approach that involves understanding the architecture, monitoring the right metrics, and leveraging the tools provided by the cloud platform. Azure offers a robust set of tools and services designed to assist in this task, making it easier to identify, diagnose, and resolve common networking issues.

Navigating the intricacies of cloud storage can be daunting, especially when striving to strike a balance between performance and cost. Azure, a cloud platform equipped with versatile storage services, presents a suite of tools and features tailored to optimize both these aspects. Delving into the nuances of Azure's storage solutions, we can explore how you can judiciously leverage these offerings to ensure efficient data storage without compromising on budget constraints.

Firstly, understanding the type of data and access patterns your application requires is pivotal. Azure offers several storage options such as Azure Blob Storage, Azure Files, Azure Table Storage, and Azure Queue Storage, each catering to different needs. For instance, Blob Storage, which handles unstructured data, can be fine-tuned to align with performance needs using different access tiers such as hot, cool, and archive.

By astutely selecting an access tier that matches your application's usage patterns, you can optimize costs. Hot tier is suitable for frequently accessed data, while cool and archive tiers are cost-effective for infrequently accessed data. This tiered approach ensures that you only pay for the performance you need.

Azure also allows you to automate the transition of data between these tiers using lifecycle management policies. These policies can be configured to move data to a cooler tier or even delete it after a certain period, ensuring you're not paying for unnecessary storage or higher-tier costs.

Another area where optimization is possible is in data redundancy. Azure provides multiple redundancy options such as Locally Redundant Storage (LRS), Zone-Redundant Storage (ZRS), Geo-Redundant Storage (GRS), and Read-Access Geo-Redundant Storage (RA-GRS). By carefully selecting the level of redundancy that meets your application's requirements and aligns with your disaster recovery plan, you can optimize costs without jeopardizing data durability.

The choice of storage account type can also have an impact on cost and performance. Azure offers different types of storage accounts like Standard and Premium, with the latter providing high-performance solid-state drive (SSD) based storage. The choice between Standard and Premium storage should be determined by the performance requirements of your application.

For applications that rely on Azure Files, optimizing the share size and properly configuring the IOPS (Input/Output Operations Per Second) is crucial. Azure Files offers provisioned and transaction optimized shares, and the choice between them can have a direct impact on cost and performance.

Data transfer costs can be a hidden expenditure that can accumulate quickly. Leveraging Azure's Content Delivery Network (CDN) can not only enhance user experience by reducing load times but can also decrease bandwidth costs.

Azure CDN caches content at strategically placed locations to provide maximum bandwidth and reduce access latency.

Optimization isn't solely confined to cost reduction but also encompasses performance enhancement. Utilizing features such as Azure Blob Storage's Indexer can significantly speed up data retrieval times, thereby enhancing application performance.

Compressing data before storage can also lead to cost savings and performance improvements. By reducing the volume of data that needs to be stored and transferred, you can achieve faster data transfer speeds and lower storage costs.

It's also important to keep an eye on storage account limits. Each storage account has specific limits such as the total storage capacity, request rate, and bandwidth. By monitoring your application's usage, you can avoid hitting these limits and distribute your data across multiple storage accounts if necessary.

Data archiving is another strategy that can lead to significant cost savings. Archiving data that is rarely accessed but needs to be retained for compliance or other reasons can be moved to Azure Blob Storage's Archive tier, which offers the lowest cost per gigabyte.

Additionally, monitoring and analytics play a crucial role in optimizing storage performance and costs. Tools such as Azure Storage Analytics and Azure Monitor provide insights into how your storage is being used and can help identify areas for optimization.

Azure Cost Management is another tool that can be harnessed to gain insights into your spending patterns and to forecast future costs. It allows you to track resource usage and manage costs with advanced analytics and data-driven insights.

Azure's Reserved Capacity feature offers significant cost savings for storage. By committing to a specific level of usage for a one to three-year period, you can save up to 72% over pay-as-you-go pricing.

Security, while not a direct cost, should not be overlooked. Ensuring that your data is securely stored can prevent potential financial repercussions arising from data breaches. Implementing features such as Azure Storage Service Encryption for data at rest and Azure Storage Shared Access Signature for secure data access can enhance security without incurring additional costs.

Lastly, regularly reviewing and cleaning up unused or obsolete data can lead to cost savings. Periodically auditing your storage accounts to identify and delete data that is no longer needed can free up storage space and reduce costs.

Optimizing storage in Azure requires a judicious blend of understanding your application's needs, configuring the resources aptly, and continuously monitoring usage patterns and costs. By being proactive and making informed decisions, you can ensure that your storage solutions are not only cost-effective but also performant and resilient.

Through a well-thought-out strategy that encompasses tiering, data management, monitoring, and utilizing the features offered by Azure, you can effectively optimize both storage performance and costs. By staying vigilant and regularly reviewing your configurations and usage, you ensure that your storage infrastructure remains in optimal condition, offering high performance at a cost that aligns with your budget.

BOOK 4
AZURE ADMINISTRATOR EXPERTISE
PRO-LEVEL AUTOMATION AND OPTIMIZATION FOR AZ-104

ROB BOTWRIGHT

Chapter 1: Elevating Azure Administration with Automation

Automation plays a pivotal role in the efficient management of resources within the Azure cloud platform, streamlining operations and enabling organizations to achieve more with less effort. In today's fast-paced digital landscape, where businesses strive to innovate and scale rapidly, the power of automation in Azure management cannot be overstated. It empowers IT teams to focus on strategic tasks, improve resource utilization, enhance security, and maintain compliance effortlessly.

One of the primary advantages of automation in Azure management is the elimination of repetitive, manual tasks. Imagine the time and effort saved by automating routine processes like provisioning virtual machines, configuring network settings, or scaling resources based on demand. This not only boosts productivity but also reduces the risk of human errors that can lead to costly downtime or security vulnerabilities.

Automation in Azure can be achieved through various tools and technologies, such as Azure Automation, Azure Logic Apps, and Azure Functions. These services provide a versatile toolkit for creating custom automation workflows tailored to specific business needs. Whether it's deploying applications, managing infrastructure as code, or orchestrating complex workflows, Azure offers a comprehensive set of resources to get the job done efficiently.

Another crucial aspect of automation in Azure management is the ability to enforce consistent policies and ensure compliance across the organization. Azure Policy, for instance, enables you to define and enforce governance rules, ensuring that resources adhere to predefined standards and regulations. This not only reduces compliance risks but also simplifies auditing and reporting processes.

Furthermore, automation enables organizations to optimize their resource utilization and cost management. Azure Cost Management and Billing, combined with automation scripts, allow you to monitor resource consumption, set budget alerts, and implement cost-saving strategies automatically. This results in better cost control and the ability to allocate resources more efficiently, ultimately leading to significant cost savings.

Security is paramount in the cloud, and automation can significantly enhance it. By automating security tasks such as threat detection, incident response, and access management, you can proactively protect your Azure environment. Azure Security Center, for example, leverages automation to identify and remediate security vulnerabilities, ensuring that your resources remain secure and compliant.

Scaling applications and services to meet fluctuating demand is a fundamental requirement in today's dynamic business environment. Azure's auto-scaling capabilities, combined with automation, enable you to scale resources up or down based on predefined criteria. This ensures that your applications can handle traffic spikes without manual intervention, providing a seamless experience for your users.

Moreover, automation in Azure management extends to DevOps practices, fostering a culture of collaboration and continuous integration/continuous deployment (CI/CD). Tools like Azure DevOps and GitHub Actions integrate seamlessly with Azure services, allowing development and operations teams to automate the entire software delivery pipeline. This leads to faster release cycles, higher-quality code, and improved overall agility.

Azure's extensive marketplace offers a wide array of pre-built automation solutions and templates, accelerating your journey toward efficient management. Whether you need to deploy a specific application stack, set up monitoring and logging, or configure a highly available infrastructure, you can find automation solutions tailored to your requirements.

In addition to these benefits, automation in Azure management contributes to disaster recovery and business continuity planning. By automating backup and recovery processes, you can ensure that your critical data and services are protected in the event of unforeseen disruptions. Azure Site Recovery, for example, simplifies the replication and failover of virtual machines, minimizing downtime and data loss.

The flexibility and scalability of Azure's automation capabilities make it suitable for organizations of all sizes and industries. Whether you're a startup looking to accelerate your digital transformation or an established enterprise seeking to optimize your cloud operations, automation in Azure management offers a wealth of opportunities to enhance efficiency, reduce costs, and mitigate risks.

To harness the power of automation in Azure management effectively, it's essential to start with a clear strategy and roadmap. Identify the key processes and tasks that can benefit from automation, prioritize them based on business impact, and gradually implement automation solutions that align with your goals. Consider the skills and training needed to operate and maintain automated workflows, as well as the ongoing monitoring and optimization of your automation resources.

As you embark on your automation journey in Azure management, keep in mind that it's not a one-size-fits-all approach. Every organization has unique requirements and challenges, so customizing your automation solutions is key to success. Leverage the extensive documentation, tutorials, and community support available in the Azure ecosystem to gain expertise and make informed decisions.

In summary, automation in Azure management is a game-changer for organizations seeking to thrive in the digital age. It empowers businesses to optimize resource utilization, enhance security, enforce compliance, and streamline operations. By harnessing the power of automation in Azure, you can focus on innovation, accelerate your digital transformation, and stay competitive in today's rapidly evolving landscape. So, take the first step toward a more efficient and resilient Azure environment by embracing automation and unlocking its full potential for your organization.

In the world of automation, selecting the right tools for your tasks is akin to choosing the perfect instrument for a musical performance. Just as a violinist carefully selects the best violin to create beautiful melodies, you too must carefully evaluate and choose the tools that will orchestrate your automation symphony.

Before diving into the wide array of automation tools available, it's crucial to have a clear understanding of your objectives. What tasks do you want to automate? Are you aiming to streamline repetitive processes, enhance security, or optimize resource utilization? The answers to these questions will serve as your guiding light in tool selection.

One of the foundational tools for automation is scripting languages. These versatile languages, such as Python, PowerShell, and Bash, allow you to create custom automation scripts tailored to your specific needs. Whether it's automating file operations, system configurations, or data processing, scripting languages provide you with the power to automate almost anything.

For those who prefer a more visual approach to automation, workflow orchestration tools like Microsoft Flow, Apache NiFi, or Zapier offer user-friendly interfaces for designing automation workflows. These tools are excellent for automating business processes, integrating applications, and orchestrating complex sequences of actions without the need for extensive coding.

Containerization platforms like Docker and Kubernetes are invaluable for automating the deployment and management of applications. They package your applications and their dependencies into containers, ensuring consistent and portable deployments across different environments. With container orchestration, you can automate scaling, load balancing, and high availability, making it a crucial choice for modern cloud-native applications.

Configuration management tools like Ansible, Puppet, and Chef are indispensable for automating server provisioning and configuration. They enable you to define infrastructure as code, ensuring that your servers are consistently and securely configured. With configuration management, you can automate tasks such as software installation, configuration updates, and security hardening across your infrastructure.

Cloud orchestration platforms, such as AWS CloudFormation and Azure Resource Manager, are tailored for automating cloud resource provisioning and management. They allow you to define your infrastructure as code, making it easy to create, update, and delete resources in the cloud with a single automation script. Cloud orchestration is ideal for organizations looking to embrace the scalability and agility of the cloud.

When it comes to data automation, ETL (Extract, Transform, Load) tools like Apache Nifi, Talend, and Microsoft SSIS are designed to automate data integration and processing.

Whether you're working with structured or unstructured data, ETL tools can help you automate data extraction from various sources, apply transformations, and load it into your target systems efficiently.

Monitoring and alerting automation tools, such as Prometheus and Grafana, are essential for keeping an eye on the health and performance of your systems. They automate the collection of metrics, the creation of dashboards, and the generation of alerts based on predefined conditions. These tools ensure that you can proactively address issues and maintain the reliability of your services.

Security automation tools like Ansible, HashiCorp Vault, and AWS Identity and Access Management (IAM) provide the means to automate security configurations and compliance checks. You can use them to enforce security policies, rotate credentials, and respond to security incidents automatically. Security automation is critical in today's threat landscape to mitigate risks effectively.

For application release automation and continuous integration/continuous deployment (CI/CD), tools like Jenkins, GitLab CI/CD, and CircleCI automate the building, testing, and deployment of software. They enable you to establish automated pipelines that ensure code changes are tested and deployed consistently, reducing manual errors and accelerating the delivery of new features.

Database automation tools, such as Flyway and Liquibase, automate database schema migrations and version control. They allow you to manage database changes as code, making it easier to apply updates, rollbacks, and maintain database consistency across different environments.

Chatbots and virtual assistants like Dialogflow, Microsoft Bot Framework, and Rasa offer automation capabilities for customer support, information retrieval, and interaction with users. These tools leverage natural language processing and machine learning to automate conversations and provide assistance 24/7.

Machine learning and AI automation platforms, including TensorFlow, PyTorch, and Azure Machine Learning, enable you to automate the development and deployment of machine learning models. They provide tools for data preprocessing, model training, and inference deployment, making it easier to incorporate AI into your applications.

Choosing the right automation tools involves assessing your technical requirements, considering the skillset of your team, and evaluating the scalability and support provided by the tools and their communities. It's also essential to stay updated on emerging automation trends and technologies, as the field is constantly evolving.

In your quest to select the perfect tools for automation tasks, remember that it's not a one-size-fits-all scenario. Each tool has its strengths and weaknesses, and the ideal tool for one task may not be the best choice for another. Be prepared to mix and match tools to create comprehensive automation solutions that align with your organization's goals and requirements.

Ultimately, the success of your automation endeavors depends on your ability to match the right tools with the right tasks, creating a harmonious symphony of efficiency and productivity. So, embrace the world of automation, explore its myriad possibilities, and embark on a journey that will streamline your operations, enhance your security, and unlock new horizons of innovation.

Chapter 2: Mastering Azure PowerShell and Command-Line Interface (CLI)

Azure PowerShell is your gateway to the vast world of Microsoft Azure, where you can wield the power of automation and management at your fingertips. With this versatile tool, you can script, manage, and automate Azure resources seamlessly. Whether you're a seasoned Azure pro or just starting your cloud journey, Azure PowerShell is a valuable asset to have in your toolkit.

Before we dive into the intricacies of Azure PowerShell, let's understand what it is. Azure PowerShell is a module that extends the capabilities of Windows PowerShell to include Azure-specific cmdlets. These cmdlets enable you to interact with Azure services, resources, and configurations from your command line or script. It's like having a magic wand to control your Azure environment effortlessly.

To begin your journey with Azure PowerShell, the first step is to install it. It's a straightforward process. You can download and install Azure PowerShell from the official Microsoft website, ensuring that you have the necessary prerequisites, such as Windows PowerShell and the AzureRM module.

Once you have Azure PowerShell installed, the next step is to connect it to your Azure subscription. You'll need to authenticate yourself to Azure using your credentials. This authentication can be achieved through the Azure portal, service principals, or managed identities, depending on your scenario and security requirements.

With Azure PowerShell, you can perform a wide range of tasks. You can create and manage virtual machines, configure networking, provision storage, deploy web applications, and much more. The power lies in the extensive library of cmdlets at your disposal, each designed to simplify Azure management.

One of the most useful aspects of Azure PowerShell is its ability to automate repetitive tasks. Instead of manually provisioning and configuring resources, you can create scripts that define your infrastructure as code. This means you can version-control your infrastructure, replicate it across environments, and make consistent changes with ease.

Let's not forget about Azure Resource Manager (ARM) templates, another essential tool in your Azure automation arsenal. ARM templates are JSON files that describe your Azure resources and their configurations. You can use Azure PowerShell to deploy, update, and manage these templates, allowing for infrastructure-as-code practices.

Azure PowerShell also facilitates the management of Azure policy and governance. You can define policies that enforce compliance standards, security rules, and resource tagging. With Azure PowerShell, you can create and assign these policies to ensure that your resources align with organizational guidelines.

But Azure PowerShell isn't just for managing infrastructure; it's also a valuable tool for monitoring and troubleshooting. You can use it to retrieve diagnostic logs, query metrics, and set up alerts for your Azure resources. This proactive approach helps you identify and address issues before they impact your services.

Another fantastic feature of Azure PowerShell is its support for Azure DevOps and CI/CD pipelines. You can integrate Azure PowerShell scripts into your automated deployment pipelines, ensuring that your applications and infrastructure are consistently deployed and configured across different environments.

Azure PowerShell also provides support for managing Azure Key Vault, a critical component for securing your sensitive information, such as connection strings and secrets. You can use Azure PowerShell to create, manage, and retrieve secrets from Key Vault programmatically.

What's more, Azure PowerShell keeps pace with the evolving Azure ecosystem. It receives regular updates and enhancements, ensuring that you have access to the latest Azure features and services. Staying up-to-date with these updates ensures that you can leverage the full potential of Azure.

Now that we've explored the capabilities of Azure PowerShell let's take a moment to appreciate the Azure portal's graphical user interface (GUI). The portal offers a user-friendly, visual way to interact with Azure resources. While it's excellent for exploration and one-off tasks, Azure PowerShell provides a more efficient and consistent approach for managing Azure at scale.

Azure PowerShell is also a great complement to Azure CLI, another command-line tool for Azure management. While Azure CLI focuses on providing a human-friendly, cross-platform experience, Azure PowerShell offers a more extensive set of cmdlets and integration with Windows PowerShell.

As you dive deeper into Azure PowerShell, you'll discover the power of modules and extensions. Azure PowerShell modules extend the core functionality of Azure PowerShell, providing additional cmdlets for specific Azure services. Extensions, on the other hand, offer specialized capabilities for tasks like managing Azure Kubernetes Service (AKS) or Azure Functions.

To make the most of Azure PowerShell, it's essential to invest time in learning and practice. Microsoft offers comprehensive documentation and tutorials to help you get started. You can also join the Azure community, participate in forums, and attend webinars and training sessions to enhance your Azure PowerShell skills.

Remember that with great power comes great responsibility. While Azure PowerShell empowers you to automate and manage Azure resources effectively, it's crucial to follow best practices for security, compliance, and resource management. Implement role-based access control (RBAC), monitor your scripts for potential issues, and regularly review and update your automation processes.

In summary, Azure PowerShell is your trusty companion in the Azure cloud, providing you with the tools to automate, manage, and optimize your resources effortlessly. Whether you're provisioning virtual machines, deploying web applications, or enforcing compliance policies, Azure PowerShell has got your back. So, roll up your sleeves, dive into the world of Azure PowerShell, and harness its magic to unlock the full potential of Microsoft Azure.

Azure Command-Line Interface (CLI) is a versatile and powerful tool that puts the control of your Azure resources right at your fingertips. With a few simple commands, you can manage, automate, and monitor your Azure environment like a pro. In this chapter, we'll explore some tips and tricks to help you become a CLI master and make the most of your Azure experience.

First things first, let's get you set up with Azure CLI. If you haven't already installed it, head over to the official Azure CLI documentation to find instructions for your operating system. Once it's up and running, you're ready to start your Azure CLI journey.

One of the fundamental commands in Azure CLI is 'az login.' This command allows you to authenticate with your Azure subscription. When you run 'az login,' you'll be prompted to open a web page, sign in with your Azure credentials, and then return to the command line. It's a straightforward process that grants you access to your Azure resources.

Now that you're logged in, let's talk about the 'az group' command. This command is your gateway to managing Azure resource groups. You can create, delete, and list resource groups using 'az group.' Resource groups help you organize and manage your Azure resources effectively. Speaking of resource management, the 'az vm' command is your go-to for virtual machine operations. With 'az vm,' you can create, start, stop, and delete virtual machines effortlessly. You can also use it to manage virtual machine extensions and even scale your VM instances up or down.

Azure CLI supports rich filtering capabilities with the '--query' parameter. You can use this parameter to filter and format the output of commands. For example, if you want to see only the names of your virtual machines, you can run 'az vm list --query [].name.' It's a handy way to get the specific information you need.

To make your CLI experience even more efficient, consider using aliases. Aliases are shortcuts for commonly used commands or command sets. You can create your aliases to save time and reduce typing. For instance, you can create an alias like 'alias vmlist="az vm list --output table"' to list your virtual machines with a simple 'vmlist' command.

Azure CLI also offers interactive mode. To access it, use the 'az interactive' command. Interactive mode provides an interactive shell with context-aware command suggestions and inline help. It's an excellent way to explore Azure CLI capabilities and learn new commands on the fly.

If you're working with Azure Kubernetes Service (AKS), the 'az aks' command is your friend. It allows you to create, manage, and scale AKS clusters effortlessly. You can also use it to deploy and manage container applications on your AKS cluster.

For managing Azure Web Apps, the 'az webapp' command is a valuable asset. You can use it to create, configure, and deploy web applications to Azure App Service. Whether you're hosting a simple website or a complex web application, 'az webapp' has you covered.

Azure CLI supports the use of scripts to automate repetitive tasks. You can write bash scripts or PowerShell scripts that leverage Azure CLI commands to automate resource provisioning, configuration, and management. This automation can save you a significant amount of time and reduce the risk of errors.

To simplify script creation further, you can use 'azcopy' for data transfer and synchronization. 'Azcopy' is a command-line utility that makes it easy to copy data to and from Azure storage accounts. Whether you're moving files, backing up data, or syncing data between on-premises and Azure, 'azcopy' is a handy tool.

The 'az monitor' command helps you keep an eye on the health and performance of your Azure resources. You can use it to set up monitoring and diagnostics, query metrics, and create alerts based on specific conditions. It's a proactive way to ensure the reliability of your services.

Azure CLI also supports extensions that add additional functionality to the tool. You can extend Azure CLI with various extensions for specific scenarios. For example, the 'aks-preview' extension provides advanced AKS management capabilities, while the 'appservice-commands' extension enhances Azure App Service management.

Don't forget to keep your Azure CLI up to date. Azure CLI receives regular updates and improvements, so it's essential to stay current with the latest version. You can update Azure CLI by running 'az upgrade,' which ensures you have access to the latest features and bug fixes.

Azure CLI is available not only for Windows but also for macOS and Linux. It's a cross-platform tool that allows you to manage your Azure resources from your preferred operating system. Whether you're on a Windows machine or a Mac, you can harness the power of Azure CLI.

When working with sensitive information in your scripts, consider using Azure Key Vault. Azure Key Vault provides a secure way to store and manage keys, secrets, and certificates. You can access Key Vault secrets from your Azure CLI scripts without exposing sensitive data.

Azure CLI is designed to be user-friendly, with intuitive commands and clear documentation. However, if you ever find yourself in need of help, you can use the 'az --help' command or visit the Azure CLI documentation online. It's a valuable resource to answer your questions and provide guidance on Azure CLI usage.

In summary, Azure CLI is a versatile and powerful tool that empowers you to manage your Azure resources efficiently. Whether you're creating virtual machines, managing web applications, or monitoring your services, Azure CLI has the commands and capabilities you need. By mastering Azure CLI and exploring its tips and tricks, you'll unlock a world of automation and management possibilities in the Azure cloud. So, roll up your sleeves, open your command prompt, and start commanding Azure like a pro!

Chapter 3: Leveraging ARM Templates for Efficient Deployments

Imagine having a powerful tool at your disposal that allows you to define and manage your Azure infrastructure as code, ensuring consistency, scalability, and automation in your cloud environment. Well, you're in luck because Azure Resource Manager (ARM) templates and JSON syntax provide just that. In this chapter, we'll embark on a journey to explore the fundamentals of ARM templates and demystify JSON syntax.

At its core, an ARM template is a declarative way to define your Azure resources and their configurations. Think of it as a blueprint for your infrastructure, where you specify what resources you need, their properties, and their relationships, all in a structured JSON file.

Now, let's talk about JSON. JSON, short for JavaScript Object Notation, is a lightweight data-interchange format. It's easy for both humans and machines to read and write. JSON uses a simple syntax of key-value pairs, arrays, and nested objects, making it an ideal choice for defining structured data.

In the context of ARM templates, JSON serves as the language to express your infrastructure requirements. Each ARM template is a JSON file that represents your desired Azure resources and their configurations. This file acts as the source of truth for your infrastructure.

Before diving deeper into JSON syntax, let's understand the key components of an ARM template. An ARM template comprises three main sections: parameters, variables, and resources. Parameters allow you to input values when deploying the template, making it flexible and reusable.

Variables are used to store intermediate values or calculated results within the template. They can simplify complex expressions and provide consistency across your template.

The most significant part of an ARM template is the 'resources' section. Here, you define the Azure resources you want to create, configure, or manage. Each resource is specified with its resource type, name, and properties.

Resource types follow a specific format: 'Microsoft.ProviderNamespace/resourceType.' For example, 'Microsoft.Storage/storageAccounts' represents a storage account resource. The 'name' field identifies the unique name of the resource within the resource group.

Properties, on the other hand, define the configuration settings for each resource. These settings vary depending on the resource type. For a virtual machine, properties might include the size, image, and operating system settings.

Now, let's delve into JSON syntax. JSON uses key-value pairs enclosed in curly braces, like this:

jsonCopy code

```
{ "key": "value" }
```

Keys are strings enclosed in double quotes, followed by a colon, and values can be strings, numbers, booleans, objects, or arrays. Objects are enclosed in curly braces, while arrays use square brackets.

To define an ARM template parameter, you can use the following JSON syntax:

jsonCopy code

```
"parameters": { "parameterName": { "type": "string", "defaultValue": "defaultValue" } }
```

In this snippet, 'parameterName' is the name of the parameter, 'type' specifies the data type of the parameter (e.g., "string," "int," "bool"), and 'defaultValue' sets a default value if one is not provided during deployment.

Variables are defined in the 'variables' section of the template, like so:

jsonCopy code

```
"variables": { "variableName": "variableValue" }
```

Here, 'variableName' is the name of the variable, and 'variableValue' is the value assigned to it. You can use variables to store values or expressions that you'll reuse throughout your template.

The 'resources' section is where you define your Azure resources. Each resource is represented as an object within an array, like this:

jsonCopy code

```
"resources": [ { "type": "resourceType", "apiVersion": "apiVersion", "name": "resourceName", "location": "location", "properties": { // Resource-specific properties } } ]
```

In this example, 'type' specifies the resource type, 'apiVersion' determines the API version to use, 'name' sets the resource name, 'location' defines the Azure region, and 'properties' holds the resource-specific configuration.

JSON supports conditional logic using "if" statements and functions like "concat" for string concatenation. For example:

jsonCopy code

```
"variables": { "storageAccountName": "[if(equals(parameters('useExistingStorage'), 'Yes'), parameters('existingStorageAccountName'), concat(parameters('uniqueString'), 'storage'))]" }
```

In this snippet, the 'storageAccountName' variable is determined based on the 'useExistingStorage' parameter. If 'useExistingStorage' is set to 'Yes,' it uses the existing storage account name; otherwise, it concatenates a unique string with 'storage.'

Loops and iteration can also be achieved using JSON functions. For instance, you can create multiple resources of the same type by iterating through an array:

jsonCopy code

```
"resources": [ { "name": "[concat('vm', copyIndex())]", "type": "Microsoft.Compute/virtualMachines", // Other
```

properties }], "copy": { "name": "virtualMachineLoop",
"count": "[parameters('numberOfVMs')]" }

In this example, the 'copy' section specifies a loop that creates a specified number of virtual machines with unique names using the 'copyIndex()' function.

JSON comments are not supported in ARM templates. However, you can use a 'metadata' object to add descriptions or annotations to your template elements:

jsonCopy code

"parameters": { "paramName": { "type": "string", "metadata": { "description": "This parameter controls the behavior of the application." } } }

When deploying an ARM template, you can use the Azure CLI or Azure PowerShell, providing the template file and any required parameter values. Azure will then create or update the specified resources based on the template definitions.

In summary, ARM templates and JSON syntax provide a robust and flexible way to define and manage your Azure infrastructure as code. With parameters, variables, and resources, you can create templates that are reusable and adaptable to various scenarios. JSON's simplicity and readability make it an excellent choice for expressing your infrastructure requirements. By mastering ARM templates and JSON syntax, you'll have the tools to efficiently manage your Azure resources and embrace infrastructure as code principles in your cloud journey. So, let's roll up our sleeves and dive into the exciting world of ARM templates and JSON!

In the dynamic world of cloud computing, deploying resources efficiently is a top priority for organizations seeking to harness the full potential of their cloud environments. This is where Azure Resource Manager (ARM) templates come into play, providing a robust framework for defining and deploying Azure resources with precision and repeatability.

Picture ARM templates as your trusty blueprints for constructing a digital skyscraper in the Azure cloud. With these templates, you can describe the precise configuration, relationships, and dependencies of your Azure resources in a declarative manner, eliminating the guesswork and manual intervention often associated with resource deployment.

At the heart of ARM templates lies JSON, the JavaScript Object Notation. JSON's simplicity and readability make it an ideal choice for representing structured data, and in this case, the definition of your Azure resources. Each ARM template is essentially a JSON document that encapsulates your infrastructure requirements.

But what makes ARM templates truly efficient? It's their ability to empower you with the automation, repeatability, and consistency needed to streamline resource deployment. Imagine deploying the same set of resources repeatedly without the risk of human error or inconsistency – that's the power of ARM templates.

Let's break down the key components of an ARM template to understand how it all comes together. At the core, an ARM template consists of parameters, variables, and resources. Parameters are like the adjustable knobs on your blueprint, allowing you to customize your resource deployment. These parameters can represent values like names, sizes, or configuration settings that vary from one deployment to another.

Variables, on the other hand, are your workbench tools. They help you store and reuse intermediate values or expressions within the template. Variables can simplify complex calculations, provide consistency, and enhance the readability of your ARM template.

The star of the show is the 'resources' section within the ARM template. This is where you define the Azure resources you want to create or manage. Each resource is specified with its type, name, location, and properties. The 'type' is a unique identifier for the resource, and the 'name' gives it a distinct label within your Azure environment.

ARM templates support conditional logic, allowing you to adapt your resource deployment based on specific conditions. You can use functions like 'if,' 'equals,' and 'not' to make decisions within your template. For instance, you can conditionally deploy resources only if a certain parameter meets a specific requirement.

Let's take a practical example. Suppose you're deploying a web application, and you want to include additional resources like a database server only if the user specifies a database connection string. With conditional logic in ARM templates, you can achieve this effortlessly.

Loops and iterations are also within your grasp. ARM templates offer a 'copy' function that enables you to create multiple instances of the same resource. For example, if you need to deploy a fleet of virtual machines or a set of storage accounts, you can use the 'copy' function to do so efficiently.

But how does ARM make this magic happen? When you deploy an ARM template, the Azure Resource Manager takes charge. It reads your template and executes it in the desired Azure region, creating or updating resources according to the template's definitions.

Imagine having a template that defines your entire application stack – virtual machines, networking, storage, and more. With a single deployment, you can provision the entire environment consistently, ensuring that each resource is configured exactly as specified in your template.

As a bonus, Azure Resource Manager handles dependencies automatically. It ensures that resources are created in the correct order, resolving any dependencies between them. This eliminates the headache of managing resource creation sequence manually.

Now, let's explore the concept of "resource groups." Azure Resource Manager allows you to organize your resources into logical containers called resource groups. These groups provide a practical way to manage and monitor related resources as a single unit.

Consider a scenario where you're running multiple applications in your Azure environment. By grouping the resources associated with each application into separate resource groups, you can easily manage, monitor, and even delete all the resources related to a specific application in one go.

Resource groups also come in handy when it's time to clean up your environment. Rather than hunting down and deleting individual resources, you can simply delete the entire resource group, ensuring that all associated resources are removed efficiently.

Here's a friendly tip: Naming conventions matter. When working with ARM templates and resource groups, adopting a consistent naming convention can make your life much easier. It helps you quickly identify the purpose and ownership of each resource and resource group.

But wait, there's more to ARM templates. Azure provides a gallery of pre-built templates and reference architectures tailored for various scenarios. These templates are designed to kickstart your deployments, whether you're setting up a web application, a database, or a full-fledged enterprise solution.

You can browse the Azure Quickstart Templates repository on GitHub to discover a wealth of templates created and maintained by the Azure community. These templates cover a wide range of use cases and can save you significant time and effort when starting your projects.

Moreover, Azure offers Azure Resource Manager template blueprints, which allow you to define governance standards for your organization. These blueprints encompass role assignments, policies, and resource groups to ensure that your deployments adhere to specific compliance and security requirements.

When deploying resources efficiently, it's essential to consider your deployment options. Azure offers several methods for deploying ARM templates, each suited to different scenarios. The Azure Portal provides a user-friendly web interface for deploying templates interactively. It's an excellent choice for small-scale or one-off deployments.

For more automation and scalability, Azure CLI (Command-Line Interface) and Azure PowerShell provide command-line tools that allow you to deploy templates programmatically. You can script your deployments, integrate them into your CI/CD pipelines, and automate resource provisioning seamlessly.

Azure DevOps, Microsoft's integrated set of development tools, also offers robust support for ARM templates. You can leverage Azure DevOps pipelines to automate the entire application lifecycle, from development to deployment, using ARM templates as code.

But what about source control and version management for your ARM templates? Here's where Git, GitHub, Azure Repos, and other version control systems shine. By storing your ARM templates in a version-controlled repository, you can track changes, collaborate with teammates, and ensure the integrity of your infrastructure code.

Here's a practical scenario: Imagine you're working on an Azure solution with a team of developers. You've defined your infrastructure as ARM templates and stored them in a Git repository. Now, whenever a teammate wants to make changes to the infrastructure, they create a branch, make their modifications, and submit a pull request for review.

This collaborative workflow allows for code reviews, discussions, and testing before changes are merged into the main branch. It ensures that your infrastructure remains reliable, consistent, and up to date.

Moreover, by adopting Infrastructure as Code (IaC) practices with ARM templates, you're positioning yourself for better agility, scalability, and reliability in your Azure deployments.

Infrastructure as Code treats infrastructure configurations as code artifacts, subject to version control, testing, and automation.

In summary, deploying resources efficiently with ARM templates is your ticket to achieving automation, repeatability, and consistency in your Azure environment. With parameters, variables, and resource definitions in JSON syntax, you can describe your infrastructure requirements with precision.

Resource groups provide a practical way to manage, monitor, and organize your resources, while naming conventions and version control help keep your deployments organized and maintainable. Azure offers a plethora of templates and blueprints to jumpstart your projects and align with governance standards.

By mastering ARM templates and adopting Infrastructure as Code principles, you'll be well-equipped to tackle the challenges of modern cloud computing. So, roll up your sleeves, embrace the power of ARM templates, and embark on a journey of efficient resource deployment in the Azure cloud!

Chapter 4: Pro-Level Cost Management and Optimization Strategies

In the ever-evolving landscape of cloud computing, cost management remains a paramount concern for organizations of all sizes. As cloud resources become increasingly abundant and complex, mastering advanced cost management techniques becomes essential to optimize spending and ensure that your cloud investments deliver the best possible value.

One of the first steps in advanced cost management is establishing a robust cost allocation and tagging strategy. Tagging resources with meaningful labels allows you to track and attribute costs accurately. By assigning tags based on criteria such as departments, projects, or environments, you gain granular visibility into where your cloud spending occurs.

Cost allocation tags enable you to answer critical questions, such as which project or team is responsible for specific cloud expenses. This level of transparency empowers you to make informed decisions about resource optimization and budget allocation.

To take cost allocation a step further, consider implementing a chargeback or showback model within your organization. Chargeback assigns costs directly to individual departments or teams, making them responsible for their cloud expenditures. Showback, on the other hand, provides visibility into costs without actually charging departments. Both models promote accountability and encourage responsible resource usage.

Next, let's explore the concept of budgeting and forecasting. Advanced cost management involves setting clear budgets for your cloud spending and regularly monitoring your progress against these budgets. Azure Budgets and AWS Budgets are built-in tools that can help you define spending limits, set alerts, and visualize your expenditure trends.

Forecasting future cloud costs can be challenging, but it's a crucial aspect of cost management. Utilize historical data, growth patterns, and usage trends to create accurate cost predictions.

Forecasting empowers you to proactively address potential budget overruns and make adjustments to your cloud strategy as needed.

Reservations and Reserved Instances (RIs) are powerful tools for cost optimization in cloud environments. Reserving resources, such as virtual machines, databases, or storage, can lead to significant cost savings. Cloud providers offer flexible reservation options, allowing you to choose the term length and payment model that best aligns with your organization's needs.

Additionally, Azure's Azure Reserved VM Instances and AWS's EC2 Reserved Instances provide the ability to reserve virtual machines at a lower cost compared to on-demand pricing. By strategically using RIs, you can ensure cost-effective resource provisioning while maintaining flexibility.

Spot Instances and Spot VMs are another advanced cost management technique, primarily offered by AWS and Azure. These instances allow you to leverage spare capacity at a reduced cost, making them ideal for workloads that can tolerate interruptions. Spot instances provide significant savings when used strategically, but they require careful planning to ensure workload availability.

Resource scheduling and automation are essential components of advanced cost management. Implementing automation scripts, such as Azure Automation or AWS Lambda, allows you to start and stop resources based on predefined schedules or triggers. For instance, you can schedule virtual machines to power down during non-business hours, reducing costs without impacting productivity.

Moreover, utilizing serverless computing services, like Azure Functions or AWS Lambda, can lead to cost savings by eliminating the need to provision and manage servers. Serverless platforms automatically scale resources based on demand, ensuring optimal resource utilization and cost-efficiency.

Spotting idle or underutilized resources is a critical cost management technique. Regularly review your cloud environment to identify resources that are no longer needed or are running with low utilization. Cloud providers offer tools like Azure Advisor and AWS Trusted Advisor to provide recommendations for resource optimization.

Rightsizing your resources is another way to achieve cost savings. Analyze the performance and utilization of your virtual machines, databases, and storage to determine if you are overprovisioned. Downsizing or resizing resources to match your actual requirements can result in substantial cost reductions.

Implementing governance policies and cost controls is paramount in advanced cost management. Azure Policy and AWS Organizations offer robust policy management capabilities to enforce compliance with spending limits, resource quotas, and security standards. By establishing and enforcing these policies, you can prevent unnecessary spending and maintain cost discipline.

Furthermore, consider utilizing cloud cost optimization tools and third-party solutions. Azure Cost Management and Billing and AWS Cost Explorer provide insights into your cloud spending, enabling you to identify cost-saving opportunities and anomalies in your billing data. Third-party tools, such as CloudHealth, CloudCheckr, and Costly, offer advanced analytics and optimization features to enhance your cost management efforts.

Monitoring and alerting are integral components of advanced cost management. Set up monitoring and alerting mechanisms to receive notifications when specific cost thresholds or anomalies are detected. This proactive approach allows you to address cost-related issues promptly and avoid unexpected budget overruns.

Cost visualization and reporting are essential for effective cost management. Leverage the reporting capabilities provided by cloud providers or use third-party tools to create customized dashboards and reports. These visualizations offer insights into your spending patterns, trends, and cost breakdowns, facilitating informed decision-making.

Advanced cost management also involves exploring reserved capacity for database services. Azure SQL Database and Amazon RDS offer reserved capacity options that allow you to reserve database resources for a predefined duration, resulting in significant cost savings compared to pay-as-you-go pricing.

Additionally, consider exploring cloud cost optimization frameworks, such as the AWS Well-Architected Framework and the Azure Well-Architected Framework. These frameworks provide best practices, guidelines, and architectural recommendations to help you design cost-efficient and scalable cloud solutions.

In summary, advanced cost management techniques are essential for optimizing cloud spending and ensuring that your organization derives maximum value from its cloud investments. By implementing robust cost allocation, budgeting, and forecasting strategies, you can gain control over your cloud expenses.

Leveraging reservations, spot instances, resource scheduling, and automation can lead to substantial cost savings. Identifying and addressing idle or underutilized resources, rightsizing, and enforcing governance policies are crucial steps in achieving cost efficiency.

Utilizing cloud cost optimization tools, monitoring, alerting, visualization, and reporting enhances your ability to manage costs effectively. Finally, exploring reserved capacity options for database services and adopting cloud cost optimization frameworks further strengthens your cost management efforts.

With these advanced cost management techniques in your toolkit, you'll be well-prepared to navigate the complexities of cloud spending and ensure that your organization's cloud journey remains cost-effective and efficient. So, embrace these techniques, continuously monitor and optimize your cloud resources, and enjoy the benefits of cost-efficient cloud operations.

In the world of cloud computing, effective cost management is not just a one-time effort; it's an ongoing journey that requires constant attention and vigilance. One of the fundamental aspects of this journey is implementing budgets and cost alerts. These tools serve as your early warning system, helping you stay within your financial boundaries and avoid unpleasant surprises when the monthly bill arrives.

Let's start by exploring budgets. A budget is essentially a spending limit that you set for your cloud resources. It acts as a financial safety net, ensuring that you don't exceed your allocated budget for a specific period. Azure Budgets and AWS Budgets are popular cloud-native tools that enable you to define and monitor these budgets seamlessly.

Creating a budget is a straightforward process. You specify the budget amount, the timeframe (monthly, quarterly, or annually), and the budget name. This budget can encompass your entire cloud expenditure or focus on specific resource groups, departments, or projects. The flexibility to tailor budgets to your organizational structure is a powerful feature.

Once your budget is set up, it's time to configure alerts. Alerts are your proactive guardians, ready to notify you when your spending approaches or surpasses the budget threshold. These notifications can be sent via email, SMS, or integrated with your preferred communication channels, ensuring that you stay informed in real-time.

Azure Budgets and AWS Budgets allow you to define multiple alerts for a single budget. For instance, you can set up alerts to trigger when you've spent 50%, 75%, and 90% of your budget. Each alert level serves as a checkpoint, giving you the flexibility to take action at different stages of your budget utilization.

Let's dive into a practical scenario. Imagine you're managing the cloud resources for your organization's marketing department. You've created a budget for the marketing team's Azure spending, with a monthly limit of $5,000. To stay ahead of the game, you've configured alerts to notify you when spending reaches $2,500 (50% of the budget), $3,750 (75% of the budget), and $4,500 (90% of the budget).

Now, when marketing campaigns are in full swing, and resource consumption surges, you'll receive timely alerts as you approach each budget milestone. These alerts empower you to make informed decisions, such as scaling resources down, optimizing configurations, or reallocating budget to avoid exceeding your financial boundaries.

But budgets and alerts are not just about staying within limits; they're also about gaining insights. These tools provide valuable data and historical context about your spending patterns. You can analyze your spending trends, identify peak usage periods, and plan your budgets accordingly. This data-driven approach to cost management fosters efficiency and accountability.

Furthermore, budgets and alerts are not static entities. Cloud environments are dynamic, and so are your spending patterns. As your organization grows, your budget requirements may change. You can adjust your budgets and alert thresholds to align with your evolving needs. This flexibility ensures that your cost management strategy remains agile and responsive.

Now, let's talk about some best practices for implementing budgets and cost alerts effectively:

Set Realistic Budgets: When defining your budgets, consider historical spending patterns, growth projections, and seasonal variations. Setting realistic budgets ensures that you strike the right balance between resource availability and cost control.

Collaborate with Stakeholders: Cost management is a shared responsibility within an organization. Collaborate with department heads, project managers, and finance teams to set budgets that reflect the needs and goals of different parts of your organization.

Use Tags for Granular Control: Leverage tagging to segment your spending and allocate budgets with precision. Tags allow you to attribute costs to specific departments, teams, or projects, providing granular insights into your spending.

Implement Reserved Instances and Spot Instances: Explore reservation options and spot instances for cost optimization. Reserving resources can lead to substantial savings, while spot instances offer cost-effective options for workloads that can tolerate interruptions.

Establish Governance Policies: Implement governance policies and cost controls to enforce budget compliance. Azure Policy and AWS Organizations offer robust policy management capabilities to maintain spending discipline.

Regularly Review and Adjust: Don't set and forget your budgets and alerts. Regularly review your spending, analyze alerts, and adjust your budgets and thresholds as needed. Continuous monitoring ensures that your cost management strategy remains effective.

Educate and Train: Invest in educating your teams about budget management and cost awareness. Providing training on cloud cost management best practices empowers your employees to make cost-conscious decisions.

Leverage Cloud Cost Optimization Tools: Take advantage of cloud cost optimization tools and third-party solutions to gain deeper insights into your spending, identify optimization opportunities, and automate cost-saving actions.

By following these best practices, you'll be well on your way to implementing budgets and cost alerts that not only help you stay within your financial boundaries but also foster a culture of cost-consciousness and optimization within your organization.

In summary, implementing budgets and cost alerts is a fundamental step in cloud cost management. These tools provide you with the visibility, control, and insights needed to manage your cloud spending effectively. Whether you're overseeing the cloud resources for a small team or a large organization, budgets and alerts are your allies in ensuring that your cloud investments deliver value without breaking the bank. So, take charge of your cloud costs, set up your budgets, configure your alerts, and embark on a cost-conscious cloud journey!

Chapter 5: Implementing Advanced Monitoring and Alerting

In the dynamic and ever-evolving world of cloud computing, setting up comprehensive monitoring solutions is not just a good practice; it's a critical necessity. Azure, Microsoft's cloud platform, provides a wide range of services and resources, and effectively monitoring them ensures the availability, performance, and security of your applications and infrastructure.

Imagine Azure monitoring as a set of digital eyes and ears that continuously observe and listen to your cloud environment. These monitoring solutions capture data about your resources, track performance metrics, detect anomalies, and provide valuable insights that empower you to make informed decisions and take timely actions.

So, where do we begin with setting up comprehensive Azure monitoring solutions? Let's start by exploring the core components and key principles that underpin effective monitoring in Azure.

Resource Logs: Azure generates a wealth of data through resource logs, which provide detailed information about the activities and operations within your resources. These logs include information about who is doing what, when, and from where. Enabling resource logs is the foundation of monitoring in Azure.

Metrics: Metrics are essential for monitoring the performance of your Azure resources. Azure Metrics provide a wealth of data, including CPU usage, memory consumption, network throughput, and more. These metrics offer valuable insights into the health and performance of your resources.

Alerts: Setting up alerts is a proactive way to stay informed about critical events and anomalies in your Azure environment. Azure Monitor enables you to define alert rules that trigger notifications via email, SMS, or integration with your preferred communication channels when specific conditions are met.

Azure Monitor: Azure Monitor is the central hub for monitoring your Azure resources. It provides a unified view of resource logs, metrics, and alerts, giving you a holistic perspective of your cloud environment. Azure Monitor also offers advanced features like Application Insights for application-level monitoring.

Log Analytics: Log Analytics is a powerful tool within Azure Monitor that allows you to collect, analyze, and visualize data from your resource logs. It offers a query language, known as Kusto Query Language (KQL), that enables you to create custom queries and extract insights from your log data.

Azure Monitor Workbooks: Workbooks are customizable dashboards within Azure Monitor that allow you to create visualizations and reports tailored to your specific monitoring needs. You can build workbooks to track the performance of specific resources or analyze data across multiple resources.

Diagnostic Settings: Diagnostic settings enable you to route resource logs and metrics to various destinations, such as Azure Monitor, Azure Storage, or Azure Event Hubs. By configuring diagnostic settings, you can centralize your monitoring data and make it accessible for analysis and alerting.

Network Watcher: Network Watcher is a service that provides network monitoring and diagnostics capabilities for your Azure resources. It helps you identify and troubleshoot network issues, analyze traffic flows, and gain visibility into the network topology of your virtual networks.

Security Center: Azure Security Center is an essential component of comprehensive monitoring, focusing on the security of your Azure resources. It provides recommendations, threat detection, and security monitoring to help you safeguard your cloud environment.

Now, let's delve into the steps involved in setting up comprehensive Azure monitoring solutions:

Enable Resource Logs: The first step is to enable resource logs for your Azure resources. You can do this by navigating to the specific resource's settings and configuring the appropriate diagnostic settings. Enabling resource logs ensures that you capture detailed data about resource activities.

Configure Metrics: Configure metric collection for your resources. Azure Metrics provide valuable insights into resource performance and can be used to create alerts and dashboards. You can access metrics through Azure Monitor or directly from the Azure portal.

Define Alert Rules: Determine the conditions that warrant alerts in your Azure environment. Create alert rules in Azure Monitor based on metrics or resource log data. For example, you can set up alerts for high CPU usage, exceeded storage thresholds, or specific log events.

Customize Dashboards: Create customized dashboards using Azure Monitor Workbooks. Dashboards allow you to visualize data from different resources and logs in a single view. You can build dashboards that align with your specific monitoring objectives and requirements.

Utilize Log Analytics: Leverage Log Analytics to perform in-depth analysis of your monitoring data. Create queries in Kusto Query Language (KQL) to extract insights and identify trends or anomalies. Log Analytics provides the flexibility to create custom reports and visualizations.

Set Up Security Monitoring: Implement Azure Security Center to enhance your security monitoring capabilities. Configure security policies, enable threat detection, and review security recommendations to protect your Azure resources from potential threats.

Establish Alert Notifications: Configure alert notifications to receive timely information about critical events. Azure Monitor allows you to send alerts via email, SMS, or integrate with third-party incident management and communication tools.

Review and Optimize: Regularly review your monitoring solutions and adjust them as needed. Monitor the effectiveness of your alerts, dashboards, and log queries. Optimize your monitoring configuration based on evolving needs and changing resource usage patterns.

Automate Responses: Consider automating responses to alerts using Azure Logic Apps or Azure Functions. Automation can help you take immediate actions when specific conditions are met, such as scaling resources, restarting services, or sending notifications to on-call teams.

Document Your Monitoring Strategy: Document your monitoring strategy, including the types of resources being monitored, the alerts in place, and the responsible parties for responding to alerts. Having clear documentation ensures that your monitoring efforts remain organized and well-documented.

Comprehensive Azure monitoring solutions not only help you identify and address issues promptly but also provide valuable insights for optimizing your cloud resources and enhancing the overall performance and security of your Azure environment.

In summary, setting up comprehensive Azure monitoring solutions is a crucial step in managing your Azure resources effectively. By enabling resource logs, configuring metrics, defining alert rules, customizing dashboards, and utilizing tools like Log Analytics and Security Center, you can gain deep insights into your cloud environment.

Regularly review and optimize your monitoring configuration to adapt to changing needs and resource usage patterns. With a well-established monitoring strategy in place, you can ensure the availability, performance, and security of your applications and infrastructure in the Azure cloud. So, embrace the power of Azure monitoring and embark on a journey of proactive cloud management and optimization!

In the realm of cloud management, staying proactive is the name of the game, and one of the most crucial aspects of proactivity is configuring alerting and notifications. These tools act as your watchful guardians, keeping a close eye on your cloud environment and alerting you when specific conditions or events warrant your attention.

Think of alerting and notifications as your cloud's way of saying, "Hey, something needs your attention," ensuring that you can respond swiftly and effectively to any changes or issues in your Azure environment.

Let's dive right in and explore the essential elements of configuring alerting and notifications for proactive management in Azure.

Azure Monitor Alerts: Azure Monitor is your go-to hub for creating and managing alerts. It provides a centralized platform to define alert rules, set up notifications, and track alert incidents across your Azure resources. You can think of Azure Monitor as your control center for proactive monitoring.

Alert Rules: Alert rules are the heart of your alerting strategy. These rules specify the conditions that trigger alerts. For example, you can set up a rule to trigger an alert when CPU usage exceeds a certain threshold or when specific log events occur. Azure Monitor allows you to define these rules with precision.

Action Groups: Action groups are the recipients of your alert notifications. They define how and where alert notifications are sent when an alert rule is triggered. Action groups can include various notification methods, such as email, SMS, webhook calls, or integration with third-party incident management systems.

Severity Levels: Azure Monitor supports different severity levels for alerts, ranging from Low to Critical. Assigning appropriate severity levels to your alerts helps prioritize and categorize them based on their impact and urgency. This ensures that you focus on critical alerts that require immediate attention.

Dynamic Thresholds: To enhance the effectiveness of your alerting, consider using dynamic thresholds. Azure Monitor allows you to set up smart detection rules that adapt to changing patterns and anomalies in your data. Dynamic thresholds help reduce false positives and ensure that alerts are triggered when they genuinely matter.

Metric Alerts: Metric alerts are based on performance metrics and provide real-time insights into the health and performance of your Azure resources. You can configure metric alerts to trigger notifications when metrics cross predefined thresholds or exhibit specific trends.

Activity Log Alerts: Activity log alerts are another valuable type of alerting in Azure. They enable you to monitor activities and events in your Azure subscription, such as resource creation, configuration changes, and access control modifications. Activity log alerts help you track changes to your resources for security and compliance purposes.

Log Alerts: Log alerts focus on monitoring log data generated by your Azure resources. Whether it's application logs, security logs, or custom logs, you can create log alerts to trigger notifications based on specific log entries or patterns. Log alerts are particularly useful for identifying and responding to issues in your applications.

Multi-Threshold Alerts: Some scenarios may require multi-threshold alerts. In these cases, you can configure alerts with multiple thresholds to trigger notifications at different levels of severity. Multi-threshold alerts are handy for complex situations where different actions are needed based on the extent of the issue.

Time-Based Alerts: Time-based alerts enable you to schedule alerting activities during specific time windows. For instance, you can configure alerts to be active only during business hours or exclude weekends. Time-based alerts help you avoid being inundated with notifications when they are not relevant.

Customized Notifications: Tailor your notifications to suit your needs. Azure Monitor allows you to create customized alert messages, providing context and guidance for responders. You can include information about the alert trigger, recommended actions, and contact details for support teams.

Automated Responses: Consider setting up automated responses to alerts using Azure Logic Apps or Azure Functions. Automation can help you take immediate actions when specific conditions are met, such as scaling resources, restarting services, or initiating incident response workflows.

Now that we've covered the essential elements let's discuss the steps to configure alerting and notifications for proactive management effectively:

Identify Monitoring Objectives: Begin by clearly defining your monitoring objectives. What are you monitoring for? What conditions or events are critical for your Azure environment? Understanding your goals and priorities will guide your alerting strategy.

Select Relevant Resources: Determine which Azure resources you need to monitor and configure alerts for. This selection should align with your monitoring objectives and the critical components of your applications and infrastructure.

Define Alert Rules: Create alert rules that align with your monitoring objectives. Specify the conditions or criteria that trigger alerts, such as thresholds, patterns, or specific log events. Ensure that your alert rules are precise and relevant to your goals.

Configure Action Groups: Set up action groups to receive alert notifications. Decide who should be notified and how they should be notified (email, SMS, webhook, etc.). Ensure that action groups include the right stakeholders, support teams, and incident responders.

Assign Severity Levels: Assign appropriate severity levels to your alerts. Use the severity levels to prioritize alerts based on their impact and urgency. This helps ensure that the most critical alerts receive immediate attention.

Test Alerting Configurations: Test your alerting configurations to verify that alerts are triggered correctly and notifications are delivered to the intended recipients. Testing helps you identify and address any issues or misconfigurations.

Monitor and Refine: Continuously monitor your alerts and refine your alerting strategy as needed. Regularly review the effectiveness of your alerts, adjust thresholds, and update action groups based on changing requirements or resource usage patterns.

Educate and Train: Educate your teams about alerting and notifications. Ensure that team members are aware of alerting policies, notification procedures, and their roles in responding to alerts. Training promotes effective incident response and coordination.

Document Your Alerting Strategy: Document your alerting strategy, including the types of alerts, conditions, severity levels, and notification procedures. Clear documentation ensures that your alerting efforts remain organized and well-documented.

By following these steps and principles, you'll be well-prepared to configure alerting and notifications for proactive management in Azure effectively. Proactive monitoring and timely responses to alerts are key to maintaining the availability, performance, and security of your Azure resources.

In summary, configuring alerting and notifications is a crucial aspect of proactive cloud management in Azure. These tools empower you to stay ahead of issues, respond promptly to critical events, and ensure the reliability of your cloud environment.

Whether you're managing a single resource or a complex cloud infrastructure, the ability to configure alerts and notifications effectively is essential for achieving proactive monitoring and maintaining the resilience of your Azure applications and services. So, embrace the power of alerting and notifications, and take control of your Azure environment with confidence!

Chapter 6: Automation and Integration: Third-Party Tools and Extensions

In the ever-evolving landscape of cloud computing, automation has emerged as a fundamental enabler of efficiency, scalability, and productivity. While cloud providers like Azure offer robust automation solutions, they also recognize the importance of integration with popular third-party tools to meet diverse automation needs.

So, let's embark on a journey to explore the realm of integrating popular third-party tools for automation in the Azure cloud environment. It's a journey that empowers you to harness the full potential of automation by seamlessly combining the capabilities of Azure with those of your preferred third-party automation tools.

Azure Logic Apps, for instance, allow you to connect and automate workflows across different applications and services, both within and outside the Azure ecosystem. You can use Logic Apps connectors to integrate with a wide range of third-party services, such as Salesforce, Slack, and Dropbox, to orchestrate complex workflows that span multiple systems.

Another powerful integration tool in the Azure arsenal is Azure Functions, which enables serverless compute for running code in response to events. Azure Functions can seamlessly connect with various third-party services, databases, and APIs, making it a versatile choice for automation tasks that require event-driven processing.

Imagine a scenario where you need to automate the process of processing customer orders from an e-commerce platform, updating inventory in a database, and notifying the shipping team via a messaging platform. Azure Logic Apps can orchestrate this end-to-end process by integrating with the e-commerce API, the database, and the messaging service, all while running serverless Azure Functions for specific data processing tasks.

For organizations that rely on configuration management and infrastructure as code, tools like Terraform and Ansible have gained popularity. These third-party automation tools provide the ability to define and provision infrastructure resources and manage configurations in a declarative manner.

Azure recognizes the importance of these tools in the automation ecosystem and offers seamless integration. You can use Terraform with Azure to define and deploy infrastructure resources in Azure using HashiCorp Configuration Language (HCL). Similarly, Ansible allows you to automate provisioning, configuration management, and application deployment in Azure through a collection of Azure modules.

Whether you're managing virtual machines, container orchestrators, or other cloud resources, the integration of Terraform and Ansible with Azure simplifies resource provisioning, configuration, and maintenance tasks, ensuring consistency and repeatability in your automation workflows.

Azure DevOps, another integral part of the Azure ecosystem, provides a comprehensive set of tools for end-to-end DevOps automation. It offers features like source code management, continuous integration and continuous delivery (CI/CD), and agile project management.

However, Azure DevOps also recognizes the need for interoperability with third-party tools. It provides integration capabilities with popular version control systems like Git, allowing teams to use their preferred source code repositories while leveraging the automation capabilities of Azure DevOps pipelines.

Moreover, Azure DevOps integrates with a wide range of third-party CI/CD tools and services, including Jenkins, Travis CI, and CircleCI. This flexibility enables organizations to tailor their CI/CD pipelines to meet their specific needs while benefiting from the collaborative and project management features of Azure DevOps.

Imagine a software development team that uses GitLab as its primary source code repository and Azure DevOps for CI/CD. Through seamless integration, the team can trigger Azure DevOps pipelines from GitLab commits, ensuring automated build and deployment processes while maintaining their preferred source code management workflow.

For organizations seeking advanced orchestration and workflow automation, tools like Apache Airflow and Kubernetes are indispensable. Apache Airflow, an open-source platform for orchestrating complex workflows, can be deployed on Azure Kubernetes Service (AKS) to manage and automate data pipelines, data processing, and data workflows.

By harnessing the power of Kubernetes, you can deploy and manage containerized applications at scale. Azure Kubernetes Service simplifies the deployment and orchestration of containerized workloads, making it a valuable platform for organizations adopting containerization and microservices architectures.

Azure provides a seamless experience for integrating these powerful tools into your automation workflows. Whether you're orchestrating data pipelines with Apache Airflow on AKS or managing containerized workloads with Kubernetes on Azure, you can take advantage of Azure's infrastructure and services to enhance scalability, security, and management.

The ability to integrate popular third-party automation tools with Azure is not limited to specific use cases; it extends across a wide spectrum of automation scenarios. For example, if your organization relies on ServiceNow for IT service management and incident tracking, Azure Logic Apps can facilitate seamless integration between Azure services and ServiceNow, automating incident resolution and service request fulfillment.

In addition to the tools mentioned, Azure also provides connectors and extensions for integrating with various other third-party services and platforms, including data analytics and visualization tools, monitoring and alerting solutions, and identity and access management providers.

Consider the scenario where an organization uses Tableau for data visualization and Power BI for business intelligence. Azure Logic Apps connectors for Tableau and Power BI enable automated data extraction, transformation, and loading (ETL) processes. You can automate the extraction of data from Azure data sources, transform it as needed, and load it into Tableau or Power BI for real-time reporting and visualization.

Furthermore, Azure integrates seamlessly with popular identity and access management providers such as Okta and Ping Identity. This integration enables organizations to leverage their existing identity solutions while ensuring secure access to Azure resources and applications.

As you embark on your journey of integrating popular third-party tools for automation in the Azure cloud environment, consider the following best practices:

Define Clear Objectives: Clearly define your automation objectives and the specific tasks you want to automate using third-party tools. Having a clear understanding of your goals is essential for successful integration.

Choose the Right Tools: Select third-party tools that align with your automation needs and organizational requirements. Evaluate the compatibility, features, and scalability of the tools to ensure they meet your objectives.

Leverage Azure Services: Take advantage of Azure services and features that enhance the integration of third-party tools. Azure Logic Apps, Azure Functions, and Azure DevOps pipelines provide powerful capabilities for orchestration and automation.

Follow Security Best Practices: Implement security best practices when integrating third-party tools with Azure. Ensure that access controls, authentication, and authorization mechanisms are in place to protect your Azure resources.

Monitor and Maintain: Regularly monitor your automation workflows and maintain the integrations. Keep your third-party tools and Azure services up to date to address any security vulnerabilities or compatibility issues.

Document and Train: Document your integration processes, configurations, and workflows. Provide training and guidance to your teams to ensure they can effectively use and maintain the integrated automation solutions.

Stay Informed: Stay informed about updates and changes to both Azure services and the third-party tools you integrate. This awareness helps you adapt to new features and improvements that enhance your automation capabilities.

In summary, integrating popular third-party tools for automation in the Azure cloud environment unlocks a world of possibilities for organizations seeking to streamline processes, enhance productivity, and optimize their operations.

Whether you're automating workflows, managing infrastructure, orchestrating data pipelines, or implementing DevOps practices, Azure's integration capabilities provide the flexibility and extensibility to meet your automation needs.

So, embrace the synergy of Azure and third-party automation tools, and embark on a journey of enhanced efficiency, scalability, and innovation in your cloud automation endeavors.

In the ever-evolving landscape of cloud computing, the Azure Marketplace stands as a treasure trove of solutions, offering a vast array of applications, services, and extensions that can be seamlessly integrated into your Azure environment. These marketplace extensions are the key to extending Azure's capabilities, enabling you to unlock new features, enhance functionality, and streamline your cloud operations.

Imagine the Azure Marketplace as a bustling marketplace, teeming with vendors and offerings tailored to meet your diverse needs. Whether you're looking to bolster your security, optimize your data analytics, or simplify your DevOps processes, the Azure Marketplace has a solution waiting for you.

One of the significant advantages of using marketplace extensions is the speed and simplicity they bring to the table. Rather than building custom solutions from scratch or navigating complex integrations, you can quickly find and deploy pre-configured extensions that align with your objectives.

For instance, if you're tasked with strengthening the security posture of your Azure environment, you can turn to the Azure Marketplace to discover a plethora of security extensions. These extensions encompass everything from threat detection and vulnerability management to identity and access management.

By selecting a security extension from the marketplace, you can expedite the deployment of critical security controls, protect your resources against threats, and fortify your compliance efforts. The Azure Marketplace simplifies the process of securing your cloud environment, allowing you to focus on proactive threat mitigation rather than the intricacies of setup.

Moreover, marketplace extensions often come with a user-friendly interface and documentation, making them accessible to a wide range of users, from cloud administrators to developers. This accessibility ensures that you can harness their capabilities without the need for specialized expertise.

Consider the scenario where your organization aims to enhance its data analytics capabilities in Azure. Rather than embarking on a time-consuming data engineering project, you can explore the Azure Marketplace for analytics extensions. Here, you'll discover tools and services that facilitate data ingestion, transformation, visualization, and machine learning.

By selecting an analytics extension from the marketplace, you can expedite the process of building data pipelines, creating interactive dashboards, and training machine learning models. These extensions empower you to derive actionable insights from your data, drive data-driven decision-making, and fuel innovation within your organization.

Furthermore, the Azure Marketplace extends its reach to DevOps and application development. If your teams are striving to streamline their development workflows, you can explore the marketplace for DevOps extensions. These extensions encompass a wide spectrum of solutions, including continuous integration and continuous delivery (CI/CD) pipelines, code repositories, and testing frameworks.

By adopting a DevOps extension from the marketplace, you can accelerate software development, automate testing processes, and ensure the reliable delivery of applications. This streamlined approach to DevOps enhances collaboration among development and operations teams, fosters a culture of automation, and paves the way for faster time-to-market.

The Azure Marketplace also caters to specialized needs, such as IoT (Internet of Things) and edge computing. If your organization is embarking on IoT initiatives or deploying edge computing solutions, you can turn to the marketplace for IoT and edge extensions.

These extensions provide a wealth of tools and services for managing IoT devices, processing data at the edge, and building intelligent IoT solutions. By leveraging IoT and edge extensions, you can harness the potential of IoT to gain real-time insights, optimize operations, and create innovative customer experiences.

Now, let's explore how to effectively extend Azure's capabilities with marketplace extensions:

Identify Your Needs: Begin by identifying your specific requirements and objectives. What capabilities or functionalities are you looking to extend in your Azure environment? Understanding your needs is the first step in finding the right marketplace extensions.

Browse the Marketplace: Navigate to the Azure Marketplace and explore the extensive catalog of extensions. You can browse extensions by category, industry, or use case. Take your time to review the offerings and read through descriptions and documentation.

Evaluate Solutions: When you find extensions that align with your needs, evaluate them carefully. Look for features, compatibility with your Azure services, user reviews, and pricing details. Some extensions offer free trials, allowing you to test their suitability.

Deploy and Configure: Once you've selected an extension, deploy it in your Azure environment. Follow the deployment instructions provided in the marketplace. Most extensions offer straightforward setup and configuration processes.

Integrate with Your Workflows: Integrate the extension seamlessly into your existing workflows and processes. Ensure that it aligns with your Azure resources and services. Most extensions offer integration guides to assist with this step.

Test and Monitor: Thoroughly test the extension's functionality to ensure it meets your requirements. Monitor its performance and impact on your Azure environment. Be prepared to make adjustments or configurations as needed.

Optimize and Scale: As your usage of the extension grows, consider optimization and scalability. Some extensions may offer features for optimizing costs or scaling resources based on demand. Explore these options to ensure cost-effectiveness and efficiency.

Stay Informed: Keep an eye on updates and enhancements to the extension. The Azure Marketplace regularly adds new extensions and updates existing ones. Staying informed ensures that you leverage the latest features and improvements.

Educate Your Team: Train your teams on using the extension effectively. Provide documentation, training materials, and guidance to ensure that everyone can make the most of the extended capabilities.

Review and Adapt: Periodically review the extension's impact on your Azure environment and adapt its usage based on changing requirements or objectives. Consider user feedback and performance metrics when making adjustments.

In summary, extending Azure's capabilities with marketplace extensions is a strategic approach to enhancing your cloud environment's functionality, efficiency, and agility. The Azure Marketplace offers a diverse selection of extensions that cater to a wide range of needs, from security and analytics to DevOps and IoT.

By identifying your specific requirements, evaluating solutions, and following best practices for deployment and integration, you can leverage marketplace extensions to streamline operations, drive innovation, and unlock the full potential of Azure in your organization.

So, explore the Azure Marketplace with curiosity, choose the extensions that align with your goals, and embark on a journey of extending Azure's capabilities to meet your unique challenges and opportunities.

Chapter 7: Disaster Recovery and High Availability: Best Practices

In the dynamic world of cloud computing, ensuring high availability is paramount. Azure, Microsoft's cloud platform, offers a wealth of services and tools to help you design and implement high availability strategies for your applications and services. These strategies are your insurance against downtime and ensure that your systems are always accessible and reliable.

Picture high availability as a safety net for your cloud environment. It's like having a backup generator that kicks in when the power goes out, keeping your lights on and your operations running smoothly. In Azure, you can employ various strategies to achieve this level of resilience.

1. Redundancy Across Regions: One of the fundamental principles of high availability in Azure is to distribute your resources across multiple Azure regions. Azure has data centers in various geographic locations worldwide. By deploying your services and data in different regions, you safeguard against region-specific outages.

2. Availability Zones: Azure offers the concept of Availability Zones, which are unique physical locations within an Azure region. Each Availability Zone has its power, cooling, and networking, and they are isolated from each other to ensure fault tolerance. By deploying your resources across Availability Zones, you protect against hardware failures.

3. Load Balancing: Load balancing is a critical component of high availability. Azure provides various load balancing options, including Azure Load Balancer and Application Gateway. These services distribute incoming traffic across multiple instances to ensure that no single instance becomes a bottleneck.

4. Auto Scaling: Implement auto-scaling to dynamically adjust the number of resources based on demand. Azure provides services like Azure Autoscale and Virtual Machine Scale Sets, allowing your application to scale out during peak usage and scale in during low traffic, ensuring cost efficiency and performance.

5. Backup and Recovery: Regularly back up your data and configurations. Azure offers services like Azure Backup and Azure Site Recovery, which provide automated backup and disaster recovery solutions. These services enable you to recover data and applications quickly in case of unexpected failures.

6. Azure App Service Environments: For web applications, consider using Azure App Service Environments (ASE). ASEs provide a fully isolated and highly scalable environment for hosting your web apps. They offer high availability, custom domain support, and network isolation.

7. Database High Availability: If your application relies on databases, Azure offers database services with built-in high availability features. Azure SQL Database, for example, provides automatic failover and data replication to ensure continuous database availability.

8. Traffic Manager: Azure Traffic Manager is a global DNS-based traffic load balancer that allows you to distribute user traffic across multiple Azure regions. It can help you achieve high availability and low-latency access for your users worldwide.

9. Application Design: Your application architecture plays a crucial role in achieving high availability. Design your applications with fault tolerance in mind. Use stateless design patterns, implement retries and circuit breakers, and handle transient errors gracefully.

10. Monitoring and Alerts: Implement robust monitoring and alerting solutions. Azure Monitor provides a unified platform for monitoring your Azure resources. Set up alerts to proactively detect and respond to issues before they impact your users.

11. Regular Testing: Perform regular testing of your high availability configurations and disaster recovery plans. Conduct failover tests and simulate real-world scenarios to ensure that your systems can recover as expected.

12. Geographic Load Balancing: If your application serves users in different regions, consider using geographic load balancing. This strategy routes users to the nearest Azure region with available resources, reducing latency and improving performance.

13. Multi-Region Active-Active: For mission-critical applications, you can implement a multi-region active-active setup. This involves running identical instances of your application in multiple regions simultaneously. Users are routed to the closest healthy region, ensuring continuous availability even in the event of a region failure.

14. Chaos Engineering: Embrace the practice of chaos engineering, where you intentionally inject failures and disruptions into your systems to identify weaknesses and improve resilience. Tools like Azure Chaos Studio can help you carry out controlled chaos experiments.

15. Incident Response Plan: Develop a well-documented incident response plan. Define roles and responsibilities, establish communication channels, and outline procedures for responding to and recovering from incidents. Regularly review and update the plan.

16. Service-Level Agreements (SLAs): Familiarize yourself with Azure SLAs for various services. SLAs provide guarantees regarding service availability. Understanding these commitments can help you make informed decisions about your high availability architecture.

17. Disaster Recovery Drills: Conduct disaster recovery drills to validate your recovery processes. Simulate scenarios where entire regions become unavailable and ensure that your disaster recovery plans are effective.

18. Azure Resource Manager Templates: Use Azure Resource Manager (ARM) templates to define and deploy your infrastructure as code. Infrastructure as code allows you to recreate your environment consistently and efficiently, ensuring that your high availability configurations are maintained.

19. 24/7 Monitoring: Implement 24/7 monitoring and support for critical services. Having a dedicated team that can respond to incidents in real-time is essential for maintaining high availability.

20. Continuous Improvement: High availability is an ongoing process. Continuously evaluate your architecture, monitor performance, and review incident reports to identify areas for improvement. Embrace a culture of continuous improvement to stay resilient.

In summary, high availability in Azure is not a one-size-fits-all approach but rather a combination of strategies, best practices, and Azure services tailored to your specific needs and objectives. By leveraging redundancy, load balancing, auto scaling, and disaster recovery solutions, you can ensure that your applications and services are always accessible and reliable, even in the face of unexpected challenges.

So, as you embark on your journey to achieve high availability in Azure, remember that it's about designing for resilience, planning for the unexpected, and maintaining a proactive approach to cloud management. Your high availability strategy is your insurance policy against downtime, ensuring that your users have a seamless and dependable experience with your Azure-based applications and services.

Imagine this scenario: your organization relies on critical systems and data to run its operations smoothly. These systems store sensitive information, facilitate customer interactions, and support your day-to-day business activities. Now, what if the unexpected happens? A natural disaster strikes, a hardware failure occurs, or a cyberattack disrupts your infrastructure. How do you ensure that your business can recover quickly and continue operating without significant downtime or data loss? The answer lies in implementing disaster recovery solutions.

Disaster recovery is not just a buzzword; it's a crucial aspect of modern business continuity planning. It's about having a well-thought-out strategy in place to safeguard your organization's data and applications from unforeseen events that can disrupt your operations. In the world of cloud computing, like Microsoft Azure, disaster recovery solutions have become more accessible and effective than ever before.

So, let's embark on a journey to explore the realm of implementing disaster recovery solutions in Azure. We'll delve into the strategies, tools, and best practices that can help you protect your data, minimize downtime, and ensure the resilience of your Azure-based workloads.

1. Azure Site Recovery (ASR): Azure Site Recovery is your go-to solution for replicating and recovering Azure VMs and on-premises physical servers and VMs. It allows you to create a failover plan that specifies how your workloads should be recovered in the event of a disaster. ASR continuously replicates your workloads to a secondary Azure region, ensuring data consistency and minimal recovery point objectives (RPOs).

2. Backup and Restore: Azure Backup provides robust backup and restore capabilities for your data and workloads. You can back up files, folders, virtual machines, and even entire Azure SQL databases. Azure Backup allows you to set backup schedules, retention policies, and encryption options, ensuring that your data is protected and recoverable.

3. Geo-Redundant Storage: Azure offers geo-redundant storage for your critical data. When you enable geo-redundancy for Azure Storage, your data is automatically replicated to a secondary Azure region, providing data resiliency. In the event of a regional outage, your data remains accessible from the secondary region.

4. Azure DevTest Labs: Disaster recovery testing is a critical component of any disaster recovery strategy. Azure DevTest Labs allows you to create isolated testing environments that mimic your production environment. You can use these labs to simulate disaster scenarios and test your recovery plans without impacting your production workloads.

5. Azure Traffic Manager: Azure Traffic Manager is a global DNS-based traffic management solution. It allows you to distribute user traffic across multiple Azure regions. By leveraging Traffic Manager, you can achieve application-level redundancy and failover. If one region becomes unavailable, Traffic Manager automatically routes traffic to healthy regions.

6. Azure Functions: Azure Functions, a serverless compute service, can be used to automate disaster recovery procedures. You can create Azure Functions that trigger failover or recovery processes based on specific conditions or events. This automation ensures that your disaster recovery plans can be executed swiftly and reliably.

7. Azure Resource Manager (ARM) Templates: Infrastructure as code (IaC) is a best practice for disaster recovery. Azure Resource Manager templates allow you to define and deploy your Azure resources in a repeatable and automated manner. By using ARM templates, you can recreate your entire Azure environment, including virtual machines, networking, and storage, in case of a disaster.

8. Multi-Region Deployments: For mission-critical applications, consider deploying them in multiple Azure regions simultaneously. This approach, known as active-active deployment, ensures that your application remains accessible even if one region experiences an outage. Azure Traffic

Manager can be used to route traffic to the nearest healthy region.

9. Azure Security Center: Security is an integral part of disaster recovery. Azure Security Center provides threat detection and security monitoring for your Azure resources. It helps you identify and respond to security incidents that could potentially lead to a disaster. Proactive security measures can prevent disasters caused by cyberattacks.

10. Disaster Recovery Planning: Disaster recovery is not just about technology; it's about planning and preparedness. Develop comprehensive disaster recovery plans that outline roles, responsibilities, communication procedures, and step-by-step recovery processes. Regularly update and test these plans to ensure their effectiveness.

11. Compliance and Governance: Consider compliance and governance requirements when implementing disaster recovery solutions. Azure provides compliance certifications and tools like Azure Policy and Azure Blueprints to help you meet regulatory and security standards. Ensure that your disaster recovery processes align with these requirements.

12. Monitoring and Alerting: Implement robust monitoring and alerting solutions to detect issues and anomalies in real-time. Azure Monitor allows you to set up alerts based on specific conditions, such as resource health or performance thresholds. Timely alerts enable you to respond quickly to potential disasters.

13. Training and Documentation: Ensure that your team is trained in disaster recovery procedures and best practices. Document your disaster recovery plans, including step-by-step instructions and contact information. Training and documentation are essential for effective response during a disaster.

14. Regular Testing: Don't wait for a real disaster to test your recovery plans. Conduct regular disaster recovery drills and simulations to validate the effectiveness of your plans. Identify areas for improvement and adjust your strategies accordingly.

15. Communication and Coordination: Communication is key during a disaster. Establish clear communication channels and protocols for notifying stakeholders, employees, and customers in case of a disaster. Maintain open lines of communication throughout the recovery process.

16. Vendor and Partner Support: Consider leveraging Azure partners and managed service providers for additional disaster recovery support. Many Azure partners offer specialized disaster recovery solutions and expertise to enhance your resilience.

17. Continuous Improvement: Disaster recovery is an ongoing process. Continuously assess and improve your disaster recovery strategies, taking into account changes in your Azure environment, new threats, and evolving best practices.

In summary, implementing disaster recovery solutions in Azure is a strategic investment in the resilience and continuity of your business. By leveraging Azure services like Azure Site Recovery, Azure Backup, and geo-redundant storage, you can protect your data, applications, and workloads from unexpected disruptions.

Remember that disaster recovery is not a one-size-fits-all approach. Tailor your disaster recovery strategies to meet the specific needs of your organization, considering factors such as data sensitivity, compliance requirements, and budget constraints.

So, as you embark on your journey to implement disaster recovery solutions in Azure, approach it with meticulous planning, proactive monitoring, and a commitment to continuous improvement. With the right strategies and tools in place, you can ensure that your organization remains resilient in the face of adversity, safeguarding your business and maintaining the trust of your stakeholders.

Chapter 8: Advanced Troubleshooting Techniques for Azure Administrators

In the vast and intricate landscape of Azure deployments, it's not uncommon to encounter complex issues that require meticulous diagnosis and resolution. These issues can range from performance bottlenecks and application errors to connectivity problems and unexpected behavior within your Azure resources. When faced with such challenges, it's essential to have a structured approach to diagnose and address complex issues effectively.

Think of diagnosing complex issues in Azure as solving a puzzle. Each piece of information you gather and every clue you uncover brings you closer to understanding the root cause and finding the solution. In this journey, we'll explore the strategies, tools, and best practices for diagnosing complex issues in Azure, helping you navigate the intricacies of cloud troubleshooting.

1. Understand Your Environment: Begin by gaining a deep understanding of your Azure environment. Familiarize yourself with the architecture, services, and configurations in play. Document critical components, dependencies, and interactions within your deployment.

2. Define the Issue: Clearly define the issue you're facing. Is it a performance problem, an error message, an outage, or unexpected behavior? Understanding the nature of the issue is the first step in the diagnosis process.

3. Gather Data: Collect relevant data and information about the issue. This may include logs, metrics, error messages, configuration settings, and user reports. The more data you have, the better equipped you are to diagnose the problem.

4. Analyze Logs and Metrics: Dive into logs and metrics from Azure services, virtual machines, and applications. Look for patterns, anomalies, and error messages that provide clues about the issue. Azure Monitor and Application Insights are valuable tools for log and metric analysis.

5. Check Dependencies: Examine dependencies and interactions between Azure resources. A problem in one resource can have a ripple effect on others. Verify that all dependencies are functioning correctly.

6. Review Configuration: Review the configuration settings of your Azure resources. Incorrect configurations can lead to unexpected behavior. Ensure that security groups, firewall rules, and access controls are correctly configured.

7. Use Azure Resource Explorer: Azure Resource Explorer is a powerful tool for exploring and querying Azure resource data. You can use it to inspect the properties and configurations of your resources in detail.

8. Azure Network Watcher: For networking issues, Azure Network Watcher provides diagnostic and visualization tools. You can use tools like Network Performance Monitor and Connection Monitor to identify connectivity problems.

9. Application Profiling: If the issue is related to application performance, consider using application profiling tools like Azure Application Insights or third-party APM (Application Performance Monitoring) solutions. These tools can help pinpoint performance bottlenecks and code-level issues.

10. Isolate Components: Isolate components and services to identify the source of the problem. By systematically disabling or isolating parts of your deployment, you can narrow down the scope of the issue.

11. Test in Staging Environments: Whenever possible, replicate the issue in a staging or test environment that mirrors your production setup. This allows you to experiment with potential solutions without impacting your live environment.

12. Review Azure Status: Check the Azure Status page for any ongoing service incidents or outages that might be affecting your resources. Azure provides real-time status updates for its services.

13. Collaboration: Collaborate with your team and leverage Azure support resources. Sometimes, a fresh perspective or expert assistance can accelerate the diagnosis process.

14. Explore Community and Forums: Azure has a vibrant community of users and forums where you can seek advice and share experiences. Azure forums and communities often have solutions and insights into common issues.

15. Test Hypotheses: Formulate hypotheses about the root cause based on the information you've gathered. Test these hypotheses systematically to confirm or rule out potential causes.

16. Documentation: Maintain thorough documentation throughout the diagnosis process. Record your observations, tests, and findings. Documentation is invaluable for reference and sharing knowledge with your team.

17. Root Cause Analysis: Once you've identified the root cause, perform a comprehensive root cause analysis (RCA). Understand why the issue occurred and what steps can be taken to prevent it in the future.

18. Implement Solutions: Apply the necessary fixes or solutions to address the issue. This may involve adjusting configurations, updating software, or making architectural changes.

19. Monitor Post-Resolution: After implementing solutions, closely monitor your Azure environment to ensure that the issue has been fully resolved. Continuously assess the impact of the changes you've made.

20. Learn and Iterate: Complex issues often provide valuable learning opportunities. Take the time to learn from the diagnosis process and share your findings with your team. Use the knowledge gained to enhance your Azure deployment's resilience.

21. Automation and Alerts: Consider implementing automation and proactive alerting to detect and respond to

278

similar issues in the future. Azure Automation and Azure Monitor can help automate remediation tasks and set up alerting based on specific conditions.

22. Disaster Recovery Planning: As part of your diagnosis process, consider how disaster recovery plans and strategies may come into play. Ensure that your Azure environment is equipped to handle unforeseen disasters and outages.

In summary, diagnosing complex issues in Azure is a skill that combines technical expertise, systematic analysis, and a methodical approach. By understanding your environment, gathering data, analyzing logs, and collaborating effectively, you can uncover the root causes of issues and implement solutions that ensure the reliability and performance of your Azure deployments.

Remember that troubleshooting complex issues is a journey that requires patience, persistence, and a willingness to learn. Embrace each challenge as an opportunity to enhance your Azure expertise and strengthen your organization's cloud resilience. With the right strategies and tools at your disposal, you can confidently navigate the complexities of Azure troubleshooting and keep your cloud environment running smoothly.

Navigating the vast and ever-evolving landscape of Microsoft Azure can be an exciting but sometimes challenging journey, especially when you encounter complex issues, have questions, or seek to optimize your cloud environment. That's where Azure support and community resources come into play – as your trusty companions on this cloud adventure.

Picture Azure support and community resources as your friendly guides, ready to assist you in your Azure endeavors. They can provide insights, solutions, and a helping hand when you're facing challenges or striving to make the most of Azure's capabilities.

Azure Support: Azure offers a range of support plans designed to cater to different needs and budgets. Whether you're a small startup or a large enterprise, there's likely an Azure support plan that aligns with your requirements.

1. Basic Support: If you're just starting your Azure journey or have minimal support needs, the Basic Support plan is a cost-effective option. It provides access to Azure documentation, best practices, and general guidance.

2. Developer Support: Developers will appreciate the Developer Support plan, which offers technical support for application development and debugging. It's a great choice for those focused on coding and testing in Azure.

3. Standard Support: The Standard Support plan is suitable for businesses running production workloads in Azure. It includes technical support, 24/7 access to Azure experts, and response times for critical issues.

4. Professional Direct Support: For organizations that require a higher level of support, the Professional Direct Support plan offers faster response times and direct access to Azure engineers. It's ideal for mission-critical environments.

5. Premier Support: Premier Support provides personalized, end-to-end support, with a dedicated Technical Account Manager (TAM) who serves as your Azure advocate. It's the top-tier support option for enterprises with complex needs.

No matter which support plan you choose, you'll gain access to a wealth of resources and expertise to assist you in your Azure journey.

Azure Community Resources: In addition to official Azure support, the Azure community is a vibrant and collaborative ecosystem where users, experts, and enthusiasts come together to share knowledge, solve problems, and learn from one another. Let's explore some of the key community resources at your disposal:

1. Azure Forums: Azure forums are bustling hubs of activity, where users ask questions, share experiences, and provide solutions to common challenges. Whether you're troubleshooting an issue or seeking advice, the Azure forums are a valuable resource.

2. Stack Overflow: Stack Overflow is a popular platform for asking technical questions and finding answers related to Azure. You'll discover a vast repository of Azure-related questions and solutions from the community.

3. Azure Feedback Forums: If you have suggestions or feedback about Azure services or features, the Azure Feedback Forums are the place to voice your thoughts. Microsoft actively engages with the community to understand user needs and make improvements.

4. GitHub: Azure-related repositories on GitHub host open-source projects, scripts, and code samples contributed by the community. It's an excellent source for finding reusable code and collaborating on Azure-related projects.

5. Tech Communities and User Groups: Many cities and regions have Azure user groups and tech communities that hold regular meetings, webinars, and events. Joining these groups can provide opportunities for networking and learning from local experts.

6. Azure Blogs: Microsoft and Azure MVPs (Most Valuable Professionals) maintain blogs that cover a wide range of Azure topics, from best practices and tutorials to in-depth technical insights. Reading Azure blogs can help you stay informed and learn from experienced practitioners.

7. Microsoft Learn: Microsoft Learn offers a variety of free, self-paced Azure courses and tutorials. It's an interactive platform where you can build hands-on skills and gain Azure certifications.

8. Azure YouTube Channel: Microsoft's Azure YouTube channel features videos, webinars, and demos on Azure services, updates, and best practices. It's a visual and engaging way to learn about Azure.

9. Azure Podcasts: If you prefer audio content, there are Azure-focused podcasts that cover a wide range of Azure topics, including interviews with Azure experts and discussions of current trends.

10. Twitter and Social Media: Follow Azure experts, Microsoft Azure, and related hashtags on Twitter and other social media platforms to stay up-to-date with Azure news, tips, and community discussions.

11. Microsoft Tech Community: The Microsoft Tech Community is a platform where Microsoft product teams and experts engage with the community. You can participate in discussions, ask questions, and learn from Microsoft insiders.

12. Azure GitHub Discussions: Some Azure services have dedicated GitHub Discussions, where you can interact with the service's development team and other users to get support and share feedback.

13. Azure Customer Stories: Microsoft regularly publishes Azure customer stories that showcase real-world implementations of Azure solutions. These stories can provide inspiration and insights for your own projects.

14. Azure Marketplace: Explore the Azure Marketplace to discover a wide range of Azure-related solutions and integrations created by Microsoft partners and the community. You can find tools and resources to enhance your Azure environment.

15. Online Forums and Groups: Beyond official Microsoft resources, various online forums, LinkedIn groups, and communities cater to Azure enthusiasts. Joining these groups can expand your network and offer additional avenues for seeking help and advice.

When navigating Azure support and community resources, consider the following best practices:

Be Specific: When seeking assistance, provide clear and detailed information about your issue or question. Include error messages, symptoms, and relevant configurations to help others understand your context.

Search First: Before posting a new question or issue, search existing resources, forums, and documentation. Chances are, someone has already encountered a similar problem and found a solution.

Contribute and Share: As you gain experience and knowledge in Azure, consider contributing to the community by answering questions, providing insights, or sharing your own experiences. Collaboration benefits everyone.

Respect Guidelines: Follow the guidelines and etiquette of the community platforms you engage with. Respect the time and efforts of others, and maintain a positive and constructive tone in your interactions.

Stay Informed: Azure is continually evolving, with updates, new features, and best practices. Stay informed by regularly checking official Azure blogs, documentation, and announcements.

Leverage Azure Support: If you have an Azure support plan, don't hesitate to reach out to Microsoft support for assistance with technical issues. They can provide expert guidance and solutions tailored to your specific needs.

In summary, Azure support and community resources are invaluable companions on your Azure journey. Whether you're a beginner exploring the cloud or a seasoned Azure pro facing complex challenges, these resources offer a wealth of knowledge, solutions, and opportunities for collaboration.

Embrace the Azure community, contribute to its growth, and leverage Azure support when needed. By tapping into these resources, you'll not only enhance your Azure expertise but also build connections with fellow cloud enthusiasts and experts, ensuring a smoother and more rewarding Azure experience.

Chapter 9: Continuous Improvement: Analyzing and Enhancing Deployments

In the ever-evolving realm of cloud computing, the journey doesn't end with deploying resources in Azure; it continues with regularly auditing and optimizing those resources. Think of it as maintaining a finely tuned instrument. Azure offers a dynamic and flexible environment, and by conducting regular audits and optimizations, you can ensure that your resources are running efficiently, cost-effectively, and securely.

Regularly auditing and optimizing Azure resources isn't just a best practice; it's an ongoing commitment to making the most of your cloud investment. It involves a systematic approach to assess the performance, cost, and security aspects of your Azure environment. Let's dive into the strategies, tools, and considerations that can help you in this journey of continuous improvement.

1. Performance Auditing: Start by auditing the performance of your Azure resources. This involves evaluating the efficiency and responsiveness of your applications and services. Here are some key aspects to consider:

a. Resource Utilization: Monitor the utilization of your virtual machines, databases, and other resources. Identify underutilized or overutilized resources that may impact performance or cost.

b. Latency and Response Times: Measure the latency and response times of your applications. Identify bottlenecks and areas where optimization can improve user experience.

c. Application Profiling: Use profiling and monitoring tools like Azure Application Insights or third-party APM (Application Performance Monitoring) solutions to analyze application performance and identify areas for improvement.

d. Load Testing: Conduct load testing to simulate real-world traffic and assess how your applications and services handle varying levels of demand. Optimize resource scaling and configurations based on test results.

2. Cost Optimization: Cost optimization is a critical aspect of managing Azure resources effectively. It's about maximizing the value you get from your Azure spending. Consider the following:

a. Cost Analysis: Regularly review your Azure cost data. Azure Cost Management and Billing provide insights into your spending patterns. Identify areas where cost can be reduced or optimized.

b. Right-Sizing: Ensure that your virtual machines are appropriately sized to match the workload demands. Downsize or upscale VMs as needed to optimize cost and performance.

c. Reserved Instances: Explore the use of Azure Reserved Instances (RIs) to save costs on virtual machines. RIs provide significant discounts in exchange for committing to a one- or three-year term.

d. Auto Scaling: Implement auto-scaling for your resources to dynamically adjust capacity based on demand. Azure Autoscale and Virtual Machine Scale Sets allow you to optimize resource utilization and reduce costs during low traffic periods.

e. Resource Tagging: Use resource tagging to categorize and track your Azure resources. Tags can help you allocate costs more effectively and identify areas for optimization.

f. Azure Cost Alerts: Set up cost alerts to receive notifications when your spending exceeds predefined thresholds. This proactive approach can help you identify cost anomalies and take corrective actions.

3. Security Auditing: Security should never be overlooked when auditing your Azure resources. It's essential to ensure that your cloud environment remains secure and compliant. Consider these security aspects:

a. Identity and Access Management: Review Azure Active Directory (Azure AD) configurations and access controls. Ensure that only authorized users and services have access to resources.

b. Security Center: Azure Security Center provides security recommendations and threat detection for your resources. Regularly review security recommendations and take action to mitigate vulnerabilities.

c. Compliance Auditing: Verify that your Azure environment complies with industry standards and regulatory requirements.

Azure provides compliance certifications and tools to help you achieve and maintain compliance.

d. Network Security: Assess network security configurations, including firewall rules, network security groups (NSGs), and Azure Firewall settings. Ensure that your network is protected against unauthorized access.

e. Data Encryption: Verify that data at rest and in transit is encrypted using Azure encryption services. Ensure that encryption keys are managed securely.

f. Patch Management: Keep your virtual machines and Azure services up to date with security patches and updates. Implement a patch management strategy to address known vulnerabilities.

4. Resource Cleanup: Unused and redundant resources can contribute to unnecessary costs and complexity. Regular resource cleanup is essential. Consider the following:

a. Resource De-provisioning: Identify and de-provision resources that are no longer in use. This includes virtual machines, storage accounts, databases, and more.

b. Orphaned Resources: Look for orphaned or unassociated resources that are not part of any active deployments. Clean up these resources to reduce clutter and cost.

c. Resource Groups: Organize your resources into resource groups with clear naming conventions. This makes it easier to manage and track resources and enables efficient cleanup.

d. Azure Policy: Implement Azure Policy to enforce resource cleanup and management policies. You can define rules to automatically delete or archive unused resources.

5. Automation: Automation can significantly streamline auditing and optimization efforts. Consider using Azure automation tools and scripts to:

a. Schedule Audits: Schedule regular audits and assessments of your Azure environment. Automation can help ensure that audits are performed consistently and at the desired frequency.

b. Remediate Issues: Implement automation scripts that can automatically remediate common issues or optimization opportunities identified during audits.

c. Alerting: Set up alerts and notifications for critical events, such as security breaches or cost overruns. Automation can trigger predefined actions in response to alerts.

d. Compliance Scanning: Automate compliance scanning and reporting to ensure that your Azure resources adhere to security and compliance standards.

6. Training and Knowledge Sharing: Invest in training and knowledge sharing within your organization. Keep your team up to date with Azure best practices and optimization techniques. Encourage knowledge sharing and collaboration to ensure that everyone is aligned with optimization goals.

7. Regular Reviews: Lastly, conduct regular reviews and assessments of your Azure environment. Establish a cadence for audits and optimization efforts, and involve relevant stakeholders. Use the insights gained from previous audits to drive continuous improvement.

In summary, regularly auditing and optimizing Azure resources is a proactive approach to ensure that your cloud environment remains performant, cost-effective, and secure. It's an ongoing commitment to harness the full potential of Azure while managing costs and mitigating risks.

By following the strategies and best practices outlined in this journey, you can navigate the complexities of Azure resource management with confidence. Remember that cloud optimization is not a one-time task but a continuous effort that evolves alongside your organization's needs and goals. Embrace the process of regular auditing and optimization, and your Azure environment will thrive in the ever-changing world of cloud computing.

In the world of Azure, where cloud environments are dynamic and ever-evolving, staying on top of best practices, cost optimization, and security recommendations can be a challenging task. This is where Azure Advisor comes into play as your trusted advisor in the cloud. Think of it as a helpful companion on your Azure journey, providing you with tailored recommendations and insights to continuously improve your Azure resources.

Azure Advisor is more than just a tool; it's your cloud optimization and best practices partner. It offers a wide range of recommendations that span performance, cost, security, and high availability aspects of your Azure environment. Let's embark on a journey to explore how you can effectively utilize Azure Advisor for continuous improvement in your cloud deployment.

1. Performance Recommendations: Performance is a critical aspect of any cloud environment. Azure Advisor provides recommendations to help you optimize your Azure resources for better performance. These recommendations include:

a. VM Resizing: Azure Advisor can suggest resizing virtual machines to match their actual usage, ensuring you're not over-provisioned or under-provisioned.

b. Scaling: Advisor offers insights into scaling resources like Azure SQL databases and web apps to handle varying workloads more efficiently.

c. Availability Sets: It recommends distributing VMs across availability sets to ensure high availability and fault tolerance.

d. Cache Usage: Azure Redis Cache recommendations help you use caching effectively to improve application performance.

2. Cost Optimization Recommendations: Azure Advisor helps you keep your Azure spending in check with a wide array of cost optimization recommendations:

a. Right-Sizing VMs: Advisor identifies over- or underutilized virtual machines and recommends resizing them for cost savings.

b. Reserved Instances (RIs): It provides guidance on purchasing Azure Reserved Instances to get significant cost discounts for long-term workloads.

c. Unused Resources: Advisor flags resources that are underutilized or not used and suggests deleting or scaling them down to save costs.

d. Low-Utilization SQL Databases: It offers recommendations to consolidate or scale down Azure SQL databases with low utilization.

e. Underutilized App Service Plans: Advisor identifies underutilized App Service Plans and recommends consolidation or scaling.

f. Azure Blob Storage: You receive recommendations to enable cool or archive storage tiers for rarely accessed data to reduce costs.

g. Shutdown VMs: Advisor suggests scheduling the automatic shutdown of VMs during non-business hours to save on compute costs.

3. Security Recommendations: Ensuring the security of your Azure resources is paramount, and Azure Advisor provides valuable security recommendations:

a. Security Center Recommendations: Advisor integrates with Azure Security Center to offer security-related suggestions like enabling threat protection and network security groups.

b. Network Security Groups: It identifies insecure network security groups and recommends adjustments to enhance security.

c. Encryption: Advisor recommends enabling encryption at rest and in transit for storage accounts, databases, and virtual machines.

d. Identity and Access Management: It provides guidance on implementing role-based access control (RBAC) and Multi-Factor Authentication (MFA) for better identity and access management.

e. Compliance Recommendations: Advisor helps you address compliance requirements by providing suggestions to configure auditing and logging settings.

4. High Availability Recommendations: High availability is crucial for keeping your applications and services up and running. Azure Advisor offers recommendations in this area:

a. Availability Zones: Advisor suggests spreading resources across Availability Zones to ensure fault tolerance and high availability.

b. Load Balancing: It provides insights into load balancing configurations for distributing traffic evenly across multiple instances.

c. Geo-Replication: Advisor recommends enabling geo-replication for critical data stores to ensure data redundancy and disaster recovery.

d. Traffic Manager: It suggests using Azure Traffic Manager to distribute traffic across multiple regions for improved availability.

5. Continuous Monitoring and Action: Azure Advisor doesn't stop at providing recommendations; it actively monitors your Azure environment and provides updates as the situation changes. This means that you can rely on Advisor for ongoing guidance and actionable insights to keep your Azure resources optimized, secure, and available.

6. Personalized Insights: Azure Advisor tailors its recommendations to your specific Azure environment, taking into account your resource configurations, usage patterns, and objectives. This personalized approach ensures that the guidance provided is relevant and actionable.

7. Integration with Azure Policy: You can integrate Azure Advisor with Azure Policy to enforce compliance with best practices and recommendations. This helps ensure that your organization's Azure resources adhere to the guidelines set by Advisor.

8. Customization and Prioritization: Azure Advisor allows you to customize and prioritize recommendations based on your organization's goals and requirements. You can choose which recommendations to focus on and tailor them to your needs.

9. Cost Projection: Advisor provides cost projections based on its recommendations, allowing you to assess the potential cost savings or increases associated with implementing the guidance.

10. Collaboration and Sharing: You can share Advisor recommendations with your team members or stakeholders to facilitate collaboration and decision-making. This fosters a culture of continuous improvement within your organization.

11. Implementation Tracking: Azure Advisor helps you track the progress of implementing recommendations, so you can measure the impact of optimizations over time.

12. Insights for Multiple Azure Services: Advisor covers a wide range of Azure services, including virtual machines, databases, web apps, Azure SQL, storage accounts, and more. This comprehensive coverage ensures that you can optimize various aspects of your Azure environment.

In summary, Azure Advisor is your invaluable companion on the journey of continuous improvement in Azure. By leveraging its performance, cost optimization, security, and high availability recommendations, you can enhance the efficiency, reliability, and cost-effectiveness of your Azure resources.

Think of Advisor as your trusted advisor in the cloud, providing proactive guidance and actionable insights to help you make informed decisions and stay on the path of continuous improvement. Whether you're just starting your Azure journey or have a mature cloud environment, Azure Advisor is there to assist you in optimizing your Azure resources effectively.

Chapter 10: Preparing for the Future: Staying Ahead in Azure Administration

In the fast-paced world of cloud computing, staying up-to-date with Azure updates and new features is not just a good practice; it's essential for making the most of your Azure resources. Think of Azure updates as your window to innovation and improvement in the cloud. They bring enhancements, performance improvements, security patches, and exciting new features that can transform the way you work with Azure.

Keeping up with Azure updates is like keeping tabs on the latest advancements in a rapidly evolving field. It ensures that you're taking full advantage of the capabilities Azure has to offer. Let's embark on a journey to explore how you can effectively stay informed about Azure updates and leverage new features to enhance your cloud experience.

1. Azure Update Channels: Azure provides multiple channels through which you can access updates and announcements. These channels include:

a. Azure Blog: The Azure Blog is a primary source for Azure announcements. It features in-depth articles, product updates, and insights directly from the Azure team.

b. Azure Updates: Azure Updates is a dedicated platform for tracking service updates, including new features and changes to existing services. You can subscribe to specific services to receive email notifications.

c. Azure Newsletter: Azure sends out a newsletter called "Azure This Week" that summarizes the week's updates and news. Subscribing to this newsletter keeps you informed in a concise format.

d. Azure Twitter: Follow the official Azure Twitter account (@Azure) to receive real-time updates, news, and announcements about Azure services and features.

e. GitHub Releases: For open-source projects and Azure-related repositories on GitHub, releases and updates are often posted there. You can watch or star repositories to receive notifications.

2. Azure Roadmap: The Azure Roadmap provides a forward-looking view of planned updates and features. It's an invaluable resource to understand what's on the horizon for Azure services. You can filter the roadmap by service and track upcoming changes that align with your interests.

3. Azure Documentation: Azure documentation is a comprehensive source of information about Azure services. It's continuously updated to reflect the latest features, best practices, and changes. Whenever a new feature is released, you can find detailed documentation to help you understand and implement it.

4. Azure Preview Features: Azure often offers preview features that allow you to try out new capabilities before they become generally available. Enabling preview features in your Azure portal settings gives you early access to innovations.

5. Azure Webinars and Events: Microsoft regularly hosts webinars, virtual events, and conferences where Azure updates and new features are showcased. Participating in these events can provide insights and hands-on experiences with the latest Azure offerings.

6. Azure User Groups and Communities: Joining Azure user groups and communities can be an excellent way to stay informed about updates. These groups often host local or virtual meetings where members share their experiences and insights about Azure.

7. Feedback Channels: Azure values feedback from users. You can provide feedback, suggest improvements, and report issues through Azure's feedback channels. Your input can influence future updates and features.

8. Azure Marketplace: Explore the Azure Marketplace to discover third-party solutions and integrations that leverage the latest Azure features. It's a marketplace for innovative solutions built on Azure technologies.

9. Azure Certified Devices and Solutions: Azure Certified devices and solutions are validated to work seamlessly with Azure services. Exploring these offerings can help you discover new tools and technologies that enhance your Azure environment.

10. Microsoft Learn: Microsoft Learn offers free, self-paced courses and modules on Azure services. It's an interactive way to learn about new features and gain hands-on experience.

11. Azure Dev/Test Subscriptions: Consider using Azure Dev/Test subscriptions for experimentation and testing. These subscriptions often receive early access to new features, allowing you to explore and provide feedback.

12. Cloud Adoption Framework: Microsoft's Cloud Adoption Framework provides guidance on adopting Azure best practices, including staying up-to-date with Azure updates and features.

13. Stay Engaged with Azure Community: Engaging with the Azure community can be a rewarding experience. Follow Azure experts, join discussions on Azure forums and social media, and participate in conversations to exchange insights and stay informed.

14. Azure Podcasts and YouTube Channels: Azure-focused podcasts and YouTube channels offer a wealth of content about Azure updates and new features. Tune in to podcasts or watch videos to hear from experts and stay updated.

15. Prioritize and Plan for Adoption: With a steady stream of updates and features, it's essential to prioritize which updates are most relevant to your organization and plan for their adoption. Not every update may be immediately applicable to your specific needs.

16. Test and Validate: Before implementing new features in production environments, it's a good practice to test and validate them in non-production environments. This ensures that they align with your requirements and won't disrupt existing workflows.

17. Feedback and Adaptation: As you adopt new features, provide feedback to Microsoft based on your experiences. Microsoft values customer input and uses it to refine and enhance Azure services.

18. Training and Skill Development: Invest in training and skill development for your team to ensure they are well-equipped to leverage new Azure features effectively. Microsoft offers Azure certifications and training resources to help you stay current.

19. Stay Aligned with Business Goals: When evaluating new features, align them with your organization's business goals and objectives. Choose updates that have the potential to drive business value and innovation.

20. Continuous Improvement Culture: Foster a culture of continuous improvement within your organization. Encourage your team to explore and embrace new features that can enhance efficiency and competitiveness.

In summary, staying up-to-date with Azure updates and new features is not just a matter of keeping pace with technology; it's about ensuring that your Azure resources remain optimized, secure, and aligned with your evolving business needs. Azure updates bring opportunities for innovation and improvement, and by staying informed and actively exploring new features, you can harness the full potential of Azure to drive your organization's success in the ever-evolving world of cloud computing.

Embarking on a journey to master Azure, Microsoft's cloud computing platform, is a rewarding endeavor that can open doors to new possibilities, enhance your career, and empower you to build and manage powerful cloud solutions. However, the path to Azure mastery is not a sprint; it's a continuous learning marathon that requires dedication, persistence, and a well-structured plan.

Building a continuous learning plan for Azure mastery is akin to charting a course through a vast and ever-evolving landscape. It involves defining your goals, acquiring knowledge and skills, staying updated with Azure's rapid advancements, and applying what you learn to real-world scenarios. In this chapter, we'll explore the key components of an effective continuous learning plan for Azure mastery.

1. Define Your Goals: Begin your journey by clearly defining your objectives and goals. Ask yourself why you want to master Azure. Is it to advance your career, build cloud solutions, or solve specific business challenges? Understanding your motivations will guide your learning plan.

2. Assess Your Current Knowledge: Take an honest inventory of your current knowledge and skills related to Azure. What do you already know? What areas are you comfortable with, and where do you need improvement? This self-assessment will help you identify your starting point.

3. Choose Your Learning Path: Azure offers a wide range of services and technologies. Depending on your goals, choose a specific learning path that aligns with your interests and career objectives. Some common learning paths include Azure Administrator, Azure Developer, Azure Solutions Architect, and more.

4. Identify Learning Resources: Azure provides a wealth of resources for learning, including official documentation, Microsoft Learn, Azure DevOps Labs, and online courses on platforms like Pluralsight, Coursera, and edX. Identify the resources that best suit your learning style and preferences.

5. Create a Study Schedule: Learning Azure is not something you can accomplish overnight. Create a study schedule that fits your lifestyle and commitments. Consistency is key, so allocate dedicated time for studying Azure concepts and hands-on labs.

6. Set Milestones: Break down your learning journey into manageable milestones. Define what you want to achieve within a specific timeframe. For example, your first milestone might be to pass the Azure Fundamentals certification exam.

7. Hands-On Practice: Azure is best learned through hands-on practice. Set up an Azure subscription, experiment with services, and build your own projects. Whether it's deploying virtual machines, creating web apps, or setting up Azure DevOps pipelines, hands-on experience is invaluable.

8. Certification Goals: Consider pursuing Azure certifications as part of your learning plan. Microsoft offers a range of certifications that validate your Azure expertise. Certifications not only boost your resume but also serve as concrete milestones in your learning journey.

9. Stay Informed: Azure is continuously evolving with new features, services, and updates. Stay informed about Azure advancements by following the Azure blog, subscribing to newsletters, and participating in Azure webinars and events.

10. Join Azure Communities: Engage with the Azure community to connect with like-minded individuals, share knowledge, and seek advice. Azure forums, LinkedIn groups, and local user groups are great places to interact with peers and experts.

11. Seek Mentorship: Consider finding a mentor who has expertise in Azure. A mentor can provide guidance, share insights, and offer valuable advice to accelerate your learning journey.

12. Practice Continuous Learning: Azure is a dynamic platform, and learning is an ongoing process. Embrace a mindset of continuous learning, where you're always open to acquiring new skills and adapting to changes in the Azure ecosystem.

13. Real-World Projects: Apply what you learn to real-world projects. Building practical solutions on Azure not only reinforces your knowledge but also demonstrates your abilities to potential employers or clients.

14. Document Your Progress: Keep a record of your progress, including completed courses, certifications earned, and projects accomplished. This documentation serves as a testament to your dedication and achievements.

15. Embrace Challenges: Learning Azure may present challenges and occasional setbacks. Embrace these challenges as opportunities for growth. Don't be discouraged by obstacles; use them as stepping stones to success.

16. Networking and Collaboration: Azure mastery is not just about technical skills; it also involves networking and collaboration. Connect with professionals in your field, attend Azure-related conferences, and collaborate on Azure projects.

17. Evaluate and Adjust: Periodically evaluate your learning plan and adjust it based on your progress and changing goals. Be flexible and open to refining your plan as you gain experience and insights.

18. Share Your Knowledge: As you become more proficient in Azure, consider sharing your knowledge with others. Writing blog posts, giving presentations, or mentoring others can reinforce your understanding and contribute to the community.

19. Keep a Growth Mindset: A growth mindset is the belief that you can develop and improve your abilities through effort and learning. Cultivate a growth mindset to approach challenges with resilience and determination.

20. Celebrate Achievements: Don't forget to celebrate your achievements along the way. Completing a certification, launching a successful Azure project, or solving a complex problem are milestones worth acknowledging.

In summary, building a continuous learning plan for Azure mastery is a journey of self-discovery and growth. It's about setting clear goals, acquiring knowledge and skills, staying updated with Azure's rapid advancements, and applying what you learn to real-world scenarios. With dedication, persistence, and a well-structured plan, you can navigate the Azure landscape with confidence and achieve mastery in the cloud. Remember, it's not just about reaching the destination; it's about enjoying the journey of continuous improvement and learning.

Conclusion

In the ever-evolving world of cloud computing, the journey to Azure Administrator Mastery is an exhilarating and transformative experience. The four books in the "AZ-104: Azure Administrator Mastery" bundle have taken you on a comprehensive exploration of Azure, equipping you with the knowledge, skills, and expertise to navigate this dynamic landscape with confidence and proficiency.

In "Azure Essentials: A Beginner's Guide to Navigating AZ-104," you embarked on your Azure journey as a novice and built a solid foundation in Azure fundamentals. You learned how to navigate the Azure portal, create and manage resources, and understand the core concepts that underpin the Azure ecosystem.

"Mastering Identity & Resource Management in Azure: A Comprehensive Guide to AZ-104" delved deep into identity management, Azure Active Directory, and resource governance. You gained the skills to secure access to Azure resources, implement identity solutions, and enforce compliance through resource management.

"Azure Networking and Storage Mastery: Advanced Techniques for AZ-104 Administrators" elevated your expertise by delving into the intricacies of Azure networking and storage. You learned how to design resilient network architectures, optimize connectivity, and harness the power of Azure Storage for various data needs.

In "Azure Administrator Expertise: Pro-Level Automation and Optimization for AZ-104," you advanced to the level of a pro-level administrator. Automation became your ally as you optimized Azure resources for performance, cost, and security. You explored the depths of Azure PowerShell and Azure CLI to streamline operations.

As you conclude your journey through these four books, you stand as an Azure Administrator with mastery over the cloud. You possess the skills to architect robust solutions, secure identities, manage resources efficiently, optimize costs, and automate tasks with finesse.

Your Azure Administrator Mastery is not just about the knowledge you've acquired but also about the mindset you've cultivated—a mindset of continuous learning and adaptability. The cloud landscape will continue to evolve, and your ability to embrace change and innovation will be your greatest asset.

In closing, the "AZ-104: Azure Administrator Mastery" bundle has been your compass in the Azure cosmos, guiding you from the basics to the realm of expertise. Azure is a world of boundless opportunities, and your journey as a master has just begun. Whether you're forging new solutions, securing identities, optimizing resources, or automating processes, Azure will continue to be your canvas for innovation and achievement.

Embrace your Azure Administrator Mastery, keep exploring, keep learning, and keep transforming the cloud landscape with your expertise. The future of Azure is in your hands, and the possibilities are limitless. Congratulations on reaching this milestone, and may your Azure journey be a never-ending adventure of discovery and growth.